A FIRST DRAFT OF HISTORY

A First

Draft of History

Ted Poston

Edited by Kathleen A. Hauke

THE UNIVERSITY OF GEORGIA PRESS

ATHENS AND LONDON

© 2000 by the University of Georgia Press
Athens, Georgia 30602
All rights reserved
Designed by Erin Kirk New
Set in 10.5 on 13 Electra by G&S Typesetters
Printed and bound by Thomson-Shore
The paper in this book meets the guidelines for
permanence and durability of the Committee on
Production Guidelines for Book Longevity of the
Council on Library Resources.

Printed in the United States of America

04 03 02 01 00   C 5 4 3 2 1

Library of Congress Cataloging-in-Publication Data

Poston, Ted, 1906–1974.
  A first draft of history / Ted Poston ; edited by Kathleen A.
  Hauke.
     p. cm.
  Includes bibliographical references and index.
  ISBN 0-8203-2239-3 (alk. paper)
  I. Hauke, Kathleen A.   II. Title.
  AC8 .P727 2000
  070.4′4 — dc21   00-036421

British Library Cataloging-in-Publication Data available

Frontispiece: Ted Poston, ca. 1949. Photo courtesy of
The New York Post.

For those who trained me in journalism and bookmaking—
William M. Tugman, Ann T. Connell, and Rolv Harlow Schillios
of the *Eugene Register-Guard*; Dan Ryan and Myrtelle Sharpsteen
of the *Kalamazoo Gazette*; Tom Crosbie, editor of the *Cork Examiner*; and Professor Karl F. Zeisler of the University of Michigan.

CONTENTS

1950s 82

ACKNOWLEDGMENTS

Thanks to the *New York Post, Amsterdam News, Pittsburgh Courier, New Republic*, and *Editor and Publisher* for permission to republish these articles. Thanks also go to the National Endowment for the Humanities for a 1984 summer stipend that allowed me to spend one summer in New York City sleuthing out all Poston's byline stories from the *Post* microfilm collection at the New York Public Library Annex and from the *Pittsburgh Courier* and the *Amsterdam News* at the Schomburg Center for Research in Black Culture. Thanks to the *Post's* Virginia Cheteyan, Peter Faris, and former reporter Joe Kahn for making the newspaper's clipping files accessible; to Adele Hall Sweet, president of the Dorothy Schiff Foundation, for placing her mother's papers in the Manuscript Division of the New York Public Library so that they are available to scholars; and to the State Historical Society of Wisconsin for preserving James A. Wechsler's papers.

I also wish to thank the University of Rhode Island librarians who helped in the initial stages of this work, as well as Janice Steingruber of interlibrary loan at the Atlanta-Fulton Public Library and Hulda Wilson at the Woodruff Library of Atlanta University Center, who provided the use of a carrel.

Debbie Stone, like me, never met Poston, but she has shown her devotion to the idea of him by carefully reading *Ted Poston, Pioneer American Journalist* and this volume, suggesting ways to improve the manuscripts. Her aunt, Maysie Stone, sculpted a bust of Poston that is presently in the Schomburg collection.

But for Malcolm L. Call, the gentle senior editor at the University of Georgia Press, Poston's advocate there, this sheaf of papers testifying to Poston's take on a segment of the American twentieth century would have lain forever in my filing cabinet rather than on readers' shelves.

Finally, thanks to Richard L. Hauke, who underwrote my labors when I forswore teaching to devote myself full time to Poston's life and work.

EDITORIAL NOTE

The *New York Post* was not a newspaper of record, such as is the *New York Times*, which can be found today on microfilm in most libraries. Therefore, Ted Poston's effervescent prose and insider's vantage point have been largely unavailable except to assiduous researchers. Of the approximately sixteen hundred extant pieces that carried his byline, the fifty-four presented here mirror not only the era but also Poston's personality — humorous, literate, impatient, educated.

The criteria for selection of stories in this collection have been Poston's style, his unique perspective on people and events, and their historical value. Some articles have been abbreviated for economy of space. My deletions are indicated by bracketed ellipses; ellipses not in brackets are Poston's. Unless otherwise noted, comments in brackets are mine. Parenthetical material is Poston's unless identified as that of one of his editors. The few typographical errors have been silently corrected.

A supplemental bibliography lists Poston's other main writings, many of which have been annotated. Articles about him are listed next, then writings by and about his family. For the bibliography, clippings culled from the *Post* morgue lacked page numbers. Documentation of articles printed in the text has not been repeated in the supplemental bibliography.

Fourteen years of my reading, interviewing, and researching archives for traces of Poston led to the acquisition of much material on him. I have placed those materials in the archives of the Auburn Avenue Research Library on African American History and Culture, Atlanta, Georgia, and I have deposited printed copies of all Poston's extant writings at the Schomburg Center for Research in Black Culture, New York Public Library.

Ted Poston knew how to engage readers and cause them to imagine life inside his skin. For example, he wrote,

> There is a sort of tragi-comedy aspect to . . . incidents laboriously dredged up . . . as you [recollect how you] worked your way up from boot-black to janitor to dining car waiter, Pullman porter, cub reporter on Harlem's biggest weekly, and then a job on the New York Post. . . .
>
> Like the time you were sitting pretty far up on the old elevated platform at 145th St. in 1932, engrossed in a paper. You didn't notice the sign on the front of the train until the first car had come to a halt in front of you. Too lazy to take two steps forward to see if it was a Sixth Av. or a Ninth-Av. train, you approached the motorman at his booth door with the query: "Is this a Sixth or a Ninth Av. train?"
>
> "Can't you read, nigger?" he asks, drawing his head back in the window.
>
> "Naw," you snap sarcastically.
>
> "Then put down that New York Times and stop making a damned fool of yourself," he retorts laughingly as he pulls up the window and speeds the train down the track. You didn't join the laughter. . . .
>
> (Ted Poston, "The Negro in New York," *New York Post* 16 April 1956)

Looking through his incensed, jaundicedly amused, black man's eyes at a world in which an African American started out valued as "three-fifths of a person"—according to Article 1 of the Constitution[1]—Poston, the first black to "make it" in the mainstream press, spiritedly reported the news in a usually upbeat tone. He was thirty years old when he went to the *New York Post* in 1936, a year in which Franklin D. Roosevelt, with the New Deal, was elevating America from Depression; Poston was sixty-five when he left the *Post* in 1972, dispirited at the latest bellicose American racial mood.

This collection of Poston's best journalistic pieces from the *Pittsburgh Courier*, the *Amsterdam News*, the *New York Post*, *Editor and Publisher*, and

New Republic reflect a black perspective on mid-twentieth-century American history in the process of its evolution.

Poston's launching seemed inauspicious except for its date. He was born on 4 July 1906, in Hopkinsville, Kentucky. The youngest of seven children, he was educated in segregated schools — Booker T. Washington Colored Grammar School, Crispus Attucks High School, and Tennessee Agricultural and Industrial College. Both parents, Ephraim and Mollie Cox Poston, became teachers after Emancipation. The whole family, for pleasure, wrote verse. Poston enjoyed a happy, carefree, prankish childhood from ages six to twelve, which he related in short stories, *The Dark Side of Hopkinsville*. But innocent joy ended for Ted in the spring of 1917, when his mother died suddenly of kidney failure. Brother Ephraim Jr. succumbed to cancer in 1914. Sister Roberta, a 1917 graduate of Kentucky Negro Industrial Institute, died of a burst appendix in 1919. Ted's father remarried in the spring of 1924. His new wife, a teacher named Susie Forrest, seemed indifferent to Ted's emotional needs and those of his sister, Lillian, three years his senior. Lillian was committed to the state hospital for the insane in 1924 and died there of tuberculosis in 1927.

As a teenager, Ted had to earn the only money he would have. During the three-week harvest season each June, he ran eight miles every morning from Hopkinsville to Pembroke, Kentucky, to pick strawberries, then walked wearily home at the end of the day. At age sixteen, during cold weather, he earned fifty cents a week at a white dentist's home hauling in coal, setting fires in the grates of each room's hearth, and carrying out the ashes. At that position he was initiated into the wonders of sex when a female resident of the house seduced him (Hauke 13–14).

Ted's brothers, Robert Lincoln Poston and Ulysses Simpson Poston, were recruited into the U.S. Army in 1918, six months before the end of World War I. Their subsequent rhymes indicate how military service emboldened their thinking. Ulysses's persona in "Private Jack McKay" was "Dark of color and of habits / Rough as new pig iron from the mold," but "Army discipline harnessed his soul," and "Directed his aim toward the ideal goal / Of brotherhood, and to hate the storm / Of prejudice," so that now "the world has to deal with a new McKay."[2] Robert penned a more pugnacious verse, "When You Meet a Member of the Ku Klux Klan," with its directive, "Walk right up to him and hit him like a natural man. . . . Think of how he did your folks in the days of long ago. . . . Take a bat of sturdy oak and knock him down once more. / This time you may leave him where he wallows in the sand."[3] That militant admonition masked Robert's more fervent appeal for simple respect in "The Negro Prayer": "Lord God, look down on Thy poor soul / Each passing breeze says I am man. . . . I'm of Thy plan, to breathe, to think. . . . Did all alike see this, O God / I'd have no cause to seek Thee now. . . . Teach them, O God, to see my worth."[4]

Mild father Ephraim dared not challenge the status quo to the extent his soldier sons did. Ephraim's poems instead lauded exemplary blacks. For example, his "Ode to David Henry Anderson" was an encomium to the founding president of West Kentucky Industrial Institute, where Ephraim taught: "They say heights of great men reached and kept / Were not attained by smiles, but frowns. . . . Some called him crank, some called him fool. . . . [who] Now send their children to this school / Bless the man who had the knowledge / To build a West Kentucky College."[5]

When Ephraim, Robert, and Ulysses Poston launched a newspaper, the *Hopkinsville Contender*, in 1919, young Ted ran with the articles to the printer, then brought the galley proofs back posthaste. That experience provided him his opening wedge in journalism; in this field, the family figured, blacks could improve conditions for the race. The *Contender's* Democratic slant embroiled the Postons in controversy with Hopkinsville's Republican town fathers to the extent that Ulysses and Robert felt compelled to leave town. They moved the *Contender* to Nashville, Tennessee, and the National Baptist Publishing Company, then to Detroit's Paradise Valley. Mesmerized there by the visiting Marcus Garvey and his Universal Negro Improvement Association (UNIA), the Poston brothers followed the West Indian orator back to New York, became key assistants, and helped Garvey edit his internationally circulated *Negro World*.

Both brothers found brides through the UNIA. Ulysses married Sybil Bryant, his leading lady in the race drama *Tallaboo*. Robert married the dynamic sculptor and art educator Augusta Savage.[6] Robert and Augusta were expecting a child when Garvey sent Robert on a mission to Liberia to arrange for a resettlement of American descendants of former slaves. En route back from Africa, Robert died of pneumonia onboard ship in March 1924. Augusta gave birth to their daughter, Roberta, four months later, but the baby lived only a few days (Martin 78).

The love Ted Poston shared with his childhood sweetheart, Mary Duncan, whom he immortalized as the unattainable Sleeping Beauty in his much-anthologized story "The Revolt of the Evil Fairies," gave Ted's high school years stability (see Ted Poston, *Dark Side*). Ted and Mary took walks, danced at friends' parties, and held hands in the balcony at the movies. Mary's father, Dr. James Duncan, thwarted the couple's romance, however; he warned that there was "a weak strain" in the Poston family, and "genius is so close to insanity" (M. Wilson interview).

Ted graduated from high school in 1924 and set off in rags and on foot — according to an FBI report and an archivist at Tennessee State University — for Nashville and the state-supported black Tennessee Agricultural and Industrial Institute, where he majored in the family's chosen fields of interest, English and journalism.[7] He and Mary Duncan maintained an intense correspondence. When Mary graduated from Attucks High School in 1926, her father sent her not to Fisk University in Nashville, as she and Ted had planned, but to Butler University in Indianapolis. Dr. Duncan died suddenly in 1928, and Mary, at loose ends, accepted the proposal of an Indianapolis suitor, a handsome and promising University of Michigan athlete and science major, Clifford Wilson, of whom her father had approved.

Left on his own during college, Ted supported himself by working during the summers as a tobacco stemmer, shoeshine boy, and dining-car waiter and Pullman porter on the Pennsylvania, Illinois Central, and Louisville and Nashville Railroads. He learned there to dispense "brownskin service," what passengers came to expect as an "inseparable part of the cars," the porter's "gentle smile, his accommodating service, his diplomatic technique and his wide geographical knowledge."[8] In June 1928 Poston graduated and headed by train and ship for New York, where he moved in with Ulysses and Sybil and helped his brother on the *New York Contender*, now a Harlem campaign sheet that Ulysses resurrected with Democratic Party money during the election seasons of 1928 and 1932 ("Poston of the Post").

In early 1931, Ted was writing a column, "Harlem Shadows," for the black *Pittsburgh Courier* while providing brownskin service — "the best it can be done," says Allison Williams, a Hopkinsville cohort — on the railroad and immersing himself in A. Philip Randolph's drive to unionize railroad workers. In April 1931 Ted got a steady job on a Harlem weekly, the *Amsterdam News*, where he met the man who would become his lifelong best friend, Henry Lee Moon. Moon and Poston joined a group of twenty-two intellectuals, including poet Langston Hughes, on a trip to Russia in 1932 to make a motion picture on American race relations. That project was aborted when premier Joseph Stalin, seeking American diplomatic recognition for the Soviet Union, decided to refrain from offending the American government with a racial exposé.

Ted was city editor of "the *Amsterdam*" in 1935 when New York's leading news columnist, Heywood Broun of the *New York World*, bandied about the idea of starting a reporters' union. Being paid twenty-five dollars a week for his unlimited hours, Poston asked Broun whether the fledgling Newspaper Guild would include Negroes. Of course, said Broun. Ted exclaimed, "That's my kind of union!" and helped Broun get it off the ground.[9] Ted proceeded to organize the whole *Amsterdam News* staff, to the fury of its inept owner, Sadie Warren Davis. When Davis refused to recognize the union as her staff's bargaining agent, the staff went on strike. All of Harlem's clergymen and many white reporters from downtown Manhattan joined Poston, Moon, and Broun on the picket line. A comely petite Harlemite, Miriam Rivers, taken in by the glamour of it all, fell under the spell of the exciting strike leader and in November 1935 became the first Mrs. Ted Poston.

In December the strike was settled. Davis, unable to pay her creditors, had to sell the paper, and the new owners fired Poston and Moon. The two scrambled to qualify for relief and then wrote on black New York history for the Federal Writers' Project.

In 1936 Poston began contributing humorous pieces to the *New York Post*, mostly concerning the antics of Harlem characters. The respected *Post* was probably his newspaper of choice because of its liberal political bent and because the publisher, J. David Stern, a former underremunerated reporter himself, had unionized the *Post*'s editorial staff when the American Newspaper Guild was formed. Moon, the more staid of the journalistic friends, considered himself the perfect *New York Times* man and tried to get on that paper's staff, but it was not ready to hire a Negro for other than the freelance work Moon was already doing, despite its editorials on the importance of equal employment opportunity.

City editor of the *New York Post* Walter Lister held no special brief for blacks. He sought good writing and accurate reporting, and Poston offered both. When Ted had applied for a job in 1936, Lister brushed Poston aside, saying, "Well, bring me a front-page story for tomorrow's paper and we might use you on a by-the-inch basis." Poston complied, then went on to catch the flavor of Father Divine, the numbers racket, and other Harlem scams. His stories frequently appeared on page 1. So many of his articles appeared — some with byline, some without — that the copyboy, Paul Sann, one of whose jobs was to measure freelancers' inches — mentioned to Lister that Poston was earning more on a space-rate basis than he would on staff, so Lister hired Poston full time. Thus, in 1937, a black man first joined the staff of a mainstream newspaper.

Poston's marriage to Miriam Rivers disintegrated nearly as quickly as it began. The flurry and fun of the strike wore off, incompatibility replaced bliss, and the Postons were divorced by 1940.

During that pivotal year editor Robert L. Vann of the *Pittsburgh Courier* engaged Poston to tour the South, with Billy Rowe as photographer, to investigate how Negro educational institutions and businesses were faring. In the popular series that resulted — many of the articles appeared in both the *Post* and the *Courier* — Poston's former sometimes frivolous tone was tempered by a more dignified style.

On the southern trip, he and Rowe met and profiled some of the race's outstanding men, such as Robert Russa Moton, Tuskegee Institute's head. In September 1940 the *New Republic* published a long piece, "You Go South," about the southern trip. Poston was fast becoming a black power in the press, noted for writing positive yet accurate articles on blacks that simultaneously educated whites on black culture.

Following his work on the Federal Writers' Project, Moon had relocated with Robert C. Weaver to Washington, where Secretary of the Interior Harold Ickes had begun putting Negro "advisers" in place in various branches of Roosevelt's New Deal government. The traveling Poston and Rowe visited Moon in Washington, where Poston impressed Weaver and Dr. Will Alexander, President Roosevelt's informal consultant on racial affairs. As a result, while Ted filled the pages of the *Pittsburgh Courier* and the *New York Post* and war loomed, Alexander and Weaver (with nudging from Moon) invited Poston to join Weaver's staff as public relations staffer on the National Defense Advisory Commission. In that capacity Ted could pressure industrial leaders to integrate the workforce.[10]

Ted accepted Weaver's invitation. The FBI then combed every inch of Poston's trail from Hopkinsville to Harlem to Moscow and back to New York. The FBI report declared that Poston was a communist. Stunned, Ted — who had seen communism firsthand and was averse to any political *-ism* except for the New Deal — defended himself. The "informants" who had responded to the FBI's questions on Poston claimed that they had never said he was communist — that he, in fact, was very much opposed to communism. The new publishers of the *Amsterdam News* admitted to the FBI that they did not like Poston but asserted that they had never said he was a communist. Weaver and Alexander went to the Civil Service Commission and challenged the FBI report. Poston wrote an *apologia pro vita sua*. His name was finally cleared, and he became a member of Roosevelt's informal Black Cabinet (Hauke 94).

Poston was indoctrinated in the common racial indignities du jour, but, like many African Americans, he became "just accustomed to it." [11] Astute blacks learned to negotiate in both black and white worlds.

During World War II, beginning as a troubleshooter under Weaver in labor leader Sidney Hillman's National Defense Advisory Commission, Poston accompanied Weaver when he went to the War Manpower Commission. In 1943 Poston moved to head the Negro News Desk of the Office of War Information, his most prestigious government position. Southern congressmen soon halted the work of the Negro News Desk, however. They hated having taxpayers' pennies being used to publicize blacks' roles in the war effort. Poston was transferred to the White House, where he helped FDR's press secretary, Jonathan Daniels, and the president's aides for minority affairs, Dave Niles and Philleo Nash, monitor the news for incipient racial outbreaks so that the government could intercede.

Poston's bachelorhood was short-lived. On his first 1940 visit to Washington, he met and began courting a fair-skinned, convent-educated, regal and domineering civil servant on Weaver's staff, Marie Byrd Tancil. He later sent her a cartoon that showed a man saying to a waitress, "Marie, I don't come here just for the pie" (Banks interview; Lewis interview).

The flirtation was put on hold when Poston heard from the cousin of Mary Duncan Wilson, living in Indianapolis with her husband and three children, that Mary was not as happy as Ted had imagined. This news motivated Ted to travel to Indianapolis to check on his childhood sweetheart. Mary's cousin invited him, Mary and her husband, and Mary's brother's family for dinner. Ted was still enraptured by her. After dinner, Ted asked Mary to play the piano. She did, a Chopin nocturne. "Play it again," Ted begged (M. Wilson interview).

"I must have played that piece five times," Mary remembered later, and "Ted seemed in ecstasy." (Mary thought an appropriate piece for representing the turmoil in their lives was Chopin's "Revolutionary Etude" [M. Wilson interview]). There was no chance for Ted and Mary to talk alone that evening, although Mary's husband complained in later years that Ted had wanted "to take Mary upstairs to interview her" (C. Wilson interview).

The morning after the dinner, Ted called Mary from her brother's house and asked her to come over. She did. He said, "Why should we both be unhappy like this?" She explained that her mother-in-law rather than her husband was causing her grief. Poston concluded their meeting by kissing her good-bye and saying, "If you want to change the situation, let me know." Mary gave it some thought, and her husband became a wreck until she decided that for her and Ted it was just "too late"; in the ensuing years she bore two more children (M. Wilson interview). Ted returned to Washington and, as Japan bombed Pearl Harbor in December 1941, married Marie Byrd Tancil. On the dance floor, they made a handsome couple (Adams letter).

Two such high-powered individuals as Marie and Ted Poston were too much for Weaver to handle on his staff, so Marie went to the National Labor Relations Board and at war's end requested transfer to Manhattan (Weaver interview). Moon was already in New York, having departed government service in 1944 for the Congress of Industrial Organization Political Action Committee (CIO-PAC). In 1945 Marie asked Ted to return to the *Post* and bade him adieu in Washington with a "See you in New York" (Moon interview).

Poston had taken his leave of absence from the *New York Post* on 27 September 1940 and was gone for exactly five years. He returned as "somebody"—a man with a distinguished résumé. The *Post* was now owned by Dorothy Schiff, granddaughter of one of the early supporters of the National Association for the Advancement of Colored People (NAACP), Jacob Schiff.

Poston wrote to Paul A. Tierney, who had become the *Post*'s managing editor during Poston's absence, to inquire about returning: Tierney wanted Poston back. Tierney wrote to Schiff and her copublisher husband, Ted Thackrey, "Poston is a very high grade man who would be very useful to us. His government salary is $6200 a year. . . . Josephs of the *Times* is interested in him, at least $125 worth, and maybe even a little more. . . . I am equally sure Poston would be more active and happier, and feel more effective, on the *Post* than on the *Times*. . . . But the *Times*'s willingness to pay high remains a big factor." Thackrey's reply was even more positive: "I think Poston would again be an extremely valuable member of the *Post* staff and I should be shocked and chagrined if we lost him to the *Times* for any reason, including salary."[12]

In 1949 Schiff brought James Wechsler, chief of the *Post*'s Washington bureau, to New York and named him editor. With Wechsler at the helm and Schiff as publisher, the *Post* enjoyed a golden age, and Poston reigned as one of its ace reporters.

In his long career, Poston covered key events in contemporary American history from the Scottsboro boys' rape trial in 1933 through the rise and assassination of Martin Luther King Jr. and the assassinations of Medgar Evers, Malcolm X, and John F. Kennedy. Interspersed with his articles on those events were profiles on personalities who peopled the American scene and obituaries on some celebrated African Americans. His first piece in this collection, the evocative "Harlem Gasps for Cool Breath of Air," simply concerns the weather in the era before air-conditioning was commonplace — a hot Depression Harlem summer night.

Poston's happiest career day was probably 17 May 1954, when bells jangled on the teletype machines at the *Post* and the words clacked out that the U.S. Supreme Court had unanimously declared segregated education unconstitutional. Poston immediately phoned Moon at the NAACP, where Moon now directed public relations. Pandemonium in the *Post* newsroom over the announcement made thinking impossible. Poston leaped on his desk and shouted, "Will you niggers be quiet so I can write this story?" He was always trying to help whites get the feel of what it was like to be black; he took advantage of the new legal equality to try out on his peers the normal appellation to which he was accustomed.

During 1956 exciting, insightful descriptions came from Poston's typewriter concerning the Negro in New York and the Negro in Alabama. Poston's headquarters in Little Rock in 1957 for the Central High School integration story was the home of L. C. and Daisy Bates, publishers of the *Arkansas State Press*. Daisy Bates says that Poston used his bedroom at her house as his office. For that reason the Bateses renamed that bedroom "Ted's Post" (Bates 165). One of the integrating young people in Little Rock, Carlotta Walls LaNier, remembers Poston as "a caring person, laughing eyes, with a raspy voice. If he had been on radio or TV, I would have likened him to Edward R. Murrow — by his approach, carriage, professionalism" (LaNier letter).

Assignments often took Ted away from New York, much to Marie Poston's displeasure. The marriage disappointed her even more because as much as they wanted children, they failed to reproduce. During one of Ted's trips in 1956, Marie reached an intolerable level of exasperation, hired a moving van, and abandoned their Brooklyn home, taking most of its furnishings. In his subsequent retellings of her departure, Ted would say she left him "nothing but one chair to sit upon."[13]

With his second marriage ended, Poston at fifty was captivated by Ersa Hines Clinton, an assertive, confident woman of thirty-five whom he married in August 1957. Ersa, like her predecessors, enjoyed the glamour of Ted's life and associates, but since she was as talented in her field of personnel management as Ted was in journalism, her career was soaring at a time when his was leveling off.[14]

Poston was involved in a journalistic experiment using a black columnist when the *Post* engaged baseball star and civic activist Jackie Robinson in 1959. Wechsler and Schiff had already asked Poston to write a column, but he rejected the offer. He had been a columnist for the *Pittsburgh Courier* in 1931 and had disliked the terrible pressure of coming up with fresh ideas for columns regularly and on schedule.[15] When Robinson spoke to Poston of his desire to write a column — on general topics, not just sports — Poston took the ballplayer to meet Wechsler and Schiff with some sample columns that Schiff found "charming and moving."[16] So the *Post* contracted to pay Robinson one hundred dollars a week for three columns, which the *Post* would syndicate, splitting equally with Robinson any new proceeds.[17]

With the advent of the 1960s, the *Post* was restructuring and changing its focus. Schiff tinkered with her editorial management. She switched Wechsler from editor to editor of the editorial page and columnist, while Sann continued as executive editor. For the next four years, Poston functioned under a cloud when Sann put his protégé, Alvin Davis, in as managing editor and Davis decided that the *Post* had crusaded for Negroes long enough. For four prime years, then, it seemed that Davis relegated Poston's work to the back of the paper.

Poston was still writing but his articles were not all being published. He composed two long memos to Sann on how blacks were being handled under the new managing editor. One concerned "some of my ideas and the future of the *Post*," which Sann had requested. Sensitive to Sann's feelings, Poston prefaced his remarks with, "I hope my observations and opinions are accepted in the spirit in which they are given — a sincere desire to help the paper which has given me a pretty good living over the years, and, needless to say, the paper which I hope may give me an even better living in the future."[18]

During a three-month newspaper strike from December 1962 to March

1963, all the *Post* staff engaged in soul-searching. Schiff and Wechsler again broached the subject of Poston's doing a column. He penned some trial runs, but neither he nor Ersa was satisfied with them, so that idea went nowhere. One day in 1964, Schiff questioned Davis on why Poston had not been assigned to a particularly significant recent story on blacks and politics, as Nora Ephron remembers. Davis's disingenuous reply convinced Schiff that Davis was the wrong man at the top. She moved Davis to another assignment and once again the *Post* employed a cross-section of its civil rights–minded staff to delve into black news with an emphasis commensurate with the historic times and the *Post*'s readership.[19]

Also by 1964, however, Poston's spark was failing him. Arteriosclerosis, aggravated by unhealthful smoking and drinking habits, made on-the-street and out-of-town stories difficult. Henceforth Poston did most of his work by telephone. Personality "close-ups" were more suited to his late-life capabilities.

Langston Hughes's death in 1967 seemed the final turning point in Poston's life. He produced tributes to Hughes, but then the humor and zest that had marked both men's careers seemed to be cremated with Hughes's body. The 1968 assassinations of King and of Robert Kennedy sapped Poston of his remaining drive, and the progressive hardening of his arteries often clouded his thinking and made him crankish. Ersa had been promoted to confidential assistant to Governor Nelson Rockefeller and spent most of each week in Albany. Ted resented her absence, and the couple separated.

During his last few years, Poston worked on rewrite and indoctrinated such rising reporters as Robert Maynard and Pete Hamill in how to craft a news story (Maynard letter; Hamill).[20] Poston advised journalism students to beware of myths, such as of who black "leaders" really are and whether radical blacks actually have as much power as the sensation-seeking media hint. Poston retired in 1972 and died on a dreary January day two years later. None of his large family left descendants.

Poston had found racism shocking and sought creative ways of communicating its horrors while stressing in what constructive ways people could relate. Emily Dickinson said that one must tell the truth but tell it slant. In sailing, one cannot assault a headwind straight on and still progress. In his effort to get the racial story across palatably in a generally hostile milieu, Poston told the truth slant, tacking, like a sailor, against the wind.

Today journalists who socialize with their sources are suspect. In Poston's day, fraternization was considered an advantage: one picked up leads, scoops. Before tape recorders, reporters took notes, then reconstructed "quotations." The lingo of Poston's sources' "quotes" sound surprisingly like the bilingual Poston himself — conversant in black or white English as occasions demanded. Exact word-for-word sound bite was not essential. Today, a diversion from a source's exact words is practically grounds for libel. Poston's sources, conversely, were probably grateful that Poston put their ideas in his own words, because he could be counted on to phrase their thinking succinctly and colorfully. His broad background gave him a good basis for doing interpretive reporting.

Why is Poston's work important? He succeeded despite the barriers of his times, utilizing native intelligence and race pride. His parents and older brothers, coming out of the post–Civil War years, had implanted in him the idea that education was the essential first step to career viability. Ted himself had seized opportunities. Reared as a follower of Christ, he became wary of earthly messianic claims, because he had seen, for example, how his brothers suffered disillusionment after pinning their hopes on Garvey. His journalistic ambition was based on family honor: he was scion of the gifted Poston family of Kentucky.

Surveying the American scene from his vantage point within a black skin, he took as part of his mission to register the way white people regarded him and others because of color alone. White readers did not understand that odd, undermining sensation unless someone such as he articulated it. Poston expended minimal effort on hate. He, like James H. Anderson, founder of the *Amsterdam News*, could say in the end, "I am what I am. Perhaps not what I should be, perhaps no more than you believe me to be — but at least I have tried." [21] Poston tried to use his talents to educate black and white readers and, in the process, leave a record of his period from a rare insider's posture.

Joel Dreyfuss, who had worked with Poston briefly at the *New York Post*, published an appreciation in the *Washington Post* at the time of Poston's death that captured poignantly the lonely path Poston had trod for forty years as "for long periods of time the only black reporter on any major white-owned newspaper in the country," "one experience many members of my generation have been spared." From his starting line as Harlem's talented young cub, Poston climbed the professional ladder. His news reportage was a black first draft of history. This collection is the view from "Ted's Post."

Poems

Poston's byline was "T. R. Poston" until he went to the New York Post *in 1936 and became "Ted Poston." His first writing job after college was on his brother's Democratic campaign sheet, the* New York Contender. *In the spring of 1931 the* Pittsburgh Courier *began printing his column, "Harlem Shadows," for which it paid him nothing. The difficulty of life generally during the Depression led to Poston's cynical tone in some of the verses that headed his weekly column. "Our Gift, O Magi," however, expresses the thrust of his and his family's life and work — that they wanted to contribute to the building of what Martin Luther King Jr. would one day make famous as the "beloved community."*

"Our Gift, O Magi"

Pittsburgh Courier 18 April 1931

Let white men boast this civilization,
In paradoxical equations;
Some day must come the realization
That we, too, had a gift to give.
For, left without our contribution,
They could boast naught but dissolution
Abject chaos and stark confusion —
A gory land in which to live . . .

We're quite reluctant in confessing
(Admitting it, is so depressing)
That our sole gift is acquiescing
To their cruel savagery of heart . . .
We lent our ears while Negro mystics
Urged us to be idealistic —
Even while pale mobs, sadistic,
Tore our poor black souls apart . . .

And now, sectional strife's abated
Through us, the lust for blood is sated —
For We've absorbed a nation's hatred . . .
Our gift, O Magi, to America's Mart.

Pauli Murray inspired "Age Meets Youth." An early Harlem activist, Murray would later become a friend of Eleanor Roosevelt, a student of William Hastie at Howard Law School, deputy attorney general of the state of California, an Episcopal priest, and president of Benedict College in Columbia, South Carolina. She wrote two memoirs, Proud Shoes *(1956) and* Song in a Weary Throat *(1987).*[1]

"Age Meets Youth," in "Harlem Shadows"
Pittsburgh Courier 3 January 1931

I, who am aged, met Youth tonite —
    Youth — in a stripling girl;
Youth — with Ambition, Hope, and Fight —
    Youth — with Illusions unfurled . . .

When she told me her dreams, I thought of my own
    Which were shattered in ages long past;
When she spoke of her hopes, I stifled a groan —
    To think that I'd lost mine so fast . . .

But now I'm so old . . . and she is so young —
    She's hardly twenty — no more . . .
While I, from whom Hope and Ambition are flung,
    Am decrepit and old . . . twenty-four.

The sonnet form of some Poston poems reveals his classical education. The content here is the southern African American male environment. At the time of the lynching he observed, Poston was a sophomore at Tennessee State Agricultural and Industrial College (now Tennessee State University).

"I Witness My First Lynching (Nashville, Tenn.—1926)"
Pittsburgh Courier 7 March 1931

I shrank back in the shadows of the street,
As breathlessly I watched the cavalcade,

And muttered to myself, "It is not meet
That on a night like this, one's life should fade
Into mere nothingness because some men
(His brothers still, although their skins are white)
Dare take upon themselves the right to rend
The body of this poor black Son of Night. . . ."

But even then, my thoughts were not of hate —
Try as I would, I could not cry "Revenge!"
Instead, I raised my voice and railed at Fate —
Until I heard the bloody cry, "A dinge!" [2]

And bullets sped my flight from that pale crew,
Who cried "Hey! Shoot that damn black bastard, too!"

In his high school years, Poston tended fireplaces in a house in which a white woman resident sexually abused him. She threatened to tell the home's owner that Poston had raped her if he revealed to anyone her actions. Poston related details to Allison Williams at the time and often retold the story in later years, which suggests the experience's impact on him (Hauke 13–14). In this poem, a black boy accused of rape by a white woman is chased and takes refuge in a swamp. "Manhunt Fear" was published one week after two white female train passengers lodged rape accusations against nine black teenage hoboes riding a freight car in Alabama. Poston identified with the feelings of those "Scottsboro boys."

"Manhunt Fear"
Pittsburgh Courier 4 April 1931: 10

Once I was young and fearless;
I am still young —
But I fear many things . . .

I fear the night . . .
Did you ever spend a night
In a Louisiana swamp?
In a boggy swamp blacker than the night itself!
In a stinking lowland where
Slimy black things crawl over you,
Knowing that you cannot cry out?

I fear hounds . . .
Have you ever heard a bloodhound baying
In a black bayou?
Did you ever feel the hot breath
Or frenzied claws of one
As you strangled him in
The stagnant waters of the marsh?

I fear women . . .
Even more than I fear the night — or hounds . . .
For had it not been for the lies of one,
I would still fear nothing . . .

Articles

1930s

DEPRESSION HARLEM

Ted Poston left the Pittsburgh Courier *in April 1931 for the* Amsterdam News. *His days as a columnist and poet were over. The rest of his journalistic pieces of the 1930s gave him an opportunity to vent his mounting bitterness over race. "Harlem Gasps," however, calls to mind the beauty of his town on a hot summer night. Its residents have few options for relief but exploit what opportunities they have.*

"Harlem Gasps for Cool Breath of Air on Hot Nights after Weather Prophet Orders Worse: Those with Money Go to Beaches, but the Poor and Lowly Creep to Piers and Parks to Await Morning"
Amsterdam News 5 August 1931

"Local Forecast—Fair and slightly warmer tonight. Temperature yesterday—Max. 91; min. 78."

A purring cavalcade of automobiles glides slowly through the streets, pointing for the speedways, the open roads, and the Long Island driveways—bus hawks clutter the corners, pleading with passersby to hasten with them to the cooling beaches of Coney, the Rockaways, or Pelham Bay—night club owners curse silently under their breaths as they dolefully figure their losses—and Harlem faces another hot night.

But, while one-half of Harlem flees its sweltering streets for the cooling solaces of the open roads and the beaches, a less fortunate half is doomed by circumstances to remain in the confines of those sultry lowlands where "Fair and Warmer" is a nightly curse, and a trip to Rockaway is an annual event to be anticipated and planned for in the same manner in which another group might plan a trip to Europe. So let us spend tonight, tomorrow night, or any oppressive summer night with this latter group.

Let us not think, however, that because the fare to the beach is an exorbitant sum which might better be used to visit the pushcarts on Eighth Avenue or the eternal bankruptcy sales on West 125th Street, that we are going to spend the night in a noisy backroom or the kitchen-scented parlor of a walk-up apartment. Heaven (and Father Knickerbocker) forbid! Let us leave these nocturnal prisons and journey to —

The riverfronts. The Hudson River factory piers. The Harlem canal banks. The parks — Colonial, St. Nicholas, Morningside, and Mt. Morris. The rooftops. The fire escapes. The stone stoops. The one hundred and one places where thousands of Harlemites sit nightly in search of one cooling draught of fresh air — gratis.

This must be an orderly tour, however, so let us start at the piers. The Hudson River front between 125th and 135th streets draws the greater crowds. We need not visit the Fort Lee Ferry dock or the Hook and Bear Mountain ship piers — these are for pleasure seekers who can afford to purchase their comfort. We will go to the pitch black factory piers, where at the first indication of darkness a silent and bedraggled army of Harlemites congregates, pouring in a steady stream from the side streets of the community.

Faces are indistinguishable here — forms are equally hidden until some restless person stands and is silhouetted against the glittering background of Palisades Park on the Jersey side of the river. Audible conversation seems to be forbidden. Occasionally one catches the mutter of a lover's voice — an infant cries out in its sleep — or a mother calls to one of her offspring who has strayed too close to the pier's edge.

Occasionally a small red light appears — it is not a glow worm as we first supposed. It is the fire in the pipe of one of the barge captains, who seem to spend the whole night on the small covered deck of their cumbersome vessels. After the clattering noises of Harlem, the quiet here is uncanny. It is a comparative quiet, of course. One can still hear the rumble of the electric trains in the background — the music from the amusement park across the way wafts in on the breeze, and an occasional river boat bleats discordantly without warning — but no one awakens. What is a foghorn in the ears of one who was born in a second-floor apartment on Eighth Avenue?

The Harlem River banks are different. Lights from the new 155th street driveway and the old drawbridge give the scene a faint illumination. The crowds here seem younger — a little less tired. Here and there a ukelele twangs — three or four youthful swimmers are poised on the concrete ramps preparatory to plunging into the murky waters. Nearer the bridge a mother is spreading a blanket on the bare ground as the rest of the family stands around holding pillows.

Night seems to have erased the varied odors which emanate from the river during the day. The glowing black waters give one an illusion of ultimate purity. Little parties of two and three persons, each carrying a blanket or quilt, continue to come from Seventh Avenue until midnight has passed. They will remain on the banks until 4 A.M. when the pleasant breezes will suddenly cool, and the spring-like temperature will give way to the biting winds. At 4:30 A.M. the Harlem River is deserted.

The benches in the parks — so idealized by the music makers of Tin Pan Alley — are no longer monopolized by lovers. In fact, cooing couples are a small minority of the nightly inhabitants of these narrow stretches of greensward bisected by winding concrete paths. Hundreds of families journey here nightly. Children climb over the fences and pester the few lovers who have retreated to the dark shadows under the trees in the search of solitude.

The benches are occupied by middle-aged ladies whose conversations are both animated and audible.

". . . and so I says to her: 'Your place is all right with me, Clara, but I don't see why I should make no landlord rich just to be able to say I live on Sugar Hill . . .'"

Pushcart vendors of frozen ices clutter every entrance to the parks. Their efforts to outcry each other add to the bedlam caused by screaming children, screeching automobile brakes, and jabbering elders. One of the vendors is a young lady, who cries out to us as we pass: "Get your sweet ice from a sweet girl — unmarried, too!" Despite her laughing sallies, there is a note of desperation in her voice. Too much competition is often the death of trade.

The rooftops furnish the most picturesque background. Here bedraggled tenants sprawl among the veritable forests of radio aerials like wearied travelers lost and exhausted in the wilderness of some futuristic jungle. Conversations here are usually desultory, although the roof often serves as a means of acquainting neighbors with the people whom they pass daily in their rushes to and from work. A feeble "Hot, isn't it," often leads to the discovery that this is the young lady who rushes for the Lenox avenue surface car at 6:15 every morning, or that that is the mother of those brats who are always knocking something over upstairs.

All Harlemites are not granted the privilege of spending the nights on the roofs, however. Many apartment owners forbid the practice. Not a few murders have been committed on these housetops. Marauders often use the roof as a means of entering apartments to perpetrate robberies. The use of fire escapes for resting and cooling [is] likewise forbidden by law, but the practice is prevalent in Harlem.

The most pitiable of the breath seekers are to be found in the tenement sections of the side streets. Here, gaunt-faced little tots sit and lie on the concrete stoops in front of their wretched homes — their young-old faces distorted with the discomfort of their unyielding beds. A discomfort, however, which rises to a questionable bliss when compared to the stench and vermin encountered in the crowded hovels called "home."

Here, mothers, forced to desert their offspring at the first rays of dawn so that they might support them, watch these sickly little urchins as they sleep, and possibly wonder at the life which these children must live in the future. It is from these neighborhoods that the police mark so many cards "D.O.A.," the official designation for "dead on arrival." As we pass we hear the chance remark:

". . . and when I carried her to Harlem Hospital the doctor said I had to get her out in the country pretty soon. And unless I can locate her pappy or maybe hit the numbers, I don't see . . ."

We pass on — our journey is finished — but we still wonder if the weather man has any idea what will happen to Harlem when he writes:

"Local Forecast — Fair and slightly warmer tonight."

BOXING

Poston, a natural athlete, had played on Tennessee State Agricultural and Industrial College's basketball team. At the Amsterdam News *he wrote a regular feature, "Sportopics." He was a "race man" but not to the extent of supporting the race, right or wrong. In this column he implies that a Cuban boxer, Kid Chocolate, might have thrown a fight.*

"Sportopics"
Amsterdam News 25 November 1931: 12

[. . . T]here is a pungent odor emanating from the recent fistic encounter between an Italian by the name of Antonio Cansoneri and a Cuban who was christened Eligio Sardinas [but who is known as Kid Chocolate].

[. . .] We are not the type of fight fan who yells "Thief! Robber! and Murder!" every time a black boy gets belted on the bean or loses a decision. Neither are we convinced of any innate fistic superiority of black over white. Our sole conviction lies in an overwhelming distrust of organized boxing and the necessary triumph of ability over American dollars.

Probably I am just a suspicious old man. It might be that my extended sojourn in the poolrooms and speakeasies of Harlem has removed from me my faith in human nature and robbed me of my finer sensibilities. But somehow or other I just couldn't work myself into a lather over the cute little tears which gathered in the Cuban Bon Bon's eyes when Referee Winn Lewis reached for Cansoneri's hand at the end of the fight Friday night. It may be that I've seen those tears a little too often in the last fourteen months. It may be, too, that I had a sneaking suspicion that the misty eyes and lusty hug which followed Cansoneri's victory smacked slightly of rehearsal. Else something is wrong with Chocolate.

The Kid is not a palooka. If he were, he could never have gone the route of his first 150 consecutive victories without showing it. [. . .] Yet, the lad has fallen down his last FOUR major encounters — three times, admittedly, to men who were his inferior in all departments of the game. [. . .]

Probably the fight was on the level. Probably all the other contests were on the level. But I just can't escape a creeping feeling that the Keed is becoming Americanized — which, Heaven and Harlem forbid, is the worst thing which can happen to an honest man. [. . .]

THE BLACK NEWSPAPERMAN

Black journalists started out publishing their own papers. Two black men subsequently wrote briefly for the white press, T. Thomas Fortune for the New York Sun *and Lester Walton for the* New York World *and* New York Herald Tribune. *Finally, Poston came along and held the perimeter for the onslaught of black reporters who breached the barricades following the civil rights riots of the 1960s. Because of his role in the founding of the American Newspaper Guild, the reporters' union, in 1935 and in a strike against the* Amsterdam News, *of which he served as city editor, Poston was fired. The white* New York Post *hired him and kept him until his retirement in 1972.*

Poston appreciated what the reporters inside the black press were doing and chronicles it in this background of the Amsterdam News.

"The Inside Story: Newspaper Is Mirror of People It Served Twenty-five Years"
Amsterdam News 22 December 1934, sec. 3: 3, 20

In twenty-five years The Amsterdam News has become an institution. Its friends have termed it a great one. Its enemies (and who can remain in Harlem twenty-five years without enemies?) have called it a regrettable one. None can deny its existence and its power in the community it serves.

The Amsterdam News is powerful. But only as Harlem is powerful. For the newspaper is not only a mirror of the community, a voice for the otherwise inarticulate, it is the embodiment of Harlem itself—its successes, its failures, its hopes, its disappointments, its beauty, its squalor. The strength of Harlem has been the strength of The Amsterdam News. Its impotence the impotence of its unofficial organ.

Whatever success, if any, has come to The Amsterdam News during a quarter of a century has not been accidental. The paper has existed, skirted disaster innumerable times and thrived solely because it has never entertained illusions about itself. It has realized at all times that it was of the masses and not above them. It has recognized the fact that to lead, one must be able to follow; that the problems of the average Harlemite as an individual were the problems of The Amsterdam News as an institution. Only in fighting for the community could it fight for itself.

The Amsterdam News has fought against the impoverishment of the community because the paper itself has known poverty. It has attacked discrimination and exploitation on all fronts because it has suffered from both for a quarter of a century. It has constantly exposed the evils of the community in the sincere belief that in cleansing Harlem it could cleanse itself. It has ever clamored for recognition for Negroes, for only through this could their organ be recognized.

And through it all The Amsterdam News has tried to be honest and consistent with its supporters and itself. It was among the first to demand recognition of the race on the New York City police force. And it was among the first to attack both Negro and white officers when the community suffered from police brutality. It has always favored Negro representation in elective and appointive offices, yet it has never hesitated to strike at any

Negro office holder who betrayed the trust placed in him. It has fought unrelentingly for the right of Negroes to work in the stores they support, and has openly opposed the leaders of racial groups who tried to turn the movement into a racket.

The paper, over a period of twenty-five years, has supported Republicans, Fusionists, Democrats, Socialists and Communists in movements designed to better the condition of the Negro, and over the same period it has opposed Republicans, Fusionists, Democrats, Socialists and Communists when the welfare of the race seemed threatened. In twenty-five years The Amsterdam News has made scores of enemies. Over the same period it has made thousands of friends. It has not always been right (or how could it represent Harlem?) but it at least has attempted to live up to the self-inscribed epitaph of its founder, James H. Anderson, who wrote:

"I am what I am. Perhaps not [what] I should be, perhaps no more than you believe me to be — but at least I have tried . . ."

Three men, none of whom had had any previous experience in the newspaper field, incidentally, have played important parts in the development of The Amsterdam News. The background of these individuals no doubt contributed to the policy of the paper as an organ of the Negro masses in New York. For the men, like the paper they founded, succored and developed, had no illusions about themselves.

There was James H. Anderson, a bill-poster, bellhop, sailor, and sexton who founded the paper in 1909, established its policy as a New York City paper for Negro residents and gave it its sometimes misleading name, The Amsterdam News. Next was Edward A. Warren, the clubman, promoter, photographer and awning-maker, who financed the paper during its most trying periods. Who on three separate occasions pawned a large diamond ring so that the struggling newspaper might appear on the streets.

The third was William H. Davis, present general manager of the paper, who in his early years worked as a dining car employee, a janitor and a realtor before coming to Harlem. He had also operated a laundry in Boston, had tried his hand as an inventor. He was the only Negro to have an exhibit at the Panama-Pacific Exposition in 1915 (an automatic citrus fruit press) and had tried his hand at other enterprises. Mr. Davis came to The Amsterdam News in 1927. His task was to consolidate the gains made by the paper during its first seventeen years. He had an even harder task. It was to protect the supporters of The Amsterdam News from The Amsterdam News and to protect the unwieldy newspaper from itself.

James H. Anderson — he called himself "Sober Jim" Anderson (and he was sober in those days) — founded the newspaper. For his original capital the bill-poster had an idea, $10, a lead pencil, six sheets of blank paper, a dressmaker's table, space in a Sixty-fifth Street cellar — and a colossal nerve. His idea, nerve and friends carried him through.

For on that October evening in 1909 when Anderson first started assembling material for the weekly paper he was to call The Amsterdam News (the cellar was near Amsterdam avenue in the old San Juan Hill district and every noted enterprise in the neighborhood was called Amsterdam something or other — Amsterdam Drug Store, Amsterdam Bakery, Amsterdam Laundry, etc.), he was entering a field in which he had had no experience.

Worse still, he had picked a city in which the most capable of all Negro editors, T. Thomas Fortune, had established a paper almost a quarter century before him. A paper, the New York Age, which then was flourishing under the able direction of Fred R. Moore, two years after Fortune had released ownership. There was another rising competitor in the field, a five-year-old paper called the Chicago Defender, which was making its first inroads in the New York area. The trenchant pen of Fortune and the militant race consciousness of young Robert S. Abbott had already made a name for both newspapers among Negro leaders in New York City and throughout the country.

But it was there that Anderson's idea became his salvation. He felt that in fighting the battles and reporting the activities of Negroes from coast to coast, the Age and the Defender were covering too much territory. The former bellhop and bill-poster was convinced that the average New York Negro, while incensed over the oppression of his brothers in Georgia, Alabama and Mississippi, was more personally interested in what was happening to Sam Jones, Bill Green and Sadie Smith, who lived in the Amsterdam avenue area and with whom he was in daily contact. So he patterned his paper along these lines.

The first issue of The Amsterdam News appeared on the newsstands on December 4, 1909. It was a four-page affair, largely boiler plate which had been assembled by Anderson and two boys, Elmer Davis and Arthur G. Brookes, in the Sixty-fifth Street cellar. It sold for one cent. It appeared on the newsstands that week and it remained there, for Negro New Yorkers did not become over-excited by the initial effort of the ambitious bill-poster.

And one could hardly blame them. The first issue of The Amsterdam News was a pretty sorry affair. Its front page contained four columns of dis-

play advertisements, a two-column picture and biographical sketch of Anderson, a half column of "City Briefs," a quarter column of Y.M.C.A. notes
and two columns of "Afro-American Cullings" (editorials from other papers concerning the Negro). A full column editorial calling for support of
the new paper appeared on the back page. The rest of the paper was a
hodgepodge of boiler plate material.

But Anderson was not discouraged by the lack of response to his effort.
He merely added another positiᴏ to the others he already held. Along with
being editor, reporter, financier, advertising manager and distributor, he
became promotion manager.

His activities in that capacity became immediately apparent. Small boys
began to appear at the newsstands daily demanding copies of that "great
weekly paper," The Amsterdam News. No one troubled to trace these
young purchasers back to the kindly gentleman who gave each one of them
a nickel, bade them to purchase papers at four different stands and keep
the fifth penny for themselves. Few people sought the identity either of the
thirty-six-year-old subway rider who spent hours daily going from one end
of the line to the other. This mysterious rider would seat himself next to
another Negro, elaborately open a four-page newspaper called The Amsterdam News, read it intently for a few minutes and then leave it in his seat
when he disembarked at the next station — to wait for the next train.

But still there was no concerted rush for the newsstands. So Anderson
hit upon another idea. He became a forerunner of Walter Winchell and
instituted a "Rubberneck Column" in the ensuing issues. This column,
which carried community gossip without mentioning names, made an instant hit and immediately increased the circulation. It was not really a scan-
dal column, as those who were hit insisted, it was in fact a form of social
criticism which was recorded by the Rubberneck reporter.

For instance, he would point out that Mrs. X was seen leaning out of her
front window with a red bandana around her head. Or that Madame K had
disported herself in an undignified manner at the dance Saturday night.
He would pray for a heavy rainstorm so that the dirty windows in the home
of Mrs. Z could be washed. Or he would point out that Mr. R wasn't treat-
ing his customers fairly and so on. Naturally, the victims of the Rubberneck
shafts became indignant. A few even threatened Anderson with violence,
but this only increased the popularity of the column.

The editor then initiated another feature. He approached his friend, the
Rev. Richard Manuel Bolden, then pastor of Mother A.M.E. Zion Church

on Eighty-ninth Street, and persuaded him to contribute a weekly sermon to the paper. The minister also allowed Anderson to sell the paper at the church every Sunday. As the circulation increased rapidly, the price of The Amsterdam News was raised to two cents.

The paper did not get a solid foothold, however, until 1910, when Anderson followed the uptown influx and moved his offices from the San Juan Hill district to Harlem. In 1910 the Irish and Negro residents of Harlem were just reaching a truce after more than five years of bloody conflict occasioned by the colored "invasion" of the section. Scores of Negro residents had been brutally beaten by the renegade groups of the dreaded "Kelly Gang": colored pedestrians at the time had been forbidden to walk on Seventh avenue and at least one Irishman had been killed by bricks thrown from rooftops by retaliating Negroes during this period. Although The Amsterdam News arrived in Harlem during an armistice in this guerrilla warfare, the violence was destined to break out with fatal results in the next decade.

Anderson was given desk space in the newly opened offices of Attorney J. Frank Wheaton at 17 West 135th street. In these same offices at that time was a rising young attorney, Ferdinand Q. Morton, who in later years was to become civil service commissioner and leader of Negro Democrats in New York City. Neither the young attorney nor the editor of the struggling little newspaper could foresee the bitter differences which were to arise between the paper and the prominent politician twenty years later. Neither could Ferdinand Q. Morton know that he was to be one of the best known contributors to the twenty-fifth anniversary issue of The Amsterdam News.

For Morton and Anderson both had their problems in those days. The former was fighting hard to make a bare living and the latter was doing his best to finance a rapidly-growing newspaper which, despite its mounting circulation, was running more and more into debt. Anderson was not a newspaper man. Neither was he a very good business man. So he was never able to create the necessary balance between circulation and advertising so necessary to the success of any periodical.

It was there that Edward A. Warren came to the rescue. "Easy Ed" Warren they called him because of his many contributions to struggling Harlem enterprises. Even before The Amsterdam News moved to Harlem, the clubman-promoter had been advancing weekly sums towards its expenses. He continued this practice for several months until he realized one morning that he had invested more than $2,500 in Anderson's dream.

To protect his own investment and to continue the paper, Warren formed a corporation, divided the stock with Anderson and took over the active management of The Amsterdam News. After a few weeks he closed his other enterprises and set out to learn something about this new business on which he had staked his future. He learned a lot during the next few months. And before his own personal popularity and shrewd business acumen finally placed the paper on a sound footing, Warren was destined to invest so heavily in the newspaper project that, on three occasions, he was forced to pawn a large diamond ring in order to meet the mounting debts of the paper.

But Warren possessed what Anderson had lacked — business ability. And in less than a year he had secured the quality advertising needed to assure the paper of financial success. So The Amsterdam News expanded. Its staff now had fourteen people. George W. Harris, a brilliant young Harvard graduate, became editor. Anderson was managing editor, Warren treasurer and business manager. Others included Elmer G. Davis, advertising manager; Romeo L. Dougherty, sports editor; John E. Robinson, assistant to the editor; George A. Marshall, photographer; J. Hannibal Thomas and Alex Douglas, circulation managers, and Oscar O. Thomas, traveling agent. Cyril V. [Briggs] and Richard P. Nichols were added to the staff.

Also E. J. Walters, Jersey City agent; Miss Armintha A. Hodsden, bookkeeper; Miss Vivienne A. Ward and Miss Carita V. Owens, stenographers. Dougherty and Miss Hodsden (now Mrs. Armintha A. Thorne) are still on the staff. Harris later founded the New York News, became alderman, ceased publication of his paper and then revived it. Miss Owens (now Mrs. Carita V. Reane) is at present superintendent of the Harlem office of the State Employment Service.

By 1916 the paper outgrew its 135th street headquarters and moved to its present office at 2293 Seventh avenue. From that day to this the newspaper advanced as Harlem advanced. The history of Harlem from 1916 to 1934 is the history of The Amsterdam News over the same period. When the community was prosperous, the paper was prosperous; when lean days fell on Harlem, lean days fell on The Amsterdam News also.

The influence of the paper as an organ of the people was demonstrated a few years after it opened headquarters on Seventh avenue. The Negro soldier had just returned from France and the old animosity between the Irish and colored people of Harlem had been revived. There were several minor clashes at first and then a Lenox avenue incident brought the smoldering feud to a head and threatened the community with one of the bloodiest race riots in its history.

A street car motorman and a Negro soldier had an argument at Lenox avenue and 134th street. The motorman struck the soldier with an iron lever and knocked him from the car. When the street car made a return trip from the barn at 147th street, more than 200 Negro ex-service men had assembled at 135th street to seize the motorman. Seeing the crowd, the white man leaped from the car and fled to the basement of the 135th street library. The ex-soldiers, armed with captured German pistols and their own sidearms, closed in on the building. While more than a hundred of them lined up outside and repulsed the police reserves, others went into the building to find the motorman.

Powerless, the police summoned Ed Warren and begged him to rescue the doomed man. Warren rushed to the library but arrived too late. The motorman had been cornered and stabbed eighty-seven times. He died the next morning in Harlem Hospital.

Incensed by the slaying, the remaining Irish residents of the community prepared to drive the Negroes from Harlem. News stories and editorials in the Harlem Home News (now the Bronx Home News) further incensed the whites. Negroes, remembering their years of oppression and exploitation, decided not to wait for the blow to fall. So, arming themselves with every deadly weapon they could secure (including several captured German machine guns), they prepared to take the offensive against the Irish. Bloody warfare seemed inevitable.

It was then that The Amsterdam News exhibited its power. Rallying the leaders of the community, the paper pointed out the dire consequences of violent action and begged both sides to desist. A mass meeting was held at the Lafayette Theatre at which George Harris pleaded with the Negro residents to give up their plan to wipe out the whites. Warren personally approached the leaders of the ex-soldiers and persuaded them to halt the movement. The threat of bloody warfare hung over the community for several weeks but finally passed. The influence of The Amsterdam News had been definitely established.

The paper met its first disaster in 1921 when Edward Warren dropped dead. He had suffered from high blood pressure for several years, but his death was unexpected. When he crumpled to the sidewalk in front of the offices, the diamond ring which had saved The Amsterdam News on numerous occasions was still on his finger. The stones, reset, are worn to this day by his daughter, Mrs. Odessa Warren Morse, who with his wife, Mrs. Sadie Warren, inherited his stock in the newspaper.

It was upon the shoulders of Mrs. Warren that the burden of continuing the newspaper fell. For eighteen months after the death of her husband she turned over the active management of The Amsterdam News to others. T. Thomas Fortune wrote its editorials, Jesse Shipp became managing editor, John E. Robinson was appointed editor. Nichols became business manager. Louis Garcia reported sports and George Arthur became theatrical editor.

This haphazard arrangement continued until November, 1922, when Mrs. Davis secured the services of William M. Kelley, first as advertising manager and later as editor-in-chief. Under Kelley, an experienced newspaper man who had worked on Pearson's Magazine, the New York News, the New York Dispatch, and the Champion Magazine of Chicago, The Amsterdam News made its greatest strides. Dougherty returned to take over sports and theatricals and Jack Trotter became advertising manager. In 1926 Kelley hired Miss Thelma E. Berlack, a graduate of the department of journalism at New York University. Miss Berlack became society editor and assistant managing editor of the paper.

William H. Davis purchased the stock of Anderson in 1927 and became general manager of The Amsterdam News. He immediately began to institute constructive policies, which not only affected The Amsterdam News, but Negro-owned newspapers throughout the country. Davis was one of the first men in the field to insist upon accuracy in circulation figures and to base the advertising rates of his paper on these figures computed by the standard Audit Bureau of Circulation.

Davis also has done much to eliminate the racketeering elements in Negro journalism by insisting upon raising the salaries of editorial employees on The Amsterdam News to the point where they would no longer be forced to accept gratuities from outsiders for stories appearing in the paper. The general manager instituted a modern system of bookkeeping on the paper and sought to consolidate the gains made during its reckless growth in Harlem.

During the Elks' convention in New York in 1927 The Amsterdam News experimented with a daily paper which proved quite successful. Kelley resigned from the staff in 1933 and was succeeded by Obie McCollum, city editor, who had served under the editor for five years. Under McCollum, the present editor, the paper has entered its latest stage of development. The paper now has forty-five active employees.

James H. Anderson founded The Amsterdam News as a New York City paper for Negro residents. For twenty-five years it has remained such. It has succeeded only as Harlem as succeeded. It has failed only where the community has failed. The past of The Amsterdam News has been the past of Harlem as its future will undoubtedly be the future of the greatest Negro community in the world.

RUSSIA

Poston, Henry Lee Moon, Langston Hughes, and Dorothy West were among the twenty-two black Americans invited to Russia in 1932 to make a movie on American racism. Poston and Moon were furious when the expedition came to naught. In later years, Poston turned the events of that summer into a titillating oral narrative.[1]

"Poston Thrilled by Sell-Out Editions in Moscow and New York"
Editor and Publisher 20 April 1963: 146, 148

(*Editor and Publisher* Editor's Note: Ted Poston, a Negro staff reporter of the *New York Post*, told this story recently at the 15th Headliner Banquet at Lincoln University in Missouri when he accepted a human relations citation for his newspaper.)

Last March 4, while eight other New York dailies still remained in darkness [on strike], I received an unusual thrill. For the second time in my long career, I found myself working on a newspaper which actually sold out every copy of a full day's run to a news hungry public.

The first time this happened to me was more than 30 years ago. And since it happened in the Soviet Union, I think I should hasten to assure you that the FBI has since looked into the whole matter, and is willing to testify that I have always been a loyal American — albeit a newspaperman.

Being a little bit younger and much more adventurous then, I joined my long-time friend, Henry Lee Moon, now director of public relations for the NAACP, in a journalistic journey through Europe. Armed with imposing credentials from the *Amsterdam News* and the Associated Negro Press but with no expense accounts nor cash expectancies—we set out to see how the other half of the world lives.

And, after working our way through France and pre-Hitler Germany, and anywhere else where any solvent publications were willing to buy the free lance opinions of two unexcelled experts on the Great American Depression, we found ourselves eventually in Moscow.

And to our surprise and consternation, we found our arrival there created a bit of an occasion. The late Anna Louise Strong, an early Soviet sympathizer, was then editing the *Moscow Daily News*, that country's only English language daily at that time, and Moon and I were promptly invited to become managing editor and makeup editor for one day's edition.

Of course we knew that it was a propaganda stunt, but the bait they offered us was too tempting. For anything that anybody did to that four-page English language tabloid was bound to be an improvement.

Up until that historic day, for instance, the *Moscow Daily News* had never had a front page streamer. Their picture reproductions were passable, but their choices of pictures had been rather mundane. We were reliably informed that the nearest the *Moscow Daily News* had ever come to "cheese cake" had been a stirring picture of a tractor being delivered to a collective farm in the Ukraine.

And even Anna Louise Strong had been mystified by some of the paper's practices. There was the time, she recalled, when they had carried a three-line item on the front page about coal production in the Ural Mountains. And the next day's issue had devoted three full pages of a four page tabloid to a retraction of the three-line item.

"Some day," she confided to me and Moon, "I expect the paper to carry only one story. It will be a simple statement saying: 'Our last issue was a mistake; excuse it please'."

But undaunted even by this, Moon and I set out to meet the challenge. We waded into the Tass copy and came up with a gem. We made it the *Moscow Daily News'* first streamer headline: JIMMY WALKER FORCED OUT AS N.Y. MAYOR. (Of course they changed it later to read: DANCING JIMMY, CAPITALIST DOG, KICKED OUT. But they let it remain a streamer.)

We dug up single column cuts of Jimmy Walker and his bride-to-be, Betty Compton, and balanced off the bottom of page one — at Anna Louise Strong's insistence—with a three column feature on a rally in Union Square for the Scottsboro boys.

But, all in all, though, it was a one day sensation. And Anna Louise Strong rushed to the Mininskaya Hotel the next morning to tell us that our issue of the *Moscow Daily News* had enjoyed the first complete sell-out in the paper's history.

"I'm sure it is because of the new English classes they've started in the Red Army and the secret police schools," she said. We modestly accepted her compliments.

So it came as quite a shock to me and Moon three days later when we discovered that the Moscow outlet for the Soviet Fish Trust was located next door to the offices of the *Moscow Daily News*. And that on the day our great triumph came out, the store had received a record shipment of fresh fish for immediate sale.

How were we to know that the Soviet experiment had not advanced so far at that point that neither wrapping paper nor shopping bags were available to fish-hungry customers?

So last March 5, I hastily checked the Fulton Fish Market and other New York outlets after the *Post* had made its first complete sellout in ending the almost three-month news blackout. And I was assured that not a single one of our 666,000 copies had been purchased for such nefarious purposes.

SCOTTSBORO BOYS

In this piece, Poston compares a theatrical reconstruction of the Scottsboro Boys' trial to the real thing; for him, the theatrical drama caught the suspense, trauma, and horror of the actual courtroom.

"You Don't Have to Go to Decatur to Witness the Scottsboro Trial; It Is Held Here Nightly"
Amsterdam News 28 February 1934

(*Amsterdam News* Editor's Note: T. R. Poston was The Amsterdam News representative at the third trial of Haywood Patterson at Decatur [Alabama] three months ago. In the following article the writer compares the characters and court scenes of the Theatre Guild's new play by John Wexley, "They Shall Not Die," with the prototypes from which they were drawn.)

Without endangering one hair on your head, without involuntarily cringing before the baleful stares of hundreds of bloodthirsty whites, without biting your tongue to keep from crying aloud at horrible injustice you are witnessing, it is now possible for you to attend the trial of Haywood Patterson and the other Scottsboro boys.

Patterson is being framed and tried nightly at the Royale Theatre on Forty-fifth street, where the Theatre Guild is presenting John Wexley's new play, "They Shall Not Die." For obvious reasons, the guild will not tell you that you are witnessing the story of the Scottsboro cases. The names of the characters have been changed — slightly. The scenes of the action have been shifted — a few miles. And a program note tells you that the play is the outgrowth of Mr. Wexley's "own observation of the South, brought to focus by recent events there."

But you, or any other reader of the newspapers of the last three years, will not be misled. You will know that Haywood Parsons is Haywood Patterson, that Cookesville is Scottsboro, that Dexter is Decatur and that every character in "They Shall Not Die" has a prototype in actual life.

And you, and every other witness of the stirring drama on Forty-fifth street, will leave the theatre with the same feeling of choking bitterness and soul-searing horror that the writer carried from the small courtroom in Decatur in December of last year. Except that you know that this thing has actually happened, you will be moved to mutter: "Such things could not be. Human beings could not do this thing. This is the twentieth century. We are civilized . . ."

For the horror of John Wexley's drama is almost unbearable at times. As unbearable as is the infamous Scottsboro case itself. The courtroom scene, which the writer was assigned to compare with the actual happenings at Patterson's third trial in Decatur, is dwarfed by the brutality of the first scenes in which you witness the deliberate but hysterical framing of these innocent youths whose only crime was color and existence in a system which ruthlessly destroys its weaker members — be they black or white.

After that first act laid in the jail [. . .] at Scottsboro, the director mercifully grants the audience a ten-minute intermission. But ten minutes are hardly enough. When the distressed spectator finally returns to his seat, he finds that he has not recovered — may never fully recover — from what he witnessed in that first scene of "They Shall Not Die."

Anything which happens later is necessarily an anticlimax. And no play, less true, less forceful, less significant than John Wexley's drama could have survived that opening scene. But this does survive, primarily because it is not a play. It is a picture of life, of our times — stark, brutal, savage, but a true picture, not of what can happen, but of what has actually occurred.

But this is not a review. It is to be a comparison of the trial scenes of the Theatre Guild's play with the actual trial scene at the last Decatur arraignment, and a comparison of Mr. Wexley's characters with their prototypes. [. . .]

It is easier to compare the characters. [. . . T]he Haywood Patterson of the Wexley play is not the Haywood Patterson the writer met in the dingy bull-pen of the rickety Decatur jailhouse and watched in the Morgan County Circuit courthouse. The fearless, embattled extremely intelligent youth of the stage is a character created almost entirely by the author. Patterson was intelligent, he possessed a certain boyish defiance, he resented his position, but he was little like the character admirably portrayed by Al Stokes at the local theatre.

Neither was the Leibowitz of the Royale the Leibowitz of Decatur. Although Claude Rains skillfully imitated the defense counsel's voice, and in most cases delivered the latter's exact words taken from the court records, the actor at no time really imparted the vibrant personality of Samuel S. Leibowitz. And the Lord's Prayer summation, which is still discussed reverently by every Decatur Negro who heard it, is just another theatrical speech in the mouth of a self-conscious Thespian.

The Victoria Price of Linda Watkins falls somewhere in the same category. In the frisky, very affected prosecutrix of the stage, one misses much of the physically repulsive, vindictive and guilt-revealing witness, who could hardly await the proper question before pointing to "that defenunt thar" in Judge Callahan's court.

On the other hand, the Scottsboro boys, with the exception of Haywood Patterson, were so very much the Scottsboro boys that the writer found it almost impossible to distinguish between the excellent young actors and the real characters in that sordid drama of the South. [. . .]

There will be a fourth Scottsboro trial. It will probably be held in Decatur next fall. But if you don't care to wait that long or to run the personal risk of attending it, you may witness the whole arraignment, and more, at the Royale Theatre any evening.

"BELOVED COMMUNITY" IN HARLEM

An innovative Harlemite finds a way to do good. Poston describes a typically American rugged individualist working effectively for the benefit of his fellow citizens. Unusual for Poston, this article also decries directly what the race sees as placid indifference of whites to black struggles just to survive. Poston ends by comparing Joe Elder's ideals to those of Jesus Christ and Karl Marx, the only reference to Marx found in any of Poston's writings.

"Shantytown: Harlem Riverfront Settlement Is Real Community Center"
Amsterdam News 25 August 1934: 9, 15

Way back during the Depression [. . .] they devoted reams of copy to Joe Elder and his National Negro Boat Terminal at 133d street and the Harlem River.

New York dailies, the Herald Tribune, Sun, News, Post; national magazines, the Literary Digest and Time, and many other periodicals devoted columns of space to the unique community on the Harlem riverfront, where hundreds of jobless men, under the benevolent direction of Joe Elder, carried on a communal existence and beat the Big Bad Wolf from their shanty and houseboat doors.

Supercilious white writers, unconsciously expressing their gratification that members of their own group were different, described the daily routine of Joe Elder's commune and "praised" the residents of the shanty settlement for their industry, ingenuity and resourcefulness. Equally supercilious Negro hacks, aping their white masters, wrote too of the ramshackle community, its outer squalor, inner beauty and its struggling inhabitants.

But none of them — at least none whose clippings are pasted in Joe Elder's voluminous scrapbook — have described the magnitude of the undertaking, its ramifications, the extent of its influence in the neighborhood, the real character of its residents and the philosophy of its patron saint, Joe Elder, musician, mechanic, sage and humanitarian.

They are not to be blamed for this, however. [. . .] For, as the Sage of Shantytown himself put it as he discussed the project with this writer aboard the largest barge, a 110-foot barn-like covered affair:

"You can't really describe it. It's too big. It reaches too far and in too many directions. It's so much more than four barges, a few ramshackle cabins, and a couple of hundred men. It's even more than a community house for the east side, a meeting place for the people of the neighborhood, a recreation center for their children, a new starting point for the down-and-almost-outers. It's —," he searched vainly for the proper word and shrugged futilely when he failed to find it. "It's just too big."

And Joe Elder is right. You can't really describe it. Oh, anyone can paint a word picture of the four abandoned barges, with five little houses built on their rough decks, of the floating barn-like boat which contains a real community house with playground apparatus for children, dance floors for elders, assembly hall for neighborhood clubs and winter sleeping quarters for the 200 men who live in the settlement. Of the broken down trucks and little shanties which house the summer residents, and of the apparent squalor which greets the eyes of the morning commuters who pass the city on the New York Central Railroad daily.

Yet, who can describe the fierce pride of the residents, their primitive independence, yet advanced interdependence upon their community efforts? Their scorn of relief agencies (none of the men has applied for or accepted city relief). Their resentment at being called "bums" (each resident practices his own trade or has created a self-supporting trade of his own) or the implication that they are poverty-stricken (more than half of the men have postal savings accounts). Who can describe all this in a mere newspaper article? No one. It is a thing to feel when you talk to the men, and, having felt it, you go your way, knowing in your heart that you really can't describe it to others.

The National Negro Boat Terminal, the name given it by Joe Elder six years ago when he founded the place as a possible terminal for small yachts and boats which he hoped Negroes would buy (but which, of course, they never did), is located at the foot of 133d street, just off upper Park avenue. It is known now, more truthfully, as the National Negro Civil Association and has an itinerant population of about 200 residents, with only two family groups — Joe Elder, his wife, and two children, and Mr. and Mrs. William Smith. The other residents, who live on the river bank in the summer and in the large covered barge in the winter, are all men.

The community is strictly communal and self-supporting. The men ply their trades when they have one and when there is an opportunity (There are electrical engineers, trained mechanics, carpenters, pipe-fitters, brick masons, house painters and artists in the group.) and pool their resources and finances in building the community itself. Where the men are untrained they have created their own trades. Most of them have rigged up little pushcarts with which they scour the city for discarded materials, old shoes, clothes, paper, rags, metal, automobile tires, motor parts or whatever they can find. They sell most of these articles for cash and turn the rest into the community "treasury." In the winter they cut firewood from two deserted barges given Elder by the government and peddle it from their pushcarts.

The men have divided themselves into small groups and each group makes a "pool" from which they purchase food and feed themselves. In the summer they cook for the most part under the towering structure of the New York Central Railroad; in the winter on the covered barge and in the cabins. When a member becomes sick the others care for him until he recovers. They bathe at the 134th street natatorium and most of them heed Joe Elder's advice to "save a little" by opening small accounts in the postal banks. When they have accumulated enough or secured regular jobs they move away to rented rooms or apartments to make room for others. The yearly turnover of the community is almost fifty per cent, but the population always ranges from 150 to 200 persons.

In their spare time the men help Joe Elder in installing the comforts of home on the barges. Three years ago Elder installed his own electric plant which lighted all the boats. It was made from an old automobile engine and a generator purchased from the city. It operated successfully until last week, when an inspector objected to the wiring and caused its builder to rip out the lines. The boats have their own water closets, installed by a Tuskegee Institute graduate who was a temporary resident; kitchen sinks, an ornate drinking fountain (they buy their water from New York City and pump it to each barge) and kerosene cooking stoves in each cabin.

Four large oil paintings adorn the latticed inside walls of the 110-foot covered barge which Elder calls the "community house." These paintings, skillfully executed and cleverly lighted, were drawn by Arthur Tucker, a non-resident, but other paintings, on the large barge and in the other cabins, were executed by itinerant artists. There are three pianos on the barges and cases full of books in Elder's home. John Galsworthy, W. Somerset Maugham, S. S. Van Dine, Laura Jean Libbey and others are represented in these files.

The activities of the community are by no means confined to the residents, however. The place is in truth a community center for the upper east side. Children make use of the playground apparatus. Grown-ups seek the summer cool on the barges and civic and political groups hold mass meetings in the large assembly hall. Democrats, Republicans, Communists and others have met there. [. . .] A children's party this year brought more than 200 youngsters there from Sugar Hill, upper and lower Harlem and gave impetus to the Parents Club which is being sponsored by the founder.

The community value of the settlement is attested by letters of endorsement which Elder has been given by [such people as] James H. Hubert of the Urban League, [and] Roy Wilkins of the National Association for the Advancement of Colored People. [. . .] So wide are these activities that Elder has been trying to find backers to purchase the old Y.M.C.A. building on 135th street as a new community center.

One hesitates to essay a description of Joe Elder, the kindly, almost saint-like little musician who neglected his profession and started this settlement six years ago. The founder himself will give you little help. "Ask the people of the neighborhood," he'll tell you. "Find out what they think of Joe Elder. That's what really counts." Probably the best indication of the kind of man Joe Elder is, however, may be found in the fact that he, the founder, possesses no more, and in many cases, even less than any other member of the settlement. Others have postal savings accounts. Elder has turned every cent of his earnings back into the settlement.

And now it seems that his sacrifice may have been in vain. For the National Negro Boat Terminal (or the National Negro Civic Association) is threatened with destruction. White commuters, passing the site daily on their trips from and to their comfortable suburban homes, have complained to the Dock Department that the settlement is an "eyesore." They have enlisted the aid of the Outdoor Cleanliness League, a white organization, who are attempting to wipe the community out.

Their efforts seem to be bearing fruit. Officials of the Dock Department have visited the place and are considering closing it. The light inspector has complained of the electric wiring. Police have been stationed for hours on the scene despite the fine record of the residents. (There has never been an arrest nor a serious disorder in the settlement during its existence. Recently, William Smith and three other residents risked their lives to capture a murderer who had strangled and assaulted a woman on upper Park avenue.)

And Joe Elder, for the first time in six years, is becoming discouraged. He suffered a serious accident which incapacitated him for several months last spring. He has fallen slightly behind in the rent he pays the city for the site. He has received almost no support from Harlem, the community he sought to benefit, and he is beginning to be troubled by the future of little two-year-old Alice, his daughter, and little eleven-months-old Jacob, his son. Only through them can Joe Elder think of himself.

Harlem still can save the project for which this unusual little man has given six of the forty-five years of his life. Readers could deluge the office of Commissioner of Docks John McKenzie at Pier 1, North River, with letters showing the value of the settlement to the community. Clubs and other organizations could find Joe Elder's assembly hall more novel and practical for their affairs than many of the halls and ballrooms they now patronize. A visit to the place will convince anyone of the necessity of such action.

But whether or not Harlem proves itself ungrateful again, as it has done in innumerable instances, Joe Elder has built himself a monument which time cannot destroy. He has helped thousands of men to regain their self-respect. He has given hundreds of oppressed people a brief moment of relaxation. He has momentarily lightened the dreary childhood of scores of Harlem youngsters. And he has proved that at least two men, Jesus Christ and Karl Marx, were not merely impractical dreamers.

RACE RIOT 1935

A journalist as historian on the scene, Poston lays out the background of the Harlem riot of 19 March 1935. This is Poston's last story for the Amsterdam News *and the last to appear under the "T. R. Poston" byline. For unionizing the staff, he and Moon were fired by the paper's new owners.*

"One Year Ago: Next Thursday Is First Anniversary of Harlem Upheaval"
Amsterdam News 14 March 1936: 13, 19

One year ago Thursday a 16-year-old youth walked into the S. H. Kress store on 125th street and attempted to steal a 10-cent pocket knife. Had Lino Rivera accomplished this act undetected it is possible that this story might never have been written.

It is possible also that five persons, now dead, would still be living; that $500,000 worth of Harlem property would not have been destroyed, and that New York City would still have regarded Harlem as an interesting Negro Mecca of night clubs, house rent parties, shuffling tap-dancers and mammy singers.

On the other hand, it is equally possible that more people might have died, that more property might have been destroyed, and that stolid New Yorkers might have been shocked even more by the events which followed reports that Lino Rivera had been beaten to death and his body hidden in the basement of the 125th street store.

For serious students of the March 19 outbreak insist that no "riot" occurred. Rather, they say, it was an economic upheaval, a spontaneous outburst, a smouldering resentment which burst into flame when a spark was applied to the powder barrel of exploitation and discrimination which characterized the daily existence of a large sector of the community's 204,000 Negro residents. And any spark, even more trivial than the exaggerated Rivera incident, might have caused a similar outbreak.

This opinion was supported by the Mayor's Commission, thirteen prominent Negro and white citizens appointed to probe the upheaval while hundreds of reserve policemen still made Harlem an armed camp. The commission held open hearings at Heights Court—heated, boisterous hearings in which an indignant public participated.

And when the smoke of bitter charges and recriminations had cleared away the Mayor's Commission and all New York City knew what thousands of disillusioned Harlemites had known and resented for decades—what was in the minds of hundreds of usually law-abiding citizens of the community when they stormed through the streets of Harlem on the night of March 19—what one of their number epitomized at the corner of 128th street and 7th avenue when he seized a brick, aimed it at a large plate glass window and yelled: "This is for Scottsboro!"

The probing body found out that Harlem, instead of being a Negro Mecca, was really a metropolitan concentration camp with colored citizens hemmed into a restricted area and exploited by unscrupulous landlords and employers; that similar discrimination and segregation extended to every quarter of their daily existence—in their schools, home relief bureaus, in their relations with the city, state, and federal government, in their fruitless search for jobs.

The commission found out that Negro citizens had been subjected to a minor reign of terror by the police, that their civil rights had been ruthlessly violated, that unarmed suspects had been beaten, killed by men sworn to uphold the law. It was testified that politically, socially, economically, the Negro's existence here was so circumscribed that an upheaval, outburst, explosion of some sort was practically inevitable.

The findings of the commission were given widespread publicity. New York City, the state, the country took on a new "Harlem consciousness." And progressive leaders of the community expressed the hope that something beneficial — a Negro New Deal perhaps — might emerge from the chaos and confusion which was Harlem on the night of March 19.

Were their hopes justified? Who can say?

Surely many subsequent developments in the community were influenced in part, if not wholly, by the events of that hectic outburst.

The housing situation, for instance. Hardly had the echoes of the upheaval died on the streets of Harlem than Governor Lehman presented his 13-point housing program to the Legislature — a program designed to protect the rights of tenants against unscrupulous landlords and to abolish the firetraps and hovels which had claimed so many lives in this and other communities.

The Assembly sought to temporize on this legislation, but finally, faced with a proposed rent strike of 5,000 Negro tenants sponsored by the Consolidated Tenants' League, the two houses passed and the governor signed several of the important measures. These included the much-disputed multiple dwellings law which calls for the immediate demolition or renovation of thousands of New York City firetraps.

And on July 2, 1935, three months after that fateful night, Mayor LaGuardia announced that the federal government had appropriated $4,700,000 for the construction of a Harlem low-cost housing project. The effect of this project, now the subject of heated debate in the community, is problematical, but no one will hardly deny that its authorization was influenced somewhat by the events of March 19.

Then there is the school situation. For years militant, but widely-separated, groups had attempted to call attention to the disgraceful educational conditions in the community, to the antiquated buildings, the lack of facilities, the discrimination against Negro teachers, the lack of representation on important bodies.

Those conditions still obtain, but Harlem is no longer fighting for improvements on widely-separated fronts. A direct product of the revelations of the Mayor's Commission, the Provisional Committee for Better Schools in Harlem is now presenting a united front for changed conditions in the community and will hold its first important conference on March 19 (the anniversary of the outbreak) at St. Martin's Chapel, 230 Lenox avenue.

And already results are in sight. Mayor LaGuardia has approved the construction of two new school buildings in Harlem for 1936 — the first in twenty-seven years.

The home relief picture has changed somewhat too. Although the individual budgets of Harlem clients are not believed to have undergone any changes as a result of the upheaval, Negro relief workers have been given more recognition during the past year. Where on the night of March 19 Mrs. Vivian Mason[2] was the only Negro administrative head of a local bureau, two others, Edward Wilson and Henry W. Pope, now occupy similar positions. Mrs. Olive Streator has also been made a case supervisor, the only Negro to hold that position. [. . .]

Politically, too, the community has undergone changes in the last year. The election of Herbert L. Bruce as Democratic leader of the Twenty-first Assembly district and the almost successful attempt to name a Negro leader in the Nineteenth were undoubtedly influenced by the militant race consciousness aroused on March 19.

The job situation, however, does not seem to have undergone any appreciable changes. At the commission's hearings it was testified that local merchants, the public utilities of the city, state and federal government all discriminated against Negroes in the matter of employment. The Rev. Adam C. Powell, militant young minister; Norman Thomas, noted Socialist, and other witnesses urged the people of Harlem to indulge in widespread picketing and boycotting as a means of combatting this condition. [. . .]

It is difficult to gauge the effect of the outbreak on the police situation. Since March 19, 1935, there have been fewer reported cases of police brutality, less indignation over the reputed violation of civil rights. On the other hand, the residents of this community have seen more uniformed police during the past year than at any other period in its history. A Joe Louis fight, or any other demonstration, has been attended by displays of police strength seemingly out of proportion to the danger represented.

All in all, however, the community has been definitely influenced by the events of March 19, 1935. The Mayor's Commission agreed that the outbreak was the result of years of oppression suffered by thousands of American citizens in the greatest metropolitan center in the world. What lasting effect this upheaval will have on the future of these citizens can only be determined by their own efforts, in the ensuing years, to rectify the conditions so glaringly exposed one year ago next week.

HARLEM CHARACTER

Prophet Martin, like Elder of the riverboat shantytown, was another positive Harlem character. Poston's work, now published regularly in the New York Post, *reaches a broader, multiracial readership.*

"Beloved Prophet Martin Makes Last Plea to Harlem: Hundreds Heed Death Bed Appeal of Barefooted Giant for Burial Fund"
New York Post 20 July 1937: 12

Prophet Martin, the beloved bewhiskered, barefooted giant who preached the gospel for half a century on the street corners of America, made a last appeal to Harlem today.

Barefooted in death, as in life, his bushy head resting on a royal purple cushion, the eighty-six-year-old evangelist lay in state at the E. Florence Brown Funeral Parlor, 64 West 132d Street, today, as hundreds of Harlemites heeded a last message pinned to a box resting on his chest.

The appeal, written in his own shaking hand as he lay dying in Harlem Hospital last week, read:

"Help bury the Prophet."

Since early yesterday morning, the undertaker revealed, hundreds of persons to whom the evangelist was a familiar figure have visited the parlors and left a few pennies to answer the last appeal.

Thousands of others are expected to pay their last respects and increase the burial fund tomorrow when services are held at the Metropolitan Baptist Church, 128th Street and Seventh Avenue.

For Prophet Martin was more than a familiar figure on the streets of Harlem — he was an institution.

Habitually attired in a flowing, homespun shroud, his large brown feet unshod in snowy as well as hot weather, the tall gaunt preacher carried the Word daily to stranger places than Harlem street corners.

In gin mills, cabarets, bars and buffet flats, patrons were seldom surprised to see the "Prophet" enter, quote a few passages of Scripture, take up a small collection and vanish into the night.

Small children followed him on the streets, touching his robe for "good luck." Worried parents stopped him on corners and sought advice about their wayward offspring. Hustlers and numbers runners treated him with respect and unsmilingly accepted his benedictions.

An intoxicated white celebrant in a Harlem night club was once floored by a waiter when he attempted to tweak the flowing beard of the "Prophet."

"The Old Man was regular," a flashily dressed young man said this morning as he dropped a coin in the burial box, "[. . .] he never cussed a man out no matter what he knew he was doing."

Many Harlemites were surprised, though, that a collection was necessary to bury the evangelist. Since many gave freely to his daily appeals, the legend had grown that the "Prophet" was wealthy. It was rumored that he owned several apartment houses and that he traveled over the country in an expensive automobile.

His forty-year-old widow, Mrs. Mary J. Martin, dispelled these theories in an interview in their simply furnished walkup apartment at 106 West 127th Street.

"The Prophet never took up much money," she said, as her four grown daughters and nine-year-old son attempted to console her in her grief, "and what he made, he never kept for himself. We have been on relief for many months, and all we own is what you see in this house.

"If the Prophet had ever accepted a church, we might have accumulated something. But he felt that his call was for him to preach on the street corners, and he did that for fifty years — in twenty-eight States of the Union."

Mary Martin married Clayton Martin twenty-five years ago when she was fifteen. Their little son, Samuel, celebrated his ninth birthday last Friday — a few hours before the "Prophet" died in Harlem Hospital.

Early reports of his death, circulated yesterday, caused much indignation in the community. The story was passed from lip to lip that the evangelist had been stabbed by robbers, who found only $1 on his person.

Mrs. Martin could not account for these reports. Her husband had been ill for six months, she said, and confined to Harlem Hospital since June 20.

Martin was born in Henry County, Va., in 1851. He became a street corner evangelist in his youth and adopted his unusual garb a half-century ago. He did not wear shoes or any other footwear for forty-eight years, his widow said.

EASY MONEY

Creative down-home schemers tried to strike it rich through the "policy" or the "numbers" racket at the expense of their "homeboys" in the city. The num-

bers stories gave Poston freelance inches in the Post, *mainstream exposure, and thus journalistic power. These stories gave the* Post *sidebar pieces with color to accompany the serious Harlem rackets exposés for which Thomas E. Dewey, the 1944 and 1948 Republican presidential candidate, became famous. Now the numbers have become legal lotteries that operate throughout the United States.*

"Country Cousins Plot Cleanups in Numbers Racket: They Concoct Crooked Schemes to Get Square with 'Fixers'"
New York Post 6 September 1938

Harlem's country cousins — the boys who were left behind in Georgia, Kentucky, and points south — [are] all set to wreak vengeance on the policy racketeers who "fixed" the numbers.

[. . . T]he country cousins are going to do a little "fixing" of their own if their New York friends will co-operate.

This widespread plot, which came to light recently when several Harlemites were discussing the sudden increase in their daily mail, seems to have become a spontaneous development in such widely separated centers as Richmond, Va.; Nashville, Tenn.; Louisville, Ky.; Cincinnati, Ohio, and Atlanta, Ga. And the mail carriers might enter a protest any day now. As one fellow said:

"I start getting these letters from cats I done forgot existed, and they all say the same thing."

A typical letter, one of twelve examined (and of three received by the reporter) reads:

"Dear — —,

"You probably don't remember me, but I'm little Jim Jones who lived with you on Hayes Street. I got your address from your mother.

"I know you are wondering why I am writing you, so I will tell you. I just found out how we can make a lot of money if you will help me out. We play the numbers down here, you know, and this plan of mine is foolproof . . .

"They pay off here on stocks and bonds. Now, you all get them figures in New York an hour before they come out here. And now that daylight saving is on you get them two whole hours before we do.

"Well, here is how we clean up. You get the number up there the minute it comes out and telephone it to Mr. — — drug store. That's right around the corner from the numbers banker's house. I'll be waiting there at 3 o'clock, and will rush right over and put it on for the two of us.

"I know this can be done, for Sam Smith got a hot number from his nephew in Harlem last week and cleaned up big.

"Please get it for me this coming Friday. I'll be waiting.

"Lovingly yours,

"JIM JONES"

[. . . T]here is little new or original about the proposed plan. At one time, about ten years ago, it was worked effectively — so very effectively, old timers recalled today, that it practically wiped out the numbers game in Pittsburgh, and resulted in the introduction of policy wheels there.

But even policy bankers [. . .] learn a lesson occasionally and they have placed so many safeguards around their business until it is practically impossible to work the old racket — unless you are married to a clerk in Wall Street. [. . .]

One of the famous Harlem policy stories concerns a lowly clerk who cleaned up in the numbers game by double-crossing his boss. An old-timer recalled it today.

"I knew that boy well," he said, "but he was too crooked for his own good — and that's why he's rooming out in Woodlawn now.

"He got together with two other boys — one of 'em a janitor on one of the city papers and they doped out this racket. The porter would get the number from one of the newspaper guys as soon as it flashed in the office — even before they put it on the press.

"Then the porter would telephone it to the second boy and this one would rush across the street from wherever the policy bank was located. This clerk kid would come to the window and the boy would signal him what the figure was — then the smart boy would manage to ease a slip with it on it into the bunch he was sorting. The winning slip was always made out for one of his pals.

"He worked that business for months — the bankers was plenty dumb in them days — but finally he got too slick for hisself. He started making out the winning slip for his cousin, splitting the money two ways, instead of three, and telling his boys that he couldn't slip it in every now and then.

"The porter finally caught on to his jive and squealed to the banker when he wouldn't come across. The banker caught him at it the next day — and he won't do that no more. In fact, he won't never do nothing else no more."

But Harlem's country cousins probably never heard of these safeguards, which include a powerful out-of-town lobby to see that no figures leak out of Wall Street. And even several Harlemites insist that it is still possible to carry out the plan.

Detailed investigation by the reporter, however, convinced him that it can't be done these days.

So he is still writing stories — instead of his memoirs.

1940s

ENTERPRISING BLACKS

The southern pre–World War II milieu that Ted Poston inhabited was full of ideological ironies. In "You Go South," Poston injected a black consciousness into another white weekly, the New Republic, *but he bemoaned the passive attitudes of some African American religious folk and their failure of personal responsibility in making citizens' arrests such as he made in New York and as his brother, Robert Lincoln Poston, had made in Detroit when Robert and Ulysses Poston edited the* Detroit Contender *in 1920–21.[1] The Duke University student as well as the South's "quality colored folks" in this essay mouthed forward-thinking ideals but then failed to act on them.*

Poston and Billy Rowe — publicist for Joe Louis, partner in the Rowe-Louis Enterprises public relations firm, and columnist for the Pittsburgh Courier — *set out by train in the spring of 1940 but because of the filthy and humiliating Jim Crow car switched to Rowe's new automobile. The two men would tour the South under the* Courier's *auspices, with Poston as reporter and Rowe as photographer and columnist.[2]*

Here Poston points out how black life is improving under President Franklin Delano Roosevelt. Poston is laying groundwork for a Washington job that he will take later in the month. This piece echoes Rudolph Fisher's 1920s story that black America's hometown, Harlem, is indeed the "City of Refuge" and suggests that equal money would help overcome prejudice.

"You Go South"
New Republic 9 September 1940: 348–50

You are going South. You know what it is like because you were born there. But fifteen years in Harlem have dulled your childhood memories. Nevertheless you call your Northern-born companion aside as you board the day coach in Pennsylvania Station.

"Look, Billy," you explain, "we've got a job to do and we can't forget it. There'll be times when this thing will stick in your craw. Just keep in mind, the South won the Civil War, and we haven't got time to fight it again now. You can't get your pictures and I can't get my stories in jail or Federal Court."

Your companion is Philadelphia-born and Harlem-reared, but he sees your point. A short time later you are amiably debating the race question with a Duke University student, also en route to Norfolk. You are so engrossed in the conversation that you look up blankly when the conductor taps your shoulder just after the train crosses the Virginia line. The Duke student prides himself on his liberalism and has settled the question to his own satisfaction.

"It's only a matter of education," he is saying. "If all Nigras were as intelligent as you two, there would be no problem. He has to be treated like that. Now if you get down to Catfish Row in Charleston. . . ."

Young Duke is still defending his view when the interruption comes. The conductor is very polite. His voice is pitched so low you can hardly hear him. "Won't you please move forward?" he asks.

Young Duke flashes and starts to speak. He checks himself, however, and buries his face in his magazine after nodding an uncertain farewell. You gather your luggage and stumble forward to the Jim Crow car which has been switched on at the station. The car you are leaving is air-conditioned. Its dual seats are comfortable. It is clean and well-lighted and all its equipment is modern. The Jim Crow car is filthy. Its green-backed seats are moth-eaten. Its floor is littered with dirt and tobacco juice. Its windows are streaked with soot and its air is foul.

You stand aside as thirty-six other Negroes crowd in the car which has seats for only twenty-four. A Negro minister sits in the corner and listens intently as you try to keep your companion from making a row. Finally the conductor comes. You try to speak calmly about the car's condition. You point to the four other people standing in the aisle. You insist that something be done. The conductor interrupts. "It's the law," he says. "I don't own the railroad. I just work here."

"The law says separate but equal accommodation," you say. "What's equal about this?"

The conductor doesn't answer and you press your momentary advantage. You point out that only three white people are occupying the air-conditioned car behind you. You demand that those three be transferred and the first car turned over to the Negroes.

The conductor still hesitates, and then the Negro minister reaches over and touches his arm. "It's all right, Cap'n," he says, nodding in your direction, "they're young and don't know no better. We'll make out all right."

You turn back and the conductor is gone. Your companion curses, opens his camera bag, adjusts a flashlight bulb and steps into the other car. He snaps the near-empty coach and then snaps the Jim Crow car.

The conductor and a trainman rush in and raise hell about the pictures. Your companion ignores them and calmly dismantles his camera. When the trainman pushes toward him, a large overalled Negro steps into the aisle. "They done took the pitcher now, Mister," he says softly, "so what the hell you gonna do about it?" The trainman steps back and you address the conductor. You ask his name and tell him you are going into Federal Court. You smile inwardly when his fear becomes evident. You feel a little better. But you are not going to sue. You recall that Representative Arthur W. Mitchell of Chicago did just that—to no avail. And you have neither his time, money nor influence.

Three weeks later, though, your companion has made a hurried trip back to New York and returned with his 1939 Pontiac and a car has settled some of your early difficulties. And then one day you take the wrong detour in Virginia.

Your gas only carries you to the first filling station — a country store with a gas tank — so you pull under the shed and wait. You don't sound your horn for attention; you've learned that much. Five minutes later a white woman's face appears in the grocery window. She regards you silently and then disappears. You sit quietly for a full twenty minutes before a slate-faced white man steps from the store and approaches. He spurts a splash of tobacco juice near your front wheel and wipes his mouth on his sleeve. Then he asks abruptly: "Well, what do you want?"

"I guess thirteen gallons will be enough."

The grocer almost chokes on his tobacco cud. "You say *thirteen?* Yes, suh! Coming right up. Fine car you got there."

You recall this incident a half-dozen times during your next ten days in Virginia and North Carolina. There is the time, for instance, when you hesitate about taking your laundry to a large white establishment in Hampton.

"I don't think they wash colored clothes," a passerby says. But you are in a hurry, and overnight service is advertised, so you go in anyway. The clerk receives you courteously and reaches almost eagerly for your large bundle.

And the next morning when you complain mildly over the loss of a pair of shorts he is visibly disturbed.

"I'm really sorry about that, Mr. Poston," he murmurs anxiously, "and I'll look for it right away. You come back this evening and ask for me, Mr. Poston. I'm Ed. You just ask for Ed, and I'll have it for you." [. . .]

A few days later you are sitting in the office of C. C. Spaulding in the six-story building of the $47,000,000 North Carolina Mutual Life Insurance Company in Durham. Mr. Spaulding is not only one of the wealthiest Negroes in America, he is also one of the richest residents of North Carolina. Some five years ago, however, he stopped in a Durham drugstore for a Coca Cola. The clerk waited until he had finished his drink and then smashed the drinking glass on the counter. Mr. Spaulding remonstrated and the $15-a-week white clerk knocked him down and beat him up. The clerk was arrested and convicted — and released with a suspended sentence.

So you mention your recent experiences to the white-haired financier and he smiles at your surprise.

"You've stumbled on the basic reasons for improved relations in half of the South," he tells you. "This economic competition has become so great that it's no longer profitable to be prejudiced. A Negro with a dollar is no longer a Negro; he's a customer. And thanks to the New Deal, more Negroes have dollars down here today than ever before. I'm a banker and I've not always agreed with the various New Deal set-ups. But if you consider what it has meant to our people — even in relief and WPA — you've got to give Mr. Roosevelt credit. Even more important, though, is the Southern Negro's interest in voting — strictly a New Deal development — in trade unions, in joining cooperatives. . . ."

But soon you leave North Carolina. You head south on the Jefferson Davis Highway (it was the Lincoln Highway leaving New York). And now, too often, you find that neither money, education nor manners is enough.

You are hungry, for instance, and many miles from your next scheduled stop. You pull up behind a roadside restaurant and the inevitable Negro scullery boy comes from the kitchen.

"Will you wrap us up a couple of sandwiches and two containers of coffee to take down the road?" you ask. And the boy scuffs his shoes in the dirt.

"They don't sell you nothing here," he mutters without looking up. "They don't want you stopping around here."

You question him about other places up the road and he answers hurriedly, sneaking furtive glances back at the restaurant. There is a small place eighteen miles down the road where they will slip you a sandwich — if you will buy some gas.

You find the dingy little place and order your gas in front. The owner, a middle-aged, sunburned little man, agrees willingly enough to wrap up some sandwiches. You detect his Northern accent and take a further chance. You ask if he has a restroom. He flushes beneath his sunburn.

"I got one," he murmurs, half defiantly and half apologetically, "but I can't let you use it."

You sit still and stare at him. Then the defiance is gone. "I don't believe in all this. I'm a New York man myself. But my cracker neighbors won't let me. If they see you going in there . . ."

You hand him his gas money and put your car in gear. You don't even look back when he yells, "Hey, your sandwiches." And you are on your way again. You are still more angry than hungry three hours later when you pull into Columbia, South Carolina. There is a Negro hotel, of course, and you locate it finally after countless inquiries in the Negro section. You can describe your room before you enter it. You recognize the rickety iron bed, the cracked pitcher and washbasin, the dingy toilet on the next floor and the smelly clothes-closet in the corner. But worse still, the landlady has seen your New York license plates. So you know the room will cost you $2.50. You pay the sum without comment, however, although the best white hotels in the city advertise rooms with all modern conveniences for $1.50 up. "I know the white places only charge a dollar up," one Negro hotel owner has already told you, "but *you* couldn't go there for one *hundred* dollars. And besides, they can afford it. They have plenty customers all the time."

You go deeper into South Carolina.

A Bell telephone truck rips the rear fender from your car in Orangeburg, and a dozen white loungers surround you instantly. You are clearly not at fault and a white mechanic supports your contention. A traffic cop reluctantly upholds you, but the crowd sees only your license plates.

"Them niggers is from up New York," one hanger-on mutters. "Must still think they're in Harlem."

The district manager for the telephone company repeats it. "You're smarter'n everybody else," he tells your companion. "You're a New York boy."

He stares unbelievingly at your AAA card and threatens to go to court. Finally you pay half the repair bill because the white mechanic has warned you:

"Them New York plates won't help you none if he takes this thing to the law."

A Negro acquaintance tells you you are lucky.

"If it had been over in St. Matthews," he says, "they'd have locked you up and confiscated your car to boot."

So you leave your wrecked car in a garage and buy a bus ticket for Anderson. You sit on the long back seat with an old woman and a broad-shouldered Negro youth. The machine fills rapidly with whites. The driver comes back to the rear.

"You'll have to wait for the relief bus," he tells you. "This one is all taken."

"Is this the regular bus for Anderson?" the youth asks. The driver glares at him in silence and the youth nods.

"We got our tickets; we got our seats," he says. "We ain't coming."

The driver turns without a word and leaves. He enters the bus station and comes out with the starter and another driver. The old woman grabs her bag hastily and hurries for the door. The youth looks at you steadily. "You getting off?" he asks.

You shake your head and he grins. The drivers talk heatedly, looking through your window, but the starter shakes his head. Finally they go back into the station. Your driver returns and takes his seat under the wheel. The bus pulls out for Anderson. You breathe easier.

You talk with the youth en route and find he has just completed a six-months term on the chain gang. He isn't quite sure what the charge was.

"I'm standing on this corner in Anderson," he explains, "when this white woman gets out of her car. And this cop is standing in front of me. The wind blows her dress up and this cop breaks his neck getting a gander. He turns around grinning and then he sees me. And he says, 'Nigger, what you looking at?'"

You wait for him to go on, but he only shrugs.

"That's all what happened. But it got me six months. They said I was drunk and disorderly. And I hadn't even had a Coca Cola for more'n a year."

You leave the youth in Anderson, but his desperate bitterness follows you through South Carolina, Georgia, and Florida. You detect it in the mirthless smile of a crippled Klan victim in nearby Belton. His flogging was one of thirteen Negro outrages ignored by local authorities. You see it in the eyes of an elderly Negro farmer whose home had been dynamited. He had refused to let two white youths erect a still on his property. You feel it in the sullen voice of a Savannah porter. He had been slapped for failing to remove his hat as a Confederate flag passed in a recent Memorial Day parade.

And finally you detect it in yourself. One day you find yourself in a Florida pawnshop, examining a rack of pistols. The proprietor is puzzled when you suddenly laugh and walk out without making a purchase. Your sanity has returned and you have realized that a pistol is not the solution.

But you can afford to be sane. You will soon be back in Harlem.

LABOR ORGANIZING

The hopeful ending of "The Making of Mamma Harris" is typical of Poston's positive implication that we shall prevail. In this strong-woman story, the women lead and men follow. The Congress of Industrial Organizations and American Federation of Labor in the 1930s differed in that the AFL was a craft union, organized around specific trades. The CIO was organized throughout an industry: all the workers in one plant belonged to the same union. The CIO was more amenable to the inclusion of blacks, whereas the AFL excluded blacks as long as it could. Poston's remarkable capturing of figurative language is notable here.

"The Making of Mamma Harris"
New Republic 4 November 1940: 624–26[3]

She was a scrawny hardbitten little woman and she greeted me with that politely blank stare which Negroes often reserve for hostile whites or prying members of their own race.

I had been directed to her tenement in Richmond's ramshackle Negro section by another woman, a gray-haired old grandmother whose gnarled hands had been stemming tobacco for five decades.

"The white folks down at union headquarters is all right," she had said, "and we love 'em — especially Mr. Marks. But if you want to know about us stemmers and the rumpus we raised, you better go see Mamma Harris. She's Missus CIO in Richmond."

The blank look softened on the thin dark face when I mentioned this.

"Must've been Sister Jones," she said, still standing near the door. "They all call me Mamma though. Even if I ain't but forty-nine and most of them old enough to be my grandmammy."

I edged toward a rocking chair on the other side of the bed.

"I'm a CIO man myself," I remarked. "Newspaper Guild. Our local boys just fixed up The Times-Dispatch this morning."

She yelled so suddenly that I almost missed the rocker.

"Bennie!" she called toward the kitchen, "you hear that, Bennie? CIO's done organized The Dispatch. Moved right in this morning. What I tell you? We gonna make this a union town yet!"

A hulking overalled Negro appeared in the kitchen doorway. His booming bass voice heightened his startling resemblance to Paul Robeson.

"Dispatch?" he thundered. "God Amighty, we do come on."

Mrs. Harris nodded in my direction.

"He's a CIO man from up New York. Wants to know about our rumpus out at Export. He's a Guilder too, just like the white 'uns."

Bennie limped toward the other chair.

"They give us hell," he said, "but we give it right back to 'em. And it was we'uns who come out on top. The cops was salty. Wouldn't even let us set down and rest. But I told the women, I told 'em 'Sit down' and they did. Right in front of the cops too. Didn't I, Louise?"

Mrs. Harris nodded energetically from her perch on the bed.

"You dead did. And they didn't do nothing neither. They 'fraid of the women. You can outtalk the men. But us women don't take no tea for the fever."

Bennie boomed agreement. "There was five hundred of the women on the picket line and only twenty of us mens. But we sure give 'em hell. I talked right up to them cops, didn't I, Louise? Didn't I?"

Finally Mrs. Harris got around to the beginning.

"I wasn't no regular stemmer at first," she said, "but I been bringing a shift somewhere or other since I was eight. I was took out of school then and give a job minding chillun. By the time I was ten I was cooking for a family of six. And I been scuffling ever since.

"But I don't work in no factory till eight years ago. Then I went out to

Export. Well, it took me just one day to find out that preachers don't know nothing about hell. They ain't worked in no tobacco factory."

Bennie was smiling to himself and gazing at the ceiling.

"Them cops beat up them strikers something awful out at Vaughn's," he said. "They even kicked the women around. But they didn't do it to us, huh, Louise? We stood right up to 'em."

Mrs. Harris waved aside the interruption.

"Then there was this scab," she went on, "only he ain't no scab then, cause we don't have no union. We ain't even heerd of no union nowhere then, but I knew something was bound to happen. Even a dog couldn't keep on like we was. You know what I make then? Two dollars and eighty cents a week. Five dollars was a too bad week."

"I put in eighty-two and a half hours one week," Bennie said, "and they only give me $18.25. I think about this one day when one of them cops . . ."

Mrs. Harris shushed him.

"Now this scab — only he ain't no scab then — he rides me from the minute I get to Export. He's in solid with the man and he always brag he's the ringtail monkey in this circus. He's a stemmer like the rest of us but he stools for the white folks.

"There's two hundred of us on our floor alone and they only give us four and half and five cents a pound. We don't get paid for the tobacco leaf, you know. You only get paid for the stems. And some of them stems is so puny they look like horse hairs."

Bennie was chuckling softly to himself but a glance from Mrs. Harris held the cops at bay for the moment.

"And as if everything else wasn't bad enough, there was this scab. We's cramped up on them benches from kin to can't, and he's always snooping around to see nobody don't pull the stem out the center instead of pulling the leaf down both sides separate. This dust jest eats your lungs right out of you. You start dying the day you go in."

She coughed automatically and continued.

"Well, I keep this up for six long years. And this scab is riding me ever' single day. He's always riding everybody and snitching on them what don't take it. He jump me one day about singing. Course, a stemmer's bench ain't no place for singing and I ain't got no voice nohow. But I like a song and I gotta do something to ease my mind or else I go crazy.

"But he jump me this morning and tell me to shut up. Well, that's my cup. Six years is six years, but this once is too often. So I'm all over him like gravy over rice. I give him a tongue-lashing what curled every nap on his head."

For a moment she had the same beaming look which Bennie displayed when he spoke of the cops.

"I sass him deaf, dumb and blind, and he takes it. But all the time he's looking at me kinder queer. And all at once he says 'You mighty salty all of a sudden; you must be joining up with this union foolishness going on around here.'

"You coulda knocked me over with a Export stem. I ain't even heard nothing about no union. But as soon as he cuts out, I start asking around. And bless my soul if they ain't been organizing for a whole full week. And I ain't heerd a peep."

"I ain't heerd nothing neither then," Bennie put in, "and I been there fifteen years."

Mrs. Harris caught another breath.

"Well, I don't only go to the next meeting downtown, but I carries sixty of the girls from our floor. They remember how I sass this scab and they're all with me. We plopped right down in the first row of the gallery. And when they asked for volunteers to organize Export, I can't get to my feet quick enough."

"I come in right after," Bennie remarked.

"And it ain't no time," Mrs. Harris continued, "before we got seven hundred out of the thousand what works in Export. The man is going crazy mad and the scab is snooping overtime. But they can't fire us. The boom time is on and the warehouse is loaded to the gills."

She paused dramatically.

"And then on the first of August, 1938, we let 'em have it. We called our strike and closed up Export tight as a bass drum."

Bennie couldn't be shushed this time.

"The cops swooped down like ducks on a June bug," he said, "but we was ready for 'em. I was picket captain and there was five hundred on the line. And all five hundred was black and evil."

Mrs. Harris was beaming again.

"Then this scab came up with a couple hundred others and tried to break our line," she recalled, "but we wasn't giving a crip a crutch or a dog a bone. I made for that head scab personal — but the cops wouldn't let me at 'im."

"I stayed on the line for twenty-four hours running," Bennie chuckled, "and I didn't take a inch from none of them cops."

"And we wasn't by ourselves neither," Mrs. Harris went on. "The preachers, Dr. Jackson, the Southern Aid Society and all the other union people help us. GWU [Garment Workers Union] and them garment ladies give us a hundred dollars right off the bat. Malgamate sent fifty. The ship folks down in Norfolk come through, and your white Guild boys here give ten dollars too."

"It was them white garment ladies what sent the cops," Bennie cut in. "They come out five hundred strong and parade around the factory. They got signs saying 'GWU Supports Export Tobacco Workers.'

"Them cops jump salty as hell. '*White* women,' they say, '*white* women out here parading for niggers.' But they don't do nothing. Because we ain't taking no stuff from nobody."

"We was out eighteen days," Mrs. Harris said, "and the boss was losing money hand over fist. But you know how much we spend in them eighteen days? Over seven hundred dollars."

Her awed tones made it sound like seven thousand.

"But it was worth it. We win out and go back getting ten, eleven and twelve cents a pound. And better still we can wear our union buttons right out open. We might even got them scabs fired if we wanted, but we didn't want to keep nobody out of work."

Bennie stopped smiling for the first time.

"We might be better off if we did," he said soberly. "I bet we do next time."

Mrs. Harris explained.

"They been sniping away at us ever since we win. They give the scabs all the breaks and lay off us union people first whenever they can. They give all the overtime to the scabs and even let 'em get away with stripping the stem down the center. But we ain't licked yet. We still got two hundred members left and we still got union conditions."

Her face brightened again.

"And we fixed that old scab — even if he is been there nineteen years. We moved him off our floor completely, and he ain't allowed to ride nobody.

"We got a good set of people downtown now and we're reorganizing right along. By the time our new contract comes up in June, we'll probably have the whole thousand."

"And if we strike again, and them cops jump salty" — Bennie began.

This time Mamma Harris let him pursue the subject to his heart's content.

POSTON'S BEST FRIEND

After World War II, Poston returned to the New York Post *and often profiled African Americans who were coming to the fore. Here he portrays his best friend, another struggler in the pre–Martin Luther King civil rights movement.*

"One-Man Task Force": Close-up of Henry Lee Moon
New York Post *7 June 1948, sec. 2: 1*

The National Assn. for the Advancement of Colored People, which has, on occasion, belted many a Presidential hopeful, has ordered all employees to refrain from politics during 1948.

The order applies to — and is welcomed by — Henry Lee Moon, the Association's new soft-spoken but hard-hitting director of public relations. But even this may not keep the ex-newspaperman, ex-housing expert and retired PAC [CIO political action committee] assistant director from being one of the most widely quoted persons in the coming Presidential campaign.

For Moon has written a book, and he wouldn't accept his new nonpartisan job until it was safe in the hands of his publishers. The volume, "Balance of Power: The Negro Vote," was released by Doubleday on May 20, and quite a few Presidential aspirants are likely to have more than a passing interest in its contents.

"It's about time they learned what Negroes actually think of them," the ex-labor politician remarked the other day, "instead of listening to the flattery of their sycophants."

And few of the candidates will be flattered by Moon's published observations, gathered during the four years he helped direct PAC's campaigns in every state where Negroes voted. In short, he has this to say:

WALLACE — "His popularity [among Negroes][4] rests more upon his pronouncements than upon his record of performance. He has captured the Roosevelt appeal without matching the performance."

TRUMAN — ". . . a historical paradox. On the record he has been more forthright in his demand for equal opportunity for Negroes than President Roosevelt ever was . . . [but] [5] the confidence which Roosevelt inspired has not carried over into the Truman Administration."

TAFT — "To most Negro citizens he is merely a streamlined Herbert Hoover — cold, aloof and indifferent to their urgent needs."

DEWEY — ". . . is regarded as having the best record or performance on racial issues, but has alienated many Negro voters. . . . A great many people of all races hold him suspect. More flexible than Taft, he is equally as cold."

STASSEN — "has set forth at considerable length where he stands on labor relations and foreign policy, but as late as Feb., 1948, had found little to say on racial discrimination or segregation."

IKE and DOUG [Generals Dwight E. Eisenhower and Douglas MacArthur] — "The bitter experiences of Negro servicemen have not enhanced their regard for Army leaders . . . As members of the top Army brass, they must share the blame for the Army's Jim Crow policies and for unforgotten indignities, humiliations, and discriminations suffered by Negro servicemen during the war."

In his small fifth-floor NAACP office at 40 W. 40th St., Moon hastened to point out that his book is not devoted solely to the 1948 Negro vote, but traces it from pre–Civil War days up to the present.

Roddy K. Moon, a retired government inspector who is now a realtor in Cleveland, wasted no time in making [his son,] the young Henry Lee[,] aware of the political facts of life. He subscribed to The Nation and brought home occasional copies of the New Republic.

"After watching the Cleveland Republican machine in action before the great aldermanic scandals," [Henry Lee] said, "and then observing the one-party system in action during my four years as press agent at Tuskegee Institute, Ala., I had a pretty good idea of what was what."

He quit Tuskegee in 1930 and entered the late Brookwood Labor College at Katonah, N.Y., although he already held degrees from Howard and Ohio State Universities. He left Brookwood for a job on a Harlem weekly and quit that a year later for a trip to the Soviet Union.

A non-Communist liberal who might well have developed into a fellow traveler, Moon, while still in Russia, denounced the Soviet rulers for their action in canceling a film which 23 American Negroes had been invited to [make]. He has never forgotten a scathing question put to him then by A. Piatnitsky, a Comintern official.

"That's a very courageous speech, Mr. Moon," Piatnitsky said, "but I wonder if you would be so courageous in Atlanta, Ga."

"Oh, does it take courage to speak the truth in the Soviet Union?" Moon shot back, and he's still proud of the crack.

He returned to the Harlem weekly, was fired for union activity, paused shortly on WPA, joined Nathan Straus' United States Housing Authority staff in Washington, and quit that in 1944 to join Sidney Hillman on PAC.

More the professor than the labor politician in appearance, the round-faced, balding, 47-year-old Moon has little patience with people who insist that there is no such thing as a Negro or a Jewish vote.

"Of course there are racial voting blocs in this country," he says. "Any group would be foolish not to try to protect its interests at the ballot box." [. . .]

He's elated at the NAACP ban on political activity.

"I've had my say anyway," he adds.

NAACP LAWYER

Thurgood Marshall (1908–93), a future Supreme Court justice, was a noted NAACP legal tactician. He persevered in pressing to remove discrimination from the law books.

"On Appeal in the Supreme Court: Portraying the Winner of a Recent Batch of Anti-Segregation Cases, Which Gave the NAACP One of Its Important Gains to Celebrate on Its Anniversary" [Thurgood Marshall]

Survey, January 1949: 18–21

(*Survey* Editor's Note: The National Association for the Advancement of Colored People, rewarded with many a victory and strong in the support of a host of Americans of all races, colors, and creeds, is marking this year its fortieth birthday. Thurgood Marshall, the subject of this sketch, is one of the organization's most effective younger leaders. He is presented by his friend, Ted Poston, a reporter on the *New York Post* for the past twelve years. [. . .])

Thurgood Marshall, who has directed the country's most successful frontal attacks on compulsory racial segregation in the last decade, believes that it was inevitable that he should finally have wound up with the National Association for the Advancement of Colored People, the organization which he serves as special counsel and head of the legal department.

"Some Marshall had to find out that he couldn't lick the world alone," he will tell you jocularly in the association's headquarters in New York, "not, of course, that my forebears didn't try."

There was his great-grandfather, for instance — brought back to the Eastern Shore of Maryland by an African big game hunter who had picked him up personally.

"His more polite descendants like to think that he came from the cultured tribes in Sierra Leone," Marshall contends, "but we all know that he really came from the toughest part of the Congo."

His great-grandfather, Marshall goes on with the story, didn't take at all kindly to slavery. He made his personal objections so strongly felt that his kindly master called him in one day and told him: "Look: I brought you here so I can't very well shoot you — as you deserve. On the other hand, I can't, with a clear conscience, sell anyone as vicious as you to another slaveholder. So, I'm going to set you free — on one condition. Get the hell out of this county and never come back." . . .

Others in the Marshall family believed in defending their rights, too, as witness Mrs. Annie Marshall, Thurgood's Irish-looking paternal grandmother.

"She was the bane of the census takers' existence," Marshall recalls. "She never knew her real name, her age, her parents, or her race. All she knew was that she had been raised by a Negro family in Virginia." [. . .]

Her big revolt came when the Baltimore courts ruled that a big utility company had the right to erect an electric pole on the sidewalk in front of the Marshalls' corner grocery store — in spite of her insistence that the sidewalk belonged solely to her since she had paid for it.

"The company's men showed up bright and early the next morning, but they hadn't counted on Grandmother," Marshall says. "She took a kitchen chair, placed it over the spot they had marked for the pole, and calmly seated herself. This went on for days and weeks and finally Granny Anne emerged as the victor of what may have been the first successful sitdown strike in Maryland."

Marshall regards his father, the late William Canfield Marshall, a writer and one-time steward at the Gibson Island Country Club, as being in a much milder manner one of the most insidious of all the family rebels.

"He turned me into a lawyer," he says, "without once telling me that was what he wanted me to be. He did this by teaching me to argue, by challenging my logic on every point, by making me prove every statement — even if we were only discussing the weather. I only realized later that he was trying to sharpen my mind, to convince me that I could take nothing for granted."

This ability to argue successfully — and prove his point — was to stand the younger Marshall in good stead in the years to come.

There was a time in 1938, during his first year as special NAACP counsel, when he was rushed to Dallas, Texas, after Dr. George F. Porter, a Negro physician, was kicked down the courthouse steps when he answered a summons for jury duty. A short time earlier, a white NAACP representative had been beaten up on the Texas capitol grounds at Austin.

Finding local feeling rather tense, Marshall wasted little time in field investigation. He went directly to Governor James Allred. When the executive got over his astonishment at the brash young Negro, he not only ordered out the Texas Rangers to defend the rights of Negroes to jury service, but also called in the Federal Bureau of Investigation to study the local situation — an unheard of action for a southern governor.

Another case in which Marshall's "gift of gab" stood him in good stead occurred in the town of Hugo, Oklahoma, in 1941. The NAACP Special Counsel showed up to defend W. D. Lyons, a Negro handyman accused of wiping out a white family of four and of setting their house on fire to conceal the crime.

The policy of NAACP is to defend accused persons only where the evidence indicates they are victims of racial prejudice. The organization entered this case because local Negroes were convinced that Lyons was framed to shield a local white bootleg ring thought responsible for the mass slayings.

Feeling ran high in the small community and Negro residents made elaborate plans to defend the then thirty-three-year-old Marshall. A different sleeping place was arranged for him each night and an unofficial guard was established to protect him.

"We really went to all that trouble for nothing," recalled one of the NAACP officials who was there. "On the very first day, the whites were so astonished at Marshall's presentation of his case that their hostility turned to curiosity. He'd hardly finished his opening statement before he had half of them pulling for him."

On the second day of the trial, the "unofficial" guard was forgotten — as were the secret sleeping places. And on the third day, the superintendent of schools declared a half holiday, so that the white high school students could go to court "and hear that Negro lawyer."

Marshall referred to the incident in another connection the other day.

"I think the Lyons case proves that even in the most prejudiced communities, the majority of the people have some respect for truth and some sense of justice, no matter how deeply it is hidden at times.

"They were shocked to learn that Lyons had been beaten at night in the basement jail; that the police had actually brought in the bones of the murdered persons and spread them over his body in an effort to make him confess. I think they secretly enjoyed seeing the cops put on the spot when the facts came out."

He smiled wryly. "The jurors were shocked, too, but they couldn't break altogether with their backgrounds. They found Lyons guilty and then salved their consciences by giving him life imprisonment. Had they really thought a Negro guilty of such a crime, they would surely have given him the chair."

The NAACP fought the case to the U.S. Supreme Court, where a hearing was refused on a technicality. Marshall had one consolation. The father of the slain white woman took up the fight for Lyons' freedom and eventually became the president of the Hugo branch of the NAACP.

The Association in recent years has scored its greatest victories in regard to educational opportunities. Through local, state, and federal decisions, it has brought millions of dollars to Negro teachers seeking equal salaries; has improved the facilities for Negro students in many instances from kindergarten to college; has forced southern states to accept responsibility for equal educational opportunities for all citizens. Through its branches it has helped abolish Jim Crow public schools in Hillburn, N.Y., Trenton, N.J., and other northern communities.

Thurgood Marshall has directed or conducted most of the work in the educational field. He is himself the son of a still active Baltimore teacher, Mrs. Norma A. Marshall. As a law student and assistant student librarian at Howard University in Washington, D.C., young Marshall did the research and participated in the 1932–33 conference with Charles Houston and William Hastie, two other noted NAACP attorneys, where the onslaught on educational inequalities in schools and colleges was planned.

During the Howard days Marshall first came to the attention of Walter White, executive secretary of the Association. In his recent autobiography,

"A Man Called White," he describes how the group tried the case by day in Virginia and planned strategy by night in the Howard Law School Library in Washington.

> It was a lanky, brash, young senior law student who was always present. I used to wonder at his presence and sometimes was amazed at his assertiveness in challenging positions by Charlie (Houston) and the other lawyers. But I soon learned of his great value to the case and doing everything he was asked, from research on obscure legal opinions to foraging for coffee and sandwiches. This law student was Thurgood Marshall who later became special counsel of the Association and one whose arguments were listened to with respect by the U.S. Supreme Court. [. . .]

The original NAACP conference call bitterly attacked lynching. Since that day the Association has fought this evil relentlessly. No federal anti-lynching bill has as yet passed Congress, but the merciless NAACP campaign has so spotlighted it in the last forty years that lynching has now been reduced to less than one percent of the 1909 figure.

The original call spoke of the disfranchisement of Negro voters in the South. Today, a few of these barriers still exist in isolated communities. But, in 1948, a million Negroes went to the polls in southern states alone, as a result of U.S. Supreme Court victories won by the NAACP in its long fight for unfettered elections. [. . .]

The association has successfully attacked other evils not envisioned by its original sponsors. Through the U.S. Supreme Court it has struck at residential segregation by outlawing the court enforcement of restrictive covenants. It has proved illegal the systematic exclusion of Negroes from juries, confessions by torture, and verdicts of mob-dominated trials.

It has pressed continually for a permanent Fair Employment Practice[s] Committee, patterned on the wartime FEPC for which it was partly responsible, and local NAACP branches have helped pass state FEPC laws in New York, New Jersey, Massachusetts, Indiana, Wisconsin, and Connecticut.

The forty-year-old Marshall, whose NAACP work keeps him flying around the country some 30,000 miles a year, has little time for outside activities. He still squeezes in a few losing hands of poker and occasional professional athletic contests, however.

"I like the movies and theater too," he said, "but I guess I get enough amusement out of my work."

He likes to recall the original Oklahoma State Court judge in the Ada

Sipuel suit. This jurist was astounded when the NAACP produced as witnesses outstanding law school authorities from Yale, Harvard, the University of Chicago, and similar institutions.

"Just before he made his ruling," Marshall recalled, "he took me aside and said: 'Those men have opened my eyes. They are the smartest people I've come across. They've done something to me right here,' pointing to his chest and heart.

"And having delivered himself of that informal opinion, he climbed back up on the bench and promptly ruled against us. Our arguments may have affected his heart, but he certainly didn't let them affect his decision."

He also likes to recall his first meeting with Federal Judge J. Waties Waring, the native South Carolinian who last year nailed the last nail in that state's "White Primary" coffin.

"When I took a teachers' salary case before him in 1944," Marshall says, "I regarded him as just another southern jurist who would give me the usual legal headwhipping before I went along to the Circuit Court of Appeals.

"Well, it turned out to be the only case I ever tried with my mouth hanging open half of the time. Judge Waring was so fair that I found my apprehensions totally unwarranted. He made his position clear and told them that the 14th Amendment was still in the Constitution and that it still prevailed, for all citizens, in his court."

Marshall's favorite quotation from his many legal opinions is Judge Waring's conclusion in killing the "White Primary":

"It is time for South Carolina to rejoin the union. It is time to fall in step with the other states and to adopt the American way on conducting elections."

The young lawyer, whose achievements have brought him the coveted Spingarn Medal and other awards and honorary degrees, has developed a definite philosophy of race relations as a result of his work.

"I think we make our greatest mistakes through generalizations and oversimplifications," he says. "We find it too easy to regard the South as all bad and the North as all good.

"Anyone familiar with the picture knows that we have made tremendous inroads in the South in recent years — particularly among the younger white people and the enlightened older ones. This doesn't mean, of course, that the battle is won; we must of necessity keep on driving. And not all efforts can be directed at the South. There is much to be accomplished in the North."

He believes too that the American people must be educated and regards his work as part of that task.

"A lawsuit," he says, "is an educational process in itself. It educates not only the defendants at which it is directed, but also the lawyers on the other side and even the general public in the area. Through such suits, many local residents realize for the first time that Negroes have rights as Americans which must be respected."

He is not at all pessimistic about the future.

"If we can keep up the educational process and legal suits," he contends, "Negroes will soon be voting in every community in the South; Jim Crow travel will be abolished, and segregation in public education will be broken down, first in the graduate professional schools, and later in the colleges and law institutions. I have no doubt that this will come to pass."

Marshall is a strapping physical specimen, 6 feet 1½ inches tall, 200 pounds, but he takes out his athletic interest as a fan at professional football and baseball games. [. . .]

Marshall has never played any sport himself — not successfully anyway. As he says,

"I gave up baseball when two sandlot teams down in Baltimore threatened a sitdown strike if either side had to accept me. I couldn't hit the side of a barn with a paddle or catch cold in a rainstorm."

He could out-argue any of his contemporaries, however — and he was a better cook than all of them put together.

"My maternal grandmother, Mary Eliza Williams, was responsible for the latter," he said. "She called me in the kitchen one day and said she was going to teach me how to cook.

"'I'm all with your parents in wanting you to be a professional man,' she told me, 'but I want to be sure you can always earn a dollar. You can pick up all that other stuff later, but I bet you never yet saw a jobless Negro cook.'"

Before entering Howard Law School, Marshall attended Lincoln University in Pennsylvania — and naturally he was a member of the debating team. While still a Lincoln student, he met Vivien G. Burey one day in a drug store, and two years later they were married. For years, he regaled friends with an account of the drug store meeting and insisted it was a case of love at first sight. Mrs. Marshall, whose nickname is "Buster," finally tired of the story and set him straight. "I really met you a long time before that, Thurgood," she told him. "It was in Harrison's Restaurant in Washington. But you were so busy arguing and debating with everybody at the table that you didn't even give me a second glance."

Since then, Thurgood has kept his arguments outside the home.

"You have a better chance of winning a decision in court," he believes.

The NAACP has won twenty-four of its twenty-six appeals in the U.S. Supreme Court and Marshall had a hand in more than half of them, was chief counsel in five of them. He is fighting for the twenty-fifth win this year as a fortieth anniversary present for his organization.

"If we can force the University of Texas to admit Heman Sweatt," he said, "we can knock down this whole theory of separate but equal accommodations — not only in schools but in other public endeavor as well.

"I believe we can do it — and so do the white students at the University of Texas. They have already organized a 200-member branch of the NAACP on the campus — and they are holding a membership card in it for Heman Sweatt."

FALSE ACCUSATION AND REPERCUSSIONS

Poston's "Horror in Sunny South," his Little Scottsboro series, provided compelling reading for New Yorkers during September 1949. It delineated the normal fear southern blacks endured daily before the legal and moral efforts for which history would credit Thurgood Marshall and Martin Luther King Jr. Citizens whose civil rights were obviated for several generations would spawn the racial militants of the 1960s.

The "chase" scenario in the third article, "Lynch Mob's Breath of Death," could be delineated only because Poston lived to tell about it. Other victims of race prejudice who did not live to tell their tales — Viola Liuzzo, Emmett Till, James Chaney, Andrew Goodman, and Michael Schwerner, for example — probably had similar experiences.[6]

In 1950 Poston won the Geist, Polk, and Broun Awards for this series. In 1951 he won a special NAACP honor, the Unity Award of the Beta Delta Mu fraternity and the Broun. The Post nominated him for the Pulitzer Prize, but it was denied. No Negro had yet won a Pulitzer.[7] In 1999 the Associated Press

*put the Little Scottsboro series at eighty-nine on its list of the twentieth cen-
tury's one hundred top works of American journalism.*[8]

"Horror in Sunny South: 'A Good Nigger'—but They Ruined Him, Too."

New York Post 4 September 1949: 3, 16

Tavares, Fla., Sept. 3 — Maybe this will bore you — especially if you read the story of Henry Shepherd [. . .] who was ruined for being "uppity."

But bear with me a moment. Rather, bear with Will Brunson.

That is how Franklin H. Williams of the NAACP put it to me as we sped in a moonless night some 75 miles from here through the swamps and wooded farmland.

"They'll scoff at your Henry Shepherd story," Williams said. "They'll tell you that the three-day outbreak of rioting in Groveland, Mascotte and other communities was only resentment against alleged Negro rapists. They'll say that Henry Shepherd only got his because he is Sammy's father — and not because he was too prosperous.

"But Will Brunson got his three weeks after the July rioting ended. Don't take my word for it. Ask Will." I did, an hour later, when we found his hidden cabin in the off-the-road woodlands. The work-ravished but still virile old man of 66 had been there — with two Negro women as his protection since his escape from Stuckey's Still (an all-Negro suburb of all-white Mascotte) some three weeks ago.

"I got the word way back in 1947 when I bought myself that new Hudson," I pieced together from his almost unintelligible drawl, "but I didn't pay it no mind then. I'd been around there for 49 years and scuffling to lay something aside for the time when nobody could take care of me or the old lady [his wife]."[9]

He had scuffled pretty well. On July 16, when a young white matron claimed she had been raped by four Negro youths, near Groveland, Will Brunson owned five of the 27 Negro houses in Stuckey's Still, the only country store, a 35-acre farm of rich cultivated farmland, with five full acres planted in already-bearing orange groves.

Not to mention a brand new tractor, a pick-up truck, his forbidden Hudson, couple of hundred chickens, and ducks, 30-odd hogs, two fine mules, 7 or 8 cows, and innumerable odds and ends of a prosperous citizen.

"I guess I should have known it that night," he said sadly. "When the white folks got through shooting up Groveland and burning down the colored houses, they came to Stuckey's Still. They shot through my windows and I tried to burrow my way through the floor into the ground.

"They shot my Hudson all to pieces; the bullet holes is still in my truck outside there. They scared everybody out into the woods, but still I didn't think this could happen to me."

The rioting died down in three days and some people came back home from the woods. And Will Brunson thought the worst was over.

"The white folks knew me well," he recalled wryly. "They knew how I'd scuffled since 1900 to get my little bit. They knew I'd grub-hoed their fields; that I had rattle snake marks on my legs I got working for them; they knew I wasn't no uppity Nigger."

But still the word came again — a week after the Groveland disorders. A note in the mailbox, a deputy sheriff's word to his wife, a cautious word from field hands in other planters' orange groves, but always:

"Get out. The white folks don't like your kind. Get out and stay out while you can."

Will Brunson wouldn't heed the word — not even when five younger Negro farmers received similar warnings and fled the community.

Then came the night last month when a car pulled up suddenly in front of his house and two white men doused the lights and jumped out.

Will fled to his nearby orange grove and peeked through the bushes as they ransacked his house. His wife, less trusting, had already fled the house days before, returning only during the days to run the store. "You can watch the hawk in the daytime," Will Brunson grinned in retrospect, "but only the hawk got eyes at night."

Not finding him in the house, the two whites procured searchlights and came looking for him in the barn. "My old mule brayed and warned me," he said, and he fled further back into the orange grove.

His pursuers' searchlights occasionally silhouetted each other and he saw the pistols in their hands. "I got so scared," he laughed bitterly, "that I found myself on the other side of a four-foot fence. I guess I ain't such a brave man at that."

His pursuers followed him through the high weeds even there and when he finally reached the road, he found the other carloads of white men waiting in ambush there.

The eerie chase continued all night until the unidentified pursuers gave up at 5 A.M.

Will Brunson got into his pick-up truck three hours later and he didn't go back to Stuckey's Still until yesterday.

"I only went to see the good white folks and I asked them what to do. [. . .] They said: 'Will, you was lucky to get out alive. If you want to stay alive, you'd better stay out!'"

Will Brunson is back in his woods. One friend did rescue his tractor and hid it out. The Old Lady has sold the pigs and cows and is bargaining (in daytime) for the chickens and other stuff.

Will Brunson is going to take the "good white folks'" advice to a point. He'd like to sell out everything, buy a little house "somewhere else for me and the old lady."

But Will Brunson doesn't intend to starve to death.

"If the white folks only knew what they've done to me," he said. "I done everything they wanted me to do, but I ain't going to starve. I starved enough when I scuffled so long; I wouldn't even buy clothes; I had a hungry gut all the time.

"Well, that gut ain't gonna be hungry no more — even if I have to let them fill it with lead."

Will Brunson wasn't joking.[10]

"Horror in Sunny Florida: Negro Reporter from Up North Put in 'His Place' by the South"
New York Post 7 September 1949: 2, 32

I know now how Negroes felt throughout the South on July 16 when blood-thirsty mobs swept through Groveland, Fla., and neighboring towns, burning and pillaging and striking terror into the hearts of thousands of helpless Negroes in the area.

I know now — personally — what it means to be chased through a moonlit Florida night with a motorized mob on your heels — and only the performance of a 1948 sedan between you and sudden death.

I know now — and I have always known, although 20 years in the North had dulled my memory — what it is to be less than a human being, to have no rights a white man must respect.

I know all this because I've just come back from Tavares, Fla., where I covered the trial of three Negro youths accused of raping a young white farm housewife.

None of this should have surprised me, for I was born in Kentucky, educated in Tennessee, and have worked and lived in a half dozen states below the Mason-Dixon Line.

And I was determined not to be surprised—in any way—when I stepped from a plane in Orlando, Fla., last Thursday morning.

I smiled at the impatience of Franklin H. Williams, assistant NAACP counsel, who met me, and jokingly chided him when he snatched my bag from an airline truck after the white attendant refused to serve me until all white passengers had claimed their baggage. (Williams was born in Flushing [N.Y.])

Williams was driving a 1948 sedan belonging to Horace Hill of Daytona Beach, the other Negro lawyer aiding the defense, and was anxious to get to Tavares, some 40 miles away, where Charles Greenlee, 16; Samuel Shepherd and Walter Irvin, 22-year-old veterans, were scheduled to go on trial an hour later.

I had no way of knowing, of course, that in just three days, this same car—and its owner's ability as a driver—would stand between me and death. (It mattered little that the mob which chased us then probably wanted Hill and Williams more. Had they caught us, I would have gone too, as would have Ramona Lowe, a reporter for the Chicago Defender.)

But that's getting ahead of the story.

Southern born and not altogether forgetful, I had not come without precautions. Williams had reserved a room for me at a Negro hotel in Orlando, but I had no intention of using it. Nor did I.

Orlando, a bustling, comparatively-liberal Florida community, is also the headquarters of the Orange County Ku Klux Klan. So if things really got tough (which I never expected), then I could at least put the klan to the trouble of searching for the three separate private homes in which I spent my nights.

On our way to Tavares, Williams summed up the principals in the courtroom drama to be enacted. First, he said, was Jess Hunter, the elderly but shrewd State's Attorney, who looked like Barry Fitzgerald but adopted the backwoods mannerisms and tactics of the late Eugene Talmadge.

When Alex Akerman Jr., the prominent white Republican lawyer who headed the NAACP defense, first brought Hill and Williams into the Lake County courtroom (the first Negroes ever to try a case there), Hunter quipped:

"Where is the other nigger prisoner?"

And later, during a pre-trial argument, Hunter had [remarked] that

"Maybe we'd better send some lawyers up to defend the darkies in Harlem."

He had flushed slightly when Williams retorted "We don't have darkies in Harlem, Mr. Hunter, we have Negroes." [. . .]

I smiled at the incident and at his description of Circuit Court Judge Futch, the presiding jurist who maintained his dignity by wearing his coat in a completely shirt-sleeved courtroom, but who whittled continuously with a pocket knife throughout the trial.

But I soon stop[ped] smiling when we reached the stately Lake County Courthouse (and jail) where an angry mob had gathered on July 16 in an effort to lynch the three youths accused of raping Mrs. Norma Lee Padgett, the young housewife.

First, there were swaggering deputies, more than a score of them, fingering their holstered pistols and glaring balefully at every strange face. But worse than the deputies were the unarmed "clay-eating crackers" whose slate-faced stares scanned the face of each of the 75 Negro spectators permitted to occupy the Jim Crow section of the courtroom balcony.

Working a running story, one becomes oblivious of this. But soon, a Negro becomes thirsty and goes to an unmarked fountain in the corridor for a drink. A furious white spectator — not a deputy — shoves you roughly aside, snarling "That fountain ain't fer niggers."

Okay, you go back in, but soon you're hungry, too.

You ask about for a restaurant and you find there's none in Tavares for Negroes. (A kindly housewife prepared us pork chop sandwiches for Thursday's lunch, but by the next day, grateful Negro mothers, hearing of the case, practically flooded the "colored lawyers" with chicken, ham, cakes and cold drinks.)

So, you shrug and accept it all. You even smile again at the "Colored Men's Room" on the first floor. But, after your first wire story over Western Union or a long distance call to your office, the word is out.

"He ain't working for one of them nigger papers," the snarling whispers ring in the corridors. "He's sending lies to one of them Communist sheets up North."

Then the little things start. A grinning cracker drops a soda bottle on your foot at the Coca-Cola slot [coin-operated] machine.

A deputy, lolling in the alternate jury box, suddenly crosses his legs as you go by, leaving his dusty footprint on your shirt.

You are jostled regularly on the stairs to the third floor courtroom, and finally one day two crackers suddenly trip you on the marble stairway, laughing when your glasses drop and break, admonishing you:

"Look where you're going, nigger."

But none of this is really important, you tell yourself. For you, it is only for a few days. You are more disturbed at the calm acceptance of such treatment by the Negroes who live there — even when they do what little they can to help "the colored lawyers."

(During jury selection, for instance, Negro spectators would slip to the "Colored Men's Room" to tip off the lawyers on prospective jurors; 50 tattered and impoverished farmers and their wives raised $58 for the NAACP Defense Fund one night after hearing Williams speak in a small country church; daily they did their best.)

Then, after three days of rationalizing, you suddenly find what keeps them submissive. It is fear and force.

You find out, personally — for the mob strikes at you.

"Horror for Sunny South: Lynch Mob's Breath of Death Scorches Reporter Fleeing Florida"

New York Post 8 September 1949: 2, 7, 8, 10, 18

How does it feel to be chased down a lonely moonlit Florida road — in a small car careening from side to side at a 90-mile clip — and with sudden death facing you from a possible collision ahead or a bloodthirsty mob behind?

Believe me, I had no desire to find out personally when I went to Tavares, Fla., last Thursday to cover the trial of three Negro youths accused of raping a young white housewife.

But I found out. And so did Franklin H. Williams and Horace Hill, Negro NAACP attorneys who defended the three youths, and Ramona Lowe, a Chicago Defender reporter.

I had only one purpose in going to Tavares. I wanted to cover the trial, and to record the personal stories of some of the reign-of-terror victims who had fled to the woods last July 16, when burning and pillaging mobs invaded Negro settlements in Glendale, Stuckey's Still, and the neighboring Bay Lake area.

And by 8:56 P.M. last Saturday night — an hour and 30 minutes after an all-white jury began deliberating the fate of Samuel Shepherd and Walter Irvin, 22-year-old veterans, and Charles Greenlee, 16-year-old itinerant worker — I thought I had pretty well served my purpose.

There had been irritations and limitations over the three-day period [. . .] but nothing that a Southern-born Negro couldn't survive, even having lived in the North for 20-odd years.

In fact, at 8:56 Saturday night, I was in Tavares' one long distance phone booth a half block from the stately Lake County courthouse trying to calm the fears of my Post Home News editors, who had not heard from me in a mere three hours: I thought they would be worried, even after such a short time out of touch with me, because I had been jostled by a couple of hoodlums on the courthouse steps the day before (that's when my glasses broke). I explained to the office that I had tried to phone twice since 5 P.M., but that the lines had been busy. And what proof had I that the lines had not been busy?

And could I explain to Jimmy Graham, my city editor, that the long distance operator had seemed a little miffed at our last conversation; that she had probably realized then for the first time that I was a Negro, and that she had committed the faux pas of calling me "Mr. Poston" for three days running.

Of course not. I had been more amused than irritated when she curtly called me "Ted" on my two unsuccessful calls later, so I merely told the city desk:

"Keep your shirt on. There's absolutely nothing to worry about. Tell Jimmy the verdict will be in any minute, and I'll be heading for Orlando — 40 miles away — later tonight."

I was still chuckling 10 minutes later when I went back to the press table (the Negro press table over near the railing) and Williams walked over from the other side of the room where he had been conferring with Alex Akerman Jr. and Joseph Price Jr., the two white Florida lawyers who had also defended the boys.

"Judge Futch wants us to get out of Lake County the minute this verdict is read," he whispered. "Neither he nor Jess Hunter (the State's attorney) want any more trouble or bad publicity. You watch the judge for the sign, Ramona; Ted probably won't catch it without his glasses."

Even then there was no alarm — Lake County had had enough bad publicity during the three-day rioting; no one was fool enough to risk any more.

The jury filed in three minutes later and Shepherd and Irvin were doomed to death while Greenlee was given "mercy," life imprisonment.

As the courtroom spectators, already warned by Judge Futch against any demonstration, received in stony silence the news that at least one of the boys would not be electrocuted, Williams and Hill walked rapidly to the door behind the judge's bench.

As four state troopers escorted them quickly down the corridor, Ramona and I started to follow, but hesitated when Jess Hunter started to address the audience.

"This verdict is the verdict of the people of Lake County," he was saying. "I ask you to accept the verdict and retire quietly to your homes."

I looked beyond Hunter at the courtroom and felt my first but momentary apprehension. The once-jammed room was half empty. Women, children and 75 Negroes in the Jim-Crow half of the balcony filled most of the still-occupied seats.

I touched Ramona's arm, guided her into the corridor—where we almost bumped into Mrs. Norma Lee Padgett, the 17-year-old housewife whose unsupported word had wrecked three youthful lives—and headed for the crowded third-floor stairway.

We became separated as Ramona preceded me down the steps through a hostile sea of white faces. I walked carefully—there was some slight jostling—but I intended taking no chances at this late date.

I reached the courthouse lobby without incident and headed for the rear door through which the troopers had escorted the lawyers, but an almost imperceptible nod from a departing Negro spectator sent me out the side door to the sprawling lawn where I heard Hill calling softly: "Ted?"

He had turned his 1948 sedan around, double-parked it in the wrong direction on a one-way street, doused his lights but kept his motor running. I walked swiftly across the shadowy lawn, between two of the towering royal palm trees surrounding the courthouse, and jumped in the front seat. The car was already moving.

But suddenly Frank Williams asked: "Where's Ramona?" I realized then he was on the back seat alone and opened the door to go back. Horace Hill stopped the car, but put out a hand to restrain me. "Wait a minute. . ." he stated.

"Don't argue now, Horace. Let him go," Williams snapped and Hill turned around to face him.

"Look, Frank," he spoke soberly but quickly, "you're not in New York now. These clay-eating crackers aren't joking. I know; I wasn't born down here for nothing—"

They were still arguing as I ran swiftly across the lawn again, cursing both Ramona and myself under my breath, but refusing to admit my own growing fears.

I found Ramona in the lobby, calmly talking to James Shepherd, elder brother of one of the doomed boys, and apparently oblivious of the hateful stares of the dozen white men. As I approached, Ramona cried:

"The sheriff won't let him have his car back." (James' 1942 Mercury had been a state exhibit.) "He told him to come back Tuesday—"

I ignored Ramona and spoke to James Shepherd. "You got a way to get back to Orlando tonight?" I asked. He nodded, saying "Mr. J. P. Ellis of the NAACP is—"

"Well, take it. Now." I cut him off, firmly guiding the still-protesting Ramona towards the side door. "But we can't leave him like that, Ted—" she was saying until I snapped shortly:

"The hell we can't. Come on."

Hill was really angry as we raced back to the car, although his anger had some of the quality of the fear I was admitting to myself for the first time.

"Now you've done it," he said, as Ramona scrambled through the single far-side door and I took my seat beside him. "The state patrol escort's been gone 10 minutes with the others. We'll never catch up now!"

With our lights still doused, we pulled around the corner and headed for the Orlando highway. For 10 minutes and two miles out of Tavares Hill cursed us for the "damfoolishness" which had made us miss the escort. Even Williams said at one point:

"You both should have thought of our spot. After all, we were the lawyers. They blame us for getting Greenlee out of the chair. You both might have had a chance, but not the first Negro lawyers to ever appear in Lake County Circuit Court." [. . .]

Williams started to say something, but another car suddenly appeared behind us and shot ahead, blinking its lights three times. (Even now, I can't recall whether this car had been following us or whether it dashed from one of the many dirt side roads.)

Simultaneously, [. . .] two parked cars lighted up and started diagonally across the highway. The one on the left swerved swiftly back towards the side however as Hill, stepping on the gas, drove straight towards it and almost sideswiped the signal car as we shot ahead of all three.

The other car righted itself and all three dashed up the road directly behind us, two of them almost abreast.

Williams and Ramona peered anxiously out the rear window as Hill— the sedan was now making 83 miles an hour— caught up with and passed three slow-moving cars ahead, executing an almost perfect "S" as he shot by the first on the left, the second on the right and the third on the left again.

Williams reported softly that one of the cars had remained on our tail during the whole intricate maneuver and had lost only a few yards in the process. The other two were dropping slightly behind. We were on a short straight stretch and the speedometer climbed slowly past 85.

"I think he's picking up a little bit, Horace," Williams reported, adding softly: "This might be it, after all."

Ramona was sobbing, muttering, "Oh, God. It's my fault. I got you into this. It's my fault. I should've — "

I yelled "Shut up!", more to quiet my own fears than her moaning voice. [. . .]

I was left alone with my thoughts.

What were they? How can you tell? Really scared people don't think much of anything, but getting away. You try to deny the existing situation. You tell yourself "It's only somebody trying to scare you" and you close your eyes and nurse the thought even when you know it isn't true.

You curse yourself, of course. You recall that you really didn't have to be in this spot. Hadn't the city desk three times turned down your request to cover Florida's "Little Scottsboro Case?" But, oh no, you wanted to be a big shot.

Then your anger shifts to your pursuers — even if it is only a cover-up for your stark fear? What right have they to chase you, to kill you — to make you kill yourself?

And suddenly you open your eyes to find yourself hurtling forward in a stygian blackness, lighted only by the reflection of pursuing headlights in your own rear-view mirror. You are on a long straight stretch of highway and Hill has cut off his own lights, trusting only the light of the Florida moon.

And only when Williams yells: "Straighten up, Horace!" do you realize that not only are you plunging through darkness at 85 to 90 miles an hour, but that the car is also zig-zagging from side to side on the road. Hill explains succinctly:

"Getting closer. Might shoot at tires."

You picture what this will mean and your fright is almost paralyzing. But suddenly you see the lights of Apopka, a bustling rural village, up ahead. [. . .]

The green of the first of Apopka's three traffic lights is visible only as a blur to my weak eyes, but as we shoot towards it the blur turns to red.

"For God's sake, stop, Horace," Williams yells from the back seat. "If we hit some of these crackers —"

But Hill only muttered "Naw" and sent the car hurtling through the light and the country town at 80 miles an hour, scattering a few pedestrians near what appeared to be a movie house, and missing by inches a pick-up truck which crossed our path at the third traffic light. [. . .]

No one said anything, but Hill pushed the car back up to 90.

Williams spoke again: "I got a good look back there in Apopka. There's three on the front seat. One is bare-headed."

[. . .] Williams' voice, almost detached in its seeming calmness, went on.

"I really believed that pickup truck saved us," he was saying. "One of the crackers was leaning out the front window just before we passed it. I'm sure he was aiming at our tires or this back window one . . . I believe that skidding knocked him out."

Ramona was looking out the back window. [. . .] None of us was prepared for her sudden scream:

"They're not back there now," she was yelling, "they must have turned off. They're not back there any more."

Williams fumbled for a match in his side pocket. Hill glanced briefly at the rear-view mirror but didn't slow down a bit.

Two minutes later, we hit the city limits of Orlando.

Well towards the center of the city, Hill headed the car to a lighted curb and parked.

We looked at each other in silence. There was no elation, no release from the fear which still gripped us. [. . .]

Williams broke the silence:

"Drive over to Akerman's office, Horace," he said. "We've got to get to work on that appeal."

"Horror in the Sunny South: Ted Poston Tells Neighbors' Story of Truth behind the Florida 'Rape'"

New York Post 11 September 1949: 4, 20

What really happened on a lonely country highway near Groveland, Fla., between 2:30 and 3:30 A.M. on the morning of July 16?

Willie Padgett, a 21-year-old white dirt farmer, says that four Negro youths started out by helping him push his car which was stalled and ended up by "kidnaping" his 17-year-old wife.

Mrs. Norma Lee Tyson Padgett says that the four Negro boys drove her away into the night in their own car, stopped and debated whether they should rape her near the lighted windows of another white farmer's house, and finally carried her to a secluded spot many miles away where each criminally assaulted her.

I listened to the couple — a petulant blonde with a jutting chin, and a callow youth whose long face, and protruding buck teeth give him the incongruous appearance of a grinning Buster Keaton — as they told their stories in the Lake County Courthouse at Tavares, Fla., last week.

And as a staff correspondent for the New York Post Home News, I heard an all-white jury condemn Samuel Shepherd and Walter Irvin, 22-year-old veterans, to death in Florida's electric chair, and Charles Greenlee, 16, an itinerant worker, to imprisonment for life.

The "Guilty, so say we all" verdict was made although the three-day trial record contained not one bit of evidence to support Mrs. Padgett's story. [. . .]

To get a reasonable story — at least one more reasonable than the case presented by State's Attorney Jess Hunter — I went first to the voluminous files of the National Assn. for the Advancement of Colored People, whose two Negro lawyers, Franklin H. Williams and Horace Hill, had made the first on-the-spot inquiry into the case.

Then — with either Williams or Hill or some local driver at the wheel — I drove many miles nightly through that citrus grove area to talk to individual Negroes and "the good white folks" to whom they referred me, in an effort to find out what really happened.

And I got a story [. . .] which the NAACP wished to develop further when its lawyers vainly begged Circuit Judge Futch for a delay in holding the trial.

[. . .] Norma Lee Padgett is a Tyson. The Tysons are a large and influential family in Lake County, Fla., and the name is spoken of with the same awe that a Kentuckian might employ in mentioning a Hatfield or McCoy.

"Few white men and no niggers at all would dare mess with the Tysons," a "good" white man told me one day in the very shadow of the courthouse. [. . .]

Well, Willie Padgett — whose dirt-farming relatives are classed locally as "clay-eating crackers" — married a Tyson, the 17-year-old Norma Lee, a favorite in the far-flung Tyson clan.

But the marriage didn't work (Mrs. Padgett attested to this in court after her husband had intimated a state of uninterrupted connubial bliss) and

Norma Lee went back to her father while Willie remained on his mother's farm in the same Bay Lake area.

Such was the court-admitted situation on July 15 when Padgett drove over to Norma Lee's house and persuaded her to go to a square dance with him that night in Clermont, Fla., some 20 to 30 miles away.

Celebrating on the way, he bought a half pint of liquor (she testified it was a full pint) and then went to the dance where, (again her testimony) he spent the evening drinking at a table with his estranged wife and his own in-laws. One person who attended the dance told me:

"Willie spent a lot of time fluttering around Norma. He sure seemed like he was trying to get back in his happy home."

The dance broke up at 1 A.M. and Padgett set out to drive Norma home. Enroute, he testified later, they changed their minds and decided to drive to Okahumpka — a town some 20 miles away — "to get something to eat."

They changed their minds again while on the way, he said, and stalled their car in trying to turn around on the narrow road. That is when the Negro youths came up, Padgett insists, and the start of the "kidnapping" and subsequent "rape."

Other Lake County residents — white as well as colored — tell it differently. They point to court testimony that the Padgetts drove through Groveland enroute to Okahumpka and made no effort to patronize the better all-night diner in that town — a normal action for a hungry couple.

They contend that Padgett, determined to effect a reconciliation with his estranged wife, drove not only through Groveland but also past the turn-off road to her father's farm.

They charge that, parked momentarily in a driveway off the road, Willie Padgett attempted to claim his "husbandly prerogatives," and was repulsed by his wife, who leaped from the car and fled after the resulting scuffle and fight.

Knowing the temper of the Tysons, this group contends, Willie became frightened when he couldn't find his wife after searching frantically in the dark, and then came back to his car.

According to the court record itself, he drove back through Groveland, the nearest town, and then on to Clermont where he told Curtis Howard, a filling station attendant, that "something has happened."

And what occurrence could more easily divert the anger of the dreaded Tysons from the husband to another source than a report that four Negroes had "kidnapped and raped Norma?"

Not that Padgett dared to tell the Tysons even that story himself. In his sworn testimony he reported the alleged "kidnapping" to a state patrolman, and then persuaded Howard to drive him home to "change my clothes." There is no court record that he informed the Padgetts of what had happened to Norma — at least not in his testimony.

Ironically, the same filling station attendant found Norma Lee walking down the same highway early the next morning, and the local papers reported that "she ran away" from the attendant — a white man.

Howard drove back and got Padgett and the two returned and finally persuaded Norma Lee to return to Groveland. Arriving there, all three reported that Mrs. Padgett had been raped — and a 17-year-old country girl found herself the "heroine" of the most exciting incident in Lake County history.

There is conjecture in any reconstruction of what happened on that country road on July 16. But there is no conjecture about what happened to Samuel Shepherd, Walter Irvin and Charles Greenlee soon after their arrest that same morning.

"Horror in the Sunny South: Unmerciful Beating Is Lot of Negro Arrested in Florida on Rape Charge"

New York Post 12 September 1949: 2, 17

What happens to a Negro arrested for rape in Florida, the 27th state to join the Union? Ask Samuel Shepherd. [. . .]

Ask Walter Irvin. [. . .]

Or ask Charles Greenlee. [. . .]

You'll find Sammy and Walter in the state prison death house at Raiford. There's no hurry about seeing Charles Greenlee. He's there for the rest of his natural life — unless the NAACP wins a continuing fight to save all three.

All three will be glad to tell the story which Circuit Judge Futch refused to let them tell in court. (Ernest Thomas, 27, a fourth suspect, never got a chance to tell his story. A mob of "deputies" shot Thomas' body into an unrecognizable bloody pulp 10 days after Mrs. Norma Lee Padgett, a white housewife, had allegedly been raped on July 16 — a "rape" which, incidentally, was never proven in court.)

Let Samuel Shepherd tell you, in his own words, what happened immediately after three carloads of white deputies and state patrolmen grabbed him and Walter at Irvin's house at Groveland that morning of July 16.

"They drove us four or five miles in the country — in the woods off a clay road. They took Walter out of the car and started to beating him and asking about this man's wife, and then they took me out of the car and whipped me up, too. They whipped me with their fists and billies. They must have beat us about a half a hour. . . ."

And what was happening to Irvin at the same time?

"One short guy in plain clothes who had a pistol belt grabbed me and hit me with his billy a lot of times across the head. He held me and a lot of others started to hitting me with billies and fists, and knocking me down and kicking me and picking me up and knocking me down again.

"When they were beating me, they said to me: 'Nigger, you the one that picked up this white girl last night.' I said to them, 'What white girl?' They said 'You might as well tell us you're the one did it, 'cause we gonna beat the hell out of you until you tell us you did do it . . .' but as far as I remember I always told them I was not the one . . ."

Getting no confessions they, the deputies, threw the boys back in the cars and headed for the more secure fourth-floor jail in Tavares. Walter recalls: "I was bleeding pretty bad mostly from my head . . . they made me sit on the edge of the car seat to keep from getting blood on the seat . . ."

But what of the "safety" of the Tavares jail? Charles Greenlee was there. Arrested as a hitchhiker 20 miles from the scene of the alleged rape at the approximate time that the reputed crime was being committed, he had already been cleared by Willie Padgett, husband of the alleged victim, who had viewed him in his cell in Groveland and said: "That's not one of the boys; no, he's not one of them."

But Greenlee had been carried to Tavares for "safe keeping" anyway. [. . .] Greenlee speaking:

"One of the men said: 'Boy, I believe you lying.' I said no. He told one of the other three to handcuff me. He handcuffed my hands up over my head to a pipe. My feet were just barely touching the floor. Then two men began whipping me with a rubber hose . . . They hit me across my back and legs and face. I was bleeding all over — my arms, face and all was bloody.

"As I was fixing to get in the elevator, the tall man he kicked me. I got in the elevator and turned around and faced him and he kicked me again (in the groin) and it hurt so bad I kneeled down on the floor. Then they put me in my cell . . ."

Shepherd and Irvin also arrived at Tavares and they soon learned what "safe keeping" means too — in the same jail basement. Walter said:

"They taken me down first . . . They handcuffed me over a pipe so that my feet couldn't touch the floor, then they started beating me again with a rubber hose . . . I was bleeding all the time around my head."

They handcuffed Shepherd's hands above the pipe too, and:

"They pulled off my clothes, dropped my pants around my feet and started whipping me. They beat me with a rubber hose . . . My mouth was bleeding where a front tooth went through my lip. They broke three teeth in the back of my mouth . . ."

Then word came from Groveland that a lynch mob was on its way to Tavares. [. . .]

Shepherd and Irvin were rushed outside and put into a car. Greenlee was left in his cell. [. . .]

Irvin recalls:

"I was very dizzy then. One of them had kicked me in my — — — (groin) and I was bleeding pretty bad. They put us in the car and then they took us out into the woods again.

"They didn't beat us then; they handcuffed us around a tree; I'm on one side and Sammy is on the other side . . . they parked a little ways away and listened over the radio and told us we was lucky we didn't get killed."

Later they put them back in the cars and headed for the state prison at Raiford. Irvin remembers:

"We stopped by a sheriff's house, or somebody who said he was a sheriff. This guy he comes out of the house and he said 'Where is them niggers at?'

"He had a big flashlight. We were lying down in the car and he hit Sammy with his flashlight and stomped him with his foot. Then he came around on the other side of the car and beat me across my legs and arms and head with the searchlight. Next thing I remember I was in Raiford."

They were still in Raiford on July 31 when Franklin H. Williams [. . .] finally tracked them down and interviewed them. They wore the same bloody clothes; the seat of Irvin's pants was a stiff bloody mass.

By then, however, the police had announced that Shepherd and Greenlee had confessed. And Thomas, the fourth suspect, had been shot to death in the woods 40 miles away. [. . .]

The defendants never had a chance — to tell this story.

At Williams' insistence, a doctor had examined the boys a week after he found them, but Judge Futch wouldn't let the doctor testify either.

Somehow, though, Shepherd, Irvin and Greenlee should have been allowed to tell their story — if only here.

HARLEM "MAYOR"

"Bojangles," a tap-dancing star of the 1930s, "kept hope alive," as Jesse Jackson phrases the strategy. Bojangles's conviction that "we can't let whites get us down" echoes Langston Hughes's phrase in "The Negro Artist and the Racial Mountain": "We younger Negro artists who create now intend to express our individual dark-skinned selves without fear or shame. If white people are pleased we are glad. If they are not, it doesn't matter. We know we are beautiful. And ugly too." [11]

"Taps for Bill Robinson Set for Noon Monday"
New York Post 27 November 1949: 2, 20

His famous dancing feet stilled forever, Bill Bojangles Robinson, 71, will lie in state at the Abyssinian Baptist Church, 132 W. 138th St., from 2:30 P.M. Sunday until the funeral Monday noon. Burial will be in the actors' section of Evergreen Cemetery, Brooklyn.

At Robinson's bedside when he died Friday at 7:28 P.M. at Columbia-Presbyterian Medical Center were his wife, Elaine; her sister, Mrs. Dorothy Small, and his manager, Marty Forkins.

Since Bojangles was admitted to the hospital Nov. 14 when a heart condition worsened, he received more than 5,600 wires and letters from admirers. President Truman, Cabinet members and Congressmen were among those wishing him a speedy recovery. . . .

His 60th year in show business was marked with "Bill Robinson Day" proclaimed April 29, 1946, by Mayor O'Dwyer. On that day, when his doctor said he had "the legs of a boy of 16," "Bojangles" danced his way through 24 hours of public and private functions.

The beloved dancer was born in Richmond, Va., May 25, 1878, as Luther Robinson. He was orphaned early, and went to live with his grandmother, Mrs. Bedelia Robinson, a former slave.

He always hated the name of Luther, and at the age of eight, when he got a job as stable-boy at a track near Washington, he went home, licked his big brother, Bill, and told him he was taking his name. He gave his brother the name of Percy, which he still uses.

He was given the nickname "Bojangles" by a Harlem friend, Des Williams, and Robinson himself never pretended to know what it meant.

The dancer's schooling ended when he was six, and he never had any formal dancing training. He used to earn pennies as a boy dancing on Richmond street corners.

His first "big" money was $5 a week and board he earned with Eddie Leonard, the old minstrel man, in a spectacle called "The South Before the War."

Ultra race-conscious Negro critics in the mid-20s often cited the Eddie Leonard days when objecting to Robinson's "old white gentleman and old colored man" jokes of that period. Bojangles finally gave up the minstrel jokes and developed a good-natured humor of his own as a smiling but insistent fighter for Negro rights. . . .

Appointed "Mayor of Harlem" by the late Jimmy Walker, named honorary chief or deputy sheriff by a score of police departments, Robinson was one of the country's most honored entertainers — and he loved every single honor.

One police department gave him a gold-plated pistol, and he wasted no time in putting it to use — with almost disastrous results. In Pittsburgh one night, he whipped out his pistol and chased two youths who had snatched a woman's pocketbook, and a rookie Pittsburgh cop, seeing a running man with a gun, promptly shot Bojangles. His wound wasn't serious and the Pittsburgh Police Dept. apologized profusely.

His recent heart attack prevented him from receiving in person one of his most cherished honors. The Grand St. Boys Club, of which he was the first honorary member, unveiled a plaque containing bronze casts of his dancing feet. . . .

It was inevitable that Robinson would go to Hollywood where he made 14 pictures. He cherished his deep friendship with Shirley Temple, the child star, who affectionately called him "Uncle Bill."

He taught Shirley to tap and to execute his famous staircase dance — a much-imitated routine for which Fred Stone once sent him a check "in part payment for the stair dance I stole from you." . . .

Robinson's health and vitality was a source of puzzlement to the medical profession. Even after he passed the normal three score and 10 years, he hardly looked 40. His face was unlined and there wasn't a gray hair on his close-cropped head. He could run backward faster than the ordinary man could run forward and once established a world record by back-pedaling 75 yards in 8⅕ seconds.

His youthful second wife often complained that she couldn't keep up with Bill. "I sometimes try to sleep from Friday to Monday to store up energy," she said, "but Bill gets tired and worrisome if he sleeps more than five hours a night."

Much of his earnings were spent on youngsters and school children in his continuing fight against juvenile delinquency. Death robbed him of his greatest plan for them, however. He often said, half-jokingly:

"When I'm 102 I'm going to stop dancing and start a dancing school. You see, I'm a sort of Rip Van Winkle of dancing."

"Bojangles Takes His Last Curtain Call"
New York Post 28 November 1949

Bill Robinson took his last curtain call before a packed house in Harlem today, and no one would have loved [it] more than Bojangles himself.

In a final trip from the 369th Anti-Aircraft Regiment Armory at 142d St. and Fifth Av. down through 125th St. and up to Abyssinian Baptist Church at 132 W. 138th St., Bojangles played his final scene to an estimated 500,000 persons — on sidewalks, on housetops, on stoops, windows and fire escapes.

It was Bojangles Day — the last one — and Harlem and Broadway, which were equally his, joined hands in the final tribute.

As Mayor O'Dwyer, who later delivered the eulogy, waited bareheaded outside the church, police estimated that 10,000 persons jammed 138th St. alone.

Not since Florence Mills, "the Little Blackbird," died in 1927, and Big Jim Europe, the legendary leader of the old 15th Regiment band succumbed after World War I, had there been such a turnout in Harlem.

In death, as in life, Bojangles outdrew them all.

All 3,000 seats in the church auditorium and 2,000 spaces in the overflow basement had been filled since early morning. Mourners there were led by Bo's widow, the former Elaine Dash; his brother, Percy, now blind; his first wife, Mrs. Fannie (Little Bo) Robinson and other relatives.

Marian Anderson sang "Ave Maria"; Hazel Scot[t] played Chopin's "Funeral March," and the Rev. Adam C. Powell Jr., pastor of the church and husband of the pianist, conducted the services.

O'Dwyer looked down at the bier from the pulpit and said: "Bill, New York wants me to say this farewell to you. The love and affection and joy you gave us is measured by the sorrow of seeing you go."

Bojangles, who loved to amuse people, actually drew a laugh from his mourners when Powell told them, "Bill had two sins — gambling and ice cream."

"I love the way he died," said Powell. "He made $4,000,000 and died without a cent. He could die this way because he trusted people. He knew he would be taken care of."

The crowds had started gathering at the armory at 8 A.M. . . .

More than 5,000 passed the casket this morning, in addition to the 40,000 who had viewed the body since Saturday. Men, even more than women, wept as they passed the bier, and mourners ranged from judges and other city officials to school children.

Among the scores of floral tributes to arrive this morning was a huge spray of yellow chrysanthemums carrying a card: "For Uncle Billy, from the Little Colonel — Shirley Temple." Others included just little bundles of wilted blossoms offered by less fortunate youngsters.

Led by a sergeant and six mounted policemen, the hearse, with three flower cars directly behind, proceeded first to Lenox Av. and then down to 125th St.

At 135th St., Bojangles passed for the last time the now darkened Lincoln Theatre where he was one of the first headliners. On the same street were Harlem YMCAs to which he had contributed both his talents and his ever-available cash.

The funeral march, in which high Elk officials and the 45-piece band of the Monarch Lodge participated, turned West on 125th St. and north on Seventh Av.

At 132d St. and 7th Av. Bojangles passed the stump of the Tree of Hope, that fabulous old oak in front of the now closed Lafayette Theatre which entertainers, especially Bo, had rubbed when hoping for employment.

And behind the Lafayette the pool and card rooms of the Rhythm Club was practically deserted as Bo's old pool and tonk and blackjack companions were outside watching the cortege.

And at 135th St. they passed Small's Paradise, a large nightclub which grew with Bo's assistance from a little hole-in-the-wall just three blocks away to one of the last big night clubs left in Harlem. Every step of the way was watched by hundreds of thousands of Harlemites, including school children who were given a half holiday.

Following the funeral services, the cortege retraced much of this route on its trip down to Times Sq. where Noble Sissle, president of the Negro Actors Guild, led a massed band in Duffy Square in a typical Broadway musical tribute to the stage, screen and television star.

Flags on theatres, hotels and shops in the area were at half-staff during this tribute. After this brief ceremony, the procession was dispersed and a small cortege escorted the body to Evergreen Cemetery, Brooklyn.

1950S

Evidence of the nationwide paranoia that Wisconsin's Senator Joseph Mc-Carthy engendered during the early 1950s, finding communism in every person who differed with him, this piece shows that even the patriotic were afraid to acknowledge words from the U.S. Constitution and the Declaration of Independence.

"A Poll of Fear in Our Town"
  Ted Poston and Nancy Seely
  New York Post 31 July 1951: 4, 16

(*Post* Editor's Note: On July 4, The Madison Capitol-Times, published in Sen. McCarthy's home state of Wisconsin, circulated a petition exclusively containing quotations from the Declaration of Independence and the Bill of Rights. Out of 112 persons interviewed, only one signed it. Last Friday — before President Truman referred to the Madison episode in his Detroit speech — two Post reporters circulated a similar petition in New York City. Their report follows.)

We spent a long day trying to persuade New Yorkers to sign a petition reaffirming their belief in the Declaration of Independence and the Bill of Rights.

We did so as representatives of a fictitious American Committee to Uphold the Constitution.

We met suspicion, distrust and hostility relieved by occasional wisecracks.

Out of 161 New Yorkers whom we interviewed — chosen at random in the course of their everyday pursuits — we got exactly 19 signatures.

Although the petition contained nothing except quotations from the two historic documents, the most general reaction we encountered was that we were subversives engaged in an un-American enterprise.

We also encountered underlying dread of the "consequences" which might develop from exercising the right of petition.

A truck driver said: "I don't sign nothing, but I'll tell you this: If they get all these Bolsheviks out of the country, we wouldn't have to reaffirm our faith in the Constitution."

A Wall St. broker smiled cynically as he read the document. "No thank you," he said, and handed it back. "You can't trick me on that. I happen to think they did just right by your boys."

He pointed to the section of the Bill of Rights which reads: "Excessive bail shall not be required, nor excessive fines imposed, nor cruel and unusual punishments inflicted."

"You think I don't know that this is just a trick to get low bail for those damned Commies?" he asked. "Well, you won't get away with it."

We split forces and went looking for signatures all over Manhattan — on Wall St., Madison Square Park, the Lower East Side, the New York Public Library, outside Grand Central and the Waldorf-Astoria, in the penthouse sections of Park Av.

We canvassed the West Side, talked with longshoremen on the docks, produce men in the Washington Market area, housewives in Abingdon Square, passersby in the Times Square area and pedestrians on Riverside Drive.

But East Side, West Side, uptown, downtown, the most common refrain was: "I don't sign anything." "I'm not interested." "You say it's the Bill of Rights; how do I know what you're up to?"

Scores of people wouldn't even read the petition. They just brushed by, ending any possible discussion. We didn't count them among the 142 turndowns.

A patrolman in front of the National City Bank glanced sneeringly at the petition and said: "Beat it. You guys got your nerve. Kee-rist, you're even asking cops now."

Two of four Wall St. secretaries coming down the steps of the Chase National Bank read it, and one asked:

"You wouldn't be trying to make me lose my job, would you, Mister? You put your name on something these days and it's no telling where it might show up later."

A well-dressed man who had been standing nearby suddenly snapped: "Why don't you let those ladies alone. Take your goddam Red racket somewhere else."

The pattern wasn't much different on the West Side.

One woman said: "My husband told me never to sign anything."

Another: "I signed something once and my kids gave me such heck I had to promise them never to do it again."

A man: "Last time I signed something, they sent me a Communist circular through the mail."

A priest read the document and then handed it back. "I'm afraid to sign anything," he said.

But finally, after 40 rebuffs, a signature was obtained. Andy Taylor, 310 W. 129th St., a farm labor recruiter, read the petition through twice, the second time slowly. Then he asked:

"Is this really in the Constitution, the Bill of Rights? Well, I'll sign it, and I think everybody ought to be made to sign it so they can know what's in the Bill of Rights. Maybe they'd act better then."

An earnest woman in Abingdon Square at 8th Av. and 12th St. asked the reporter to sit down and discuss it. The talk went like this:

"What organization is back of this?"

"The American Committee to Uphold the Constitution."

"Never heard of it."

"Well, it's very small."

"One of those small Communist outfits, I suppose."

"No, it has no Communist connections whatsoever."

"Why aren't these statements from the Constitution and Bill of Rights all in quotation marks?"

"Just a printer's error, I guess."

"Why isn't your organization's name on this petition? It could be anything. I agree with it, of course, but I won't sign it, since I have no way of knowing what you plan to do with it."

"We want to show our Representatives in Washington that a lot of people still believe in the Constitution as it was originally written."

"Well, for Heaven's sake," the woman concluded the exchange: "They (the Congressmen) do too, you know, and if you ever suggested to one that he didn't he would launch into a tirade that would last for at least five hours. The whole thing is too general."

Another signature was almost obtained on the steps of the New York Public Library. A stocky man read the petition thoughtfully, then slowly wrote "John Evans" on the first line. He'd started adding his address when a woman companion said: "I don't think you should do it, John. You might get in trouble these days."

He hesitated a moment, drew a line through his signature and silently handed the petition back.

A woman in the garment center area asked: "Have you been cleared by our union? Do you have credentials from them? We have to be very careful. There are so many fellow traveler organizations and so many petitions passed around and signed and then used against us."

Humor was not entirely lacking. A plump lady on Riverside Dr. listened raptly as we explained the importance of reaffirming American beliefs in the Bill of Rights.

"Oh, I never sign anything anymore, dearie," she said at the end, "but tell me something: Where did you get that dress? Gimbel's? With the material? Oh, no. Lord & Taylor's, at least."

Nor was passion altogether missing. A bartender at Chrystie St. and Rivington threatened to call a cop when a reporter persisted in discussing the petition with another customer.

"We don't allow that stuff in here," he shouted, looking around to other customers for support. "No politicking and no petitions. We know your racket."

A doorman at the Waldorf was more polite but no less firm. "I'll have to summon an officer if you persist in annoying our guests," he said.

Three of the signers had a clear conscience.

"It's nothing but quotations from the Constitution and the Bill of Rights, and they're just trying to see if people will sign it. This is safe, boys; just what they taught us in school. Let's sign." They did.

A woman pushing a baby carriage along Rivington St. read it and silently handed it back. She stopped up the street, left the carriage, came back and reached for the petition. She scrawled "Roberta Rucci, E. Houston St." and wordlessly turned away.

Many persons approached said they couldn't read English or had left their glasses at home. But a mild looking little man on a bench in Trinity Churchyard at Broadway and Rector paled visibly when the petition was explained to him.

"Please, sir," he begged in broken English. "Don't make me sign. Only six months I'm here. I don't want trouble. Please."

A stylish matron walking her dog on Park Av. near 66th St. read only half of the petition before crumpling it and then tidily looked around for a waste basket.

"They should put you in jail with the rest of them," she told the reporter. "You you you damned Communist."

Neither Sen. McCarthy (R-Wis.) or Eugene Dennis (C-Federal Prison) could have asked for more.

JACKIE ROBINSON

Twenty years after Kid Chocolate, the Depression, and World War II and after Jackie Robinson had integrated baseball in 1947, the New York Post's *sports editors would borrow Poston from news reporting to put his human-interest sights on the exhilaration baseball seemed to be stamping on the whole community, but the exhilaration resulted from the success of Robinson's team, the Brooklyn Dodgers, not from integration. As was his wont in his stories on black athletes, Poston did not focus on the cruelty that Robinson suffered but on factors with which spectators could identify — in the case of Robinson during the 1951 World Series, playing through pain, team loyalty, and family values. This article also shows a baseball player's lifestyle in the era before million-dollar salaries and chartered jets.*

On Poston's advice, in 1959 the New York Post *hired Robinson — a college graduate respected for his range of interests — as a columnist. Three times a week from 28 April 1959 until September 1960, Robinson wrote on any topic that came to mind. He explained at the time, "All during my baseball days, and after I left the game, there were times when my opinions were sought. . . . I can assure you I intend to speak out as I always have" (qtd. in Allen 216). He said that he would examine the 1960 presidential campaign and discuss politics, baseball, and international affairs.*

Robinson's column ended suddenly over politics. He had first supported the most liberal of the Democratic presidential candidates, Hubert Humphrey. When Humphrey lost in the primaries to John F. Kennedy, Robinson switched his allegiance to Republican Richard Nixon, surprising his friends, his wife, and the Democratic Post. *His widow said, "I remained a Democrat, and we argued often about that" (qtd. in Allen 220). A Robinson biographer says that the endorsement of Nixon "had two immediate consequences." Rob-*

inson was placed on leave without pay from his job as vice president for per-
sonnel at a popular coffee and fast-food sandwich chain, Chock Full o' Nuts,
and the Post precipitously dropped his column. The paper announced both
moves on 8 September 1960 in a small story on an inside page.[1]

"'Tried Not to Cry,'—Jackie Re-Lives the Terrible 12th"
New York Post 1 October 1951: 5, 14

It almost didn't happen — that two-out, game-winning homer which sent the Dodgers into today's playoff with the Giants. The man who hit it didn't think he had enough left in him to come to bat in the 14th.

"I was on the verge of asking that I be taken out," said Jackie Robinson. "After I banged myself up with that catch in the 12th, I didn't think I was pulling my weight. I didn't think it would be fair to the rest of the team to stay in. I almost asked them to send in a pinch hitter for me."

Jackie, banged-up and limping so badly from a stone bruise on his right foot that he could hardly hobble along, began discussing the dramatic homerun as he stepped from the train last night at Pennsylvania Station.

Above him, on the train arrival level, were thousands of rabid Brooklyn fans, restrained by chains and police lines and ranging in age from Rosemarie Ciarletta, 8, [. . .] to Nelson Hayden, 81. [. . .] And all were yelling "Jackie."

Beside him though was Rachel, Mrs. Jackie Robinson, her face showing none of the ravages of tears she admitted shedding for the last three innings of the Philadelphia contest.

"You can't go up there, Jackie," she said as the completely weary second baseman looked up the stairs. "You promised to be at the television station at 8, and it's practically 9 now."

Four cops and a publicity man closed in and attempted to rush him to a lower level elevator, but his injured foot restrained him to snail's pace.

"We'll go out on 33d St.," Mrs. Robinson said. "Chuck (her brother) is waiting for us with the car there. He'll rush us over to the program (Celebrity Time!)."

Chuck wasn't there, though. The cops, learning that he was waiting for Jackie, had escorted him in style to the lower 31st St. exit, so the Robinsons stood forlornly in the shadow of the darkened bus station and waited.

"It was that catch in the 12th," Jackie resumed his story. "It looked easy at first. Just a routine line drive. But it was only the split second before I dove for it that I realized it wasn't routine. It wasn't hit as hard as I thought it was, and I saw it was dropping, dropping fast.

"So I left my feet and dove for it with both hands. At the same instant I gloved it, my elbow jammed straight into my stomach. It jammed everything in me right up my chest—guts and all. Nothing has ever hit me like that.

"It wasn't just my breath, although I couldn't talk for five minutes. I even had to point at my belly when the trainer came up; couldn't talk at all. I was crying and trying not to cry and—"

An officer in a Marine's uniform walked into the shadows, peered closely at him and interrupted.

"I'm a Yankee fan," he said. "Just a Yankee fan and a nobody. But I want to tell you how I appreciate you and what you did today. I want to wish you all the luck in the world against the Giants."

Jackie thanked him and would have continued, but Mrs. Robinson was worried. The cops hadn't returned with Chuck.

"You take a cab and go on over to the television station," she said. "We'll come over later. You go now."

The cops closed in again to rush him through the bus station to 34th St. and a cab stand, but Jackie paused briefly at a lunch stand for an orange-ade. In the cab, he resumed:

"I thought then that I ought to get out, but once I could stand up, I thought I might be able to make it by resting through our side of the 13th. So I didn't say anything."

But what had he thought as he dived for the liner?

"What could I think? I knew I had to get it, so I just went out to get it.

"I felt all right when we took the field in the 13th. My stomach was still paining me like hell, but nothing like it was at first. I felt it was all right after all.

"Then Nicholson, the first man up, hits this bounder straight at me. I moved in to get it and my stomach caught me. The ball blurred, it got big and then I couldn't see it. I gloved it somehow, but I knew I was through.

"Before I could make up my mind to signal Pee Wee to take me out, Hamner hit the next one at me and the same thing happened. But with two out, I decided to try to finish the inning."

The cabbie interrupted again: "Pardon me, Mr. Robinson, for butting into your personal business, but do you fellows get paid extra for this play-off with the Giants? It's extra work, do you get paid extra?"

"No," said Jackie. "We get our salary. That's enough."

The cabbie didn't think it fair and argued the point, so Jackie couldn't take up his story again until he was in the TV studio.

"I thought I had my mind made up by the time I got to the bench in the 14th. I was washed up. It wasn't fair to the other fellows to stay in just because I wanted so badly to stay in. I was ready to ask out.

"Then Pee Wee went out and Duke went down on a pop foul and before I could say anything, there I was at the plate with a bat in my hand.

"I took a swing at the first one Roberts sent up — expecting my stomach to break in two. And nothing happened. I didn't feel the swing at all. I felt like shouting."

Did he decide then to try for the homer?

"Well, no. I was swinging. I was trying to pull the ball to the left field. I knew there was a good chance for a homer if I could pull it, but I was just trying to meet the ball."

And how did he feel when he did meet it?

"I knew. The minute I met it, I knew. I didn't even have to look at it. I knew it was gone."

Had there ever been a greater thrill in his career?

"No." Soberly. "Nowhere. That was the greatest, anywhere, in any league."

Rachel and Chuck had arrived finally, but she forestalled the inquiring reporter.

"Don't ask me anything Ted Poston," she said. "Not one question."

She smiled wearily and relented slightly.

"Call me tomorrow and I'll tell you everything, but soon as this program is over Jackie and I are going home to sleep. We both need it."

LABOR LEADER

This profile of Walter Reuther shows Poston's continuing concern for labor and its leaders — especially those who regarded blacks' needs on a par with whites'. Poston here quickly and dramatically catches the concept of an idealistic man, his family, and the labor movement.

"The Many Sides of Walter Reuther"

New York Post 7 December 1952, sec. M: 2

What sort of fellow is this Walter Philip Reuther, the flamboyant young (45) red-head who has just won the presidency of the CIO?

It's hard to say. Reuther is so many things to so many people that much depends upon whom you talk to.

"A cool customer. Cold-blooded. A young-man-in-a-hurry," say his enemies. And no one could have come as fast and as far as Reuther without a respectable contingent of enemies and articulate opponents.

"The most dynamic labor leader this century has produced. The personification of YMCA wholesomeness . . . filled with Boy Scout simplicity," say his friends and followers. And they are legion. They furnished some 3,079,000 votes at the CIO convention the other day.

"A wild-eyed radical, a dreamer, a visionary," entrenched industrialists used to roar, although most of them were forced to modify that opinion during World War II as one after the other of the well-publicized "Reuther plans" were adopted and found to be practical.

And ironically there is some element of truth in all the contentions. And the opinions are often reached through the same set of facts.

His trade union opponents have condemned him for not being a hail-fellow-well-met. He doesn't drink or smoke. He hates all-night poker sessions which delight many labor sessions.

His friends laud him for the same qualities. They point to the amount of time he spends with his wife and two daughters, to his love of pineapple sodas with chocolate ice cream, to his all-night bull sessions with his union cronies in his home where coffee, tea and cookies replace sturdier refreshments.

And few of the auto moguls who have negotiated with Reuther during his turbulent career in the CIO United Auto Workers have been able to conceal their respect for his ability even when bitterly opposing what they call his "Socialistic" ideas.

There was the time when the late William Knudsen [head of General Motors] told Reuther during a particularly bitter contract session with General Motors:

"Young man, I wish you were selling used cars for us."

And when Reuther looked puzzled, Knudsen explained: "Yes, I said used cars. Anybody can sell new cars."

And much of Reuther's undeserved reputation for being cold, calculating and ruthless, stems from the intensity of his crusades, from the single-mindedness of his particular purpose.

A vanquished opponent in his drive to the UAW presidency in 1946 explained how a man so unlike his burly brawling membership happened to rise to the top of the auto union. It also might explain how he rose to the top of the CIO. For this opponent said:

"In the absence of personal warmth on the part of Reuther, the only answer is that his obvious technical competence, his dexterity in the presentation of complex economic issues to the workers, the brilliance of his public relations . . . plus a genius for political fence building, have helped Reuther climb to the top."

There is more to it than that, of course. And much of it stems from the fact that Walter Reuther was almost a third generation labor leader from the day of his birth in Wheeling, W. Va., Labor Day eve in 1907.

His grandfather had been an international organizer for the United Brewery Workers. His father, Valentine Reuther, became president of the Ohio Valley Trades and Labor Assembly at 23.

And Valentine started his four boys on the union path early in life. Each Sunday afternoon, he would take them to the upstairs bedroom and put Walter and Victor on one side and Ted and Roy on the other (or vice versa) and let them debate the current issues of the day — child labor, prohibition, capital punishment, and the rights of labor.

It was during these arguments — which Walter usually won — that his father inculcated in him a theory that was to be regarded as one of the most controversial issues of the time when Reuther sprung it on General Motors during the 1945 contract negotiations.

This was the "ability-to-pay" theory, based on the concept that a corporation's earnings could permit wage increases without necessarily encouraging price increases; that higher wages increase consumption, thereby maintaining productivity.

Walter quit high school at 15 to learn tool and die-making in a Wheeling plant. Although he was later fired for trying to organize a strike against Sunday and holiday work, he eventually became such an expert tool and die-maker that he probably today could make more at it than the $11,250 a year he will receive as both UAW and CIO president.

He went to Detroit in 1927, worked for a number of auto firms, and by 1932 had completed his high school education at night and three years at

Wayne University where he often led fellow students out to union meetings and picket lines.

By 1932, he had become a foreman of 40 men in a division at Ford, only to be bounced for talking unionism too loudly. This was only the first of a series of clashes with Ford and although he was to be brutally beaten later by Ford goons in the "Battle of the Underpass," he was to emerge victorious in most of his future clashes.

After the 1932 firing, he and Victor (who now represents the UAW in Europe while Roy is an educational director for the UAW) took their $900 savings and went on a bicycle tour of Europe and Asia. Walter worked 18 months in a Ford-built plant in Russia, where he developed a deep love for the Russian people and a fierce hatred for their Soviet rulers.

He came back to Detroit in 1935, organized UAW's West Side Local 174, ran its membership from 78 to 30,000 in one year, and began the fabulous union career most Americans today know.

It included his leadership in the 1937 sitdown strikes, his fights with John L. Lewis over isolationism, and his steady conquest of both right and leftwing opponents while he clawed his way to the top of the UAW.

But most of all, in his evolution into a national figure, the turbulent decade included the many "Reuther plans," often greeted with derision but eventually adopted by the people who first opposed him.

There was his plan for converting the automobile industry for the production of airplanes, announced with the Reuther pamphlet, "500 Planes a Day." This was adopted in a large measure although the Office of Production Management and industry spokesmen derided it at first. His plan for standardizing tank-engine production was adopted immediately, as was his plan for management-labor committees.

After this, fewer people referred to Walter Reuther as a dreamer and a visionary.

By the end of the war, the brash young man had the reputation of the most resourceful labor leader in the U.S., with the possible exception of John L. Lewis.

And this reputation was enhanced when he led the bitter GM strike in 1945–6, the longest auto stoppage in history — and obtained an 18½ cent-an-hour wage increase, the first of a series of at least five national "rounds" of wage hikes followed nationally by other industries.

It was during the "third round" fight against the Chrysler Corp. in 1948 that an unknown and still unapprehended assassin fired a shotgun blast through the window of his Detroit home, shattering an arm which has remained useless to this day. (Just 13 months later, Victor was similarly attacked and lost an eye.)

Reuther's political career paralleled his rise in union and industry circles. A Roosevelt supporter from 1936, he also backed Truman in 1948 (after trying to nominate Supreme Court Justice Douglas) and was a forceful supporter of Gov. Stevenson, both in Democratic Party and Americans for Democratic Action circles.

Since 1936, he has been married to May Wolfe, a former schoolteacher, and lives with his wife and daughters, Linda Mae and Elizabeth Ann, in a frame and brick cottage in northwest Detroit.

Unostentatious and modest in his personal life, he is a fastidious dresser. He had to give up his hobby as an amateur carpenter after the shotgun attempt on his life but he still maintains an interest in basketball and swimming, for both of which he earned medals at Wayne.

He is an executive board member of the National Assn. for the Advancement of Colored People and of the Religion and Labor Foundation and served as co-director of the UAW-CIO Fair Employment Practices Dept.

But despite his myriad other interests, the labor movement is always uppermost in Reuther's mind.

Another President-elect found that out the other day when he met with Reuther and Allan Haywood. Gen. Eisenhower was explaining to them how he knew the problems of the working man. Hadn't he worked with his hands as a boy; hadn't he in fact worked 12 hours a day?

And the brash young Reuther had only one comment.

"General," he said, "you should have joined a union."

EFFECT OF SUPREME COURT'S DECISION

One of a series of articles, this is a follow-up to the Supreme Court's historic May 1957 decision in Brown v. Board of Education. *Poston and Kenneth B. Clark, the social psychologist whose words on the effect of segregation on schoolchildren Chief Justice Earl Warren incorporated in his decision, traveled into the South together to see whether the region was readying itself. Poston kept Clark's spirits up with his comical remarks such as the one with which he ends this story.*

"Dixie's Fight for Freedom—IV"
New York Post 27 June 1954: 4, 23

A Negro workman was sweeping in front of an almost completed ultra modern public school several miles south of Albany, Georgia. The glass and brick structure was one of many Georgia was building to "equalize" Negro school facilities before the Supreme Court lowered the boom on Jim Crow education.

The workman paused as a stranger approached him.

Had he heard of the Supreme Court decision ordering an end of segregation in public schools?

"Yeah," he said indifferently.

Was he surprised?

"Nope."

Why wasn't he surprised at such a sweeping ruling?

"Well," the workman answered wryly, with a furtive twinkle in his eye, "as soon as these white folks started building this fine new combination school for us Negroes, I knew they were going to figure out some way that they could get into it, too."

The quiet amusement and droll humor with which thousands of Southern Negroes received the high court ruling has been disconcerting to foes of integration, but heartening to those fighting for more democracy in the South.

The ruling was also taken in stride by the group supposed to suffer most if segregation was ended — the 100,000 or more Negro teachers in Jim Crow schools.

I talked to scores of these teachers during my Southern tour and I did not find one who thought that the predictions of wholesale dismissals of Negro teachers would materialize.

And most of them laughed openly when I told them of the threats Gov. Talmadge had made when I discussed the subject with him.

"Why, I'm doing you people a favor in not letting them mix up the schools in Georgia," he contended heatedly. "Had you thought what would happen to Georgia's 7,000 Nigra teachers if we mixed up the schools?

"Wipe out the separate schools and you'll wipe out them 7,000 jobs overnight. The white folks in Georgia wouldn't have it otherwise."

Unlike the Negro workman, Talmadge was quite humorless about the situation. At one point, he turned to his Negro visitor (whom he had admitted through the back door).

"You say you were born and raised in Hopkinsville, Ky." he said. "Well, I'm sure they don't have any mixed schools in Hopkinsville. And it doesn't seem to have hurt you none. You seem like a pretty smart boy."

"But, Governor," I remonstrated quietly, "I'm inhibited."

Talmadge looked slightly puzzled, and even more so when I murmured ". . . and we didn't have any football field at the Booker T. Washington Colored Grammar School."

He changed the subject suddenly and said:

"If you talk to any of our Nigra school teachers in Georgia, you be sure to tell them what I said."

I did and most of them laughed. But thanks to an extensive educational job performed by the NAACP, most of them could explain easily why there would be no wholesale dismissals among Georgia's 8,600 (not 7,000) Negro teachers, or among Negro educators elsewhere in the South.

The points they made were simple and valid:

As long as residential segregation is maintained anywhere — in the South or in Harlem — you are going to have the same segregated schools and more or less the same faculties you have now.

There is a current and increasing shortage of both white and Negro elementary school teachers in the South, and only a small surplus of high-school teachers. Any wholesale dismissal of Negro teachers would only make more acute an already pressing problem.

At least 43 per cent of the Negro teachers in the affected Southern states are protected against arbitrary dismissal by tenure laws. And the NAACP would defend those tenure rights in any case of arbitrary dismissals.

Several Negro teachers pointed proudly to a 1953 survey by the National Education Assn. which showed that in several Southern states, Negro teachers were better prepared for their jobs than white teachers. [. . .]

A Birmingham professor who studies every summer at Teachers College in New York, said:

"Why didn't you tell him that Negroes can and do hold so many more better-paying jobs in New York that many of them look down on the money they'd get as school teachers?

"The South has been lucky in that it has been able to attract the best Negro brains to the teaching profession, since there is little else down here that we can do. On the other hand, some of its worst-prepared whites have gone into teaching because it is the easiest thing a lazy mind can do."

Much of their confidence is based upon what has happened in the past when segregation was ended in public schools in other areas.

At least a half dozen teachers pointed out what had happened in southern New Jersey when Jim Crow schools were ended there — amid dire predictions of mass firings of Negro teachers.

"There were only 479 Negro teachers in New Jersey in 1946 when they had segregated schools," one said, citing an NAACP pamphlet, "but there are 615 now, an increase of 166 in eight years."

Others pointed out that in East St. Louis, Ill., scene of the most bitter post World War I race riot, and in 11 other communities in southern Illinois, Negro teachers are now working in white or integrated schools since the recent end of segregation.

"There's not much difference between southern New Jersey or southern Illinois and northern Georgia," one teacher put it, "and if they can do it up there, we'll do it down here eventually. In the meanwhile we'll go on teaching. There's not much question to that."

Of course there will be some Negro teachers — and some whites — who will lose their jobs when the program of gradual integration of schools gets underway.

Looking at the situation realistically, one must speculate on the future of many of the 500-odd Negro supervisors and 3,000 or more Negro principals who do not all enjoy the tenure rights of classroom teachers.

Many of these educators may be replaced or shifted when schools are combined or when integration becomes a reality in their communities. But, conversely, many will be retained as long as residential segregation makes educational segregation mandatory.

There will be some Negro — and white — teachers who will also lose their jobs because they should never have had them in the first place. They are not really qualified to teach children — Negro or white.

There was, however, one Negro educator who denounced the Supreme Court ruling but he avoided me when I tried to interview him. Dr. J. W. Holley, president emeritus of the Albany State College for Negroes and an old political crony of the late Gene Talmadge, told the Albany (Ga.) Herald:

"Negroes know that integration of the schools would be of great harm to both races . . . The National Assn. for the Advancement of Colored People and the Rosenwald Foundation have been the worst enemy of the Negro and of progress in the South."

Local papers throughout the South, while urging calm and caution in the face of the decision, exerted heavy pressure on local Negro educators to obtain similar statements, but few were successful.

More typical was the comment of Prof. J. S. Morgan, principal of the Cartersville, Ga., Negro schools, who told the Cartersville Tribune-News:

"Of course I am pleased over news of the Supreme Court decision, and most other Negroes are, too."

The writer left the South with only one regret. He didn't get back to see Herman Talmadge again.

For, only four days after my interview with the governor executive, the Hopkinsville, Ky., School Board announced that the elementary and high schools there will be integrated and an effort will be made to start the program next September.

I felt less inhibited already—and I wanted to tell Herman about it.

POLICE BRUTALITY, 1950s

W. J. Cash in The Mind of the South *discusses the romanticism, individualism, and classism that led to the southern white belief in the need to keep the Negro "in his place" and the races sexually apart. One Poston theme is how destructive that notion is to the civil rights of the human race. Here he gives witness to the naïveté of a black male youth who may have hoped that* Brown v. Board of Education *had killed Jim Crow. Poston sometimes quoted "good guys" in proper English and "bad guys" in vernacular, perhaps to subtly suggest that bad guys are ignorant and that education and breadth of experience might alleviate their narrow-mindedness.*

"'Just a Day's Work' to a Georgia Trooper"
New York Post 29 June 1955: 2+

A Georgia state trooper accused of brutally beating a 16-year-old Negro youth with iron handcuffs, choking him into near insensibility and threatening to kill him, today dismissed the incident with these words: "It was just an ordinary day's work and that's all I got to say about it.

"If you want anything else out of me, just come on down here to Americus, Ga., and I'll give it to you."

State Trooper J. W. Southwell was discussing with The Post charges that he beat William Henry Owens, 16, last June 14 while the Hardinsburg, Ky., high school youth was driving the family of an elderly white barber from Cloverport, Ky., to Tampa, Fla.

The incident, which took place four miles from Ellaville, Ga., was first reported to Florida public officials by the retired barber, Arthur Mattingly, 66, and his family. They said they were ordered from the scene by the trooper who said:

"I don't want no witnesses."

Mattingly, who fled the state and appealed vainly to Florida officials for action, said the officer slapped the boy several times with his open hand, knocked him down in a ditch with his fist, choked him and beat him over the head with his handcuffs apparently without any provocation at all.

The beaten youth told The Post by phone from Hardinsburg, Ky., that he thought the trooper was enraged because the barber's wife, Mrs. Zora Mattingly, and daughter, Nellie, 18, were sitting on the front seat of Mattingly's car with him when the trooper drove by.

He spent two days and two nights in the Ellaville jail before being released with a $56 fine.

The youth has given a full sworn statement of the incident to attorney James A. Crumlin of Louisville, president of the Kentucky State Conference of National Assn. for the Advancement of Colored People Branches. Similar statements are being taken from other witnesses of the incident.

According to the youth, he was asked by his Hardinsburg employer, Pete Bennett, a moving van operator, to drive the Mattinglys to Tampa — because the barber is blind in one eye and has defective vision in the other.

Mattingly was resting in the back seat of the car with his grandson, Tommy Tabeling, 14, and the two women sat in front with Owens as the trooper passed them on the road. The trooper turned his car around, drove back and ordered Owens out of the car, Mattingly said.

"He led me back behind a small trailer we were pulling," the youth said, "and asked me why I was driving on the wrong side of the road. I said I wasn't driving on the wrong side, and he said: 'Whose car is this?'

"I said: 'It belongs to the white-haired gentleman inside,' and he said: 'Who are those white women in there?' and I said: 'They're Mr. Mattingly's wife and daughter,' and he said: 'Why was you on the wrong side of the road?' and then he started beating me."

Mattingly said:

"I got out to ask him where he was taking the boy. He had knocked him up beside the trailer several times and had put him in the patrol car and the boy was standing in the door begging him to let him go but he started beating him again.

"I heard the boy say: 'Please have mercy on me. I'm a long way from home. I've got a bad heart. Please don't hit me no more.'"

He said the patrolman hit the boy with his fist then, knocking him on his back in a ditch.

"Then he got on top of the boy and choked him with both hands," said Mattingly. "The boy tried to hold his hands when he was choking but that was the only time he fought back. The boy could hardly get his breath. I could hear him choking like he was almost dead."

Mrs. Mattingly, who, with the two children, corroborated the barber's account of the incident, said:

"I couldn't believe that any human could have been that cruel. He must have been drunk or crazy."

Mattingly continued:

"William was bleeding on the face a little, then the patrolman jerked him up off the ground and hit him across the face with the handcuffs before he put them on. The boy was cut on the side and back of his head. Another man in civilian clothes came up and helped put the handcuffs on."

Mattingly said five or six other white men had gathered around and then the officer asked the boy:

"Do you want to get back in the car or do you want to die?"

"Then the officer yelled at him: 'I'll kill you! I'll kill you! I'll kill you!' He yelled it three times."

Mattingly said he begged the officer not to beat the boy any more but that the trooper turned to the whole group and said:

"All of you leave. I don't want no witnesses."

"I tried to ask him where he was taking the boy and he yelled directly at me: 'I said go and I mean go.'

"The boy was begging me not to leave him but I was afraid not to leave. I knew he was liable to do to me the same way. It was the worst thing I've ever seen happen except a hanging once."

Mattingly said that despite his defective sight, he jumped in his car and drove long into the night until he thought he was out of Georgia, and spent the night in a motel at Cottage Grove.

Finding on awakening that he still was in Georgia, he drove on to White Springs, Fla., where he contacted the mayor, the police chief, the Methodist preacher and a Florida highway patrolman.

"The Florida patrolman said his 'boss' wouldn't let him telephone back to Georgia, and then he even bragged about how he once beat a 'coon' with his flashlight," Mattingly said.

Later, Pete Bennett, Owens' employer who had trucked the Mattinglys' furniture to Tampa in a moving van, heard of the incident and went to Ellaville, Ga., to get the youth out of jail.

Schley County Sheriff Edgar DeVane told The Post today:

"The young nigger plead[ed] guilty to driving on the wrong side of the road and resisting arrest and then apologized to the officer for acting a damned fool.

"Then his boss bailed him out but he hadn't ought to. He'd never seen a nigger that crazy before.

"The whole thing was just a case of a nigger resisting arrest and the officer arrested him. That's all."

Gloster Current, NAACP director of branches, said the association would complete its investigation both in Kentucky and Georgia before deciding whether federal prosecution might be possible in the interstate incident.

SKIN SHADE'S DOWNSIDE

Langston Hughes celebrated the skin hues that God gave African Americans, calling one poem "Harlem Sweeties" (Rampersad and Roussel 245). The following autobiographical piece describes a dose of discrimination in which Poston's color was not "sweet." Poston met four friends in Richmond, Virginia, to drive with them down to the retreat of Tuskegee Institute's president at Capahosic on the York River. The adventure left Poston hungry and laughing to keep from crying. He shows that Americans in 1956 were a long way from judging people on the content of their character. Poston had trained himself to handle discrimination with cool to keep his sanity, but this article points out how racial insult is no less hurtful when conveyed in courteous language.

After this incident, Poston rarely again traveled by train, the place where, as a dining car waiter, he had schooled himself in dealing with the ways of white folks. He subsequently traveled by air.

"Dinner for Four Was OK . . . but Not for Five"
New York Post 7 October 1956: 4, 25

Richmond, Va., Oct. 6 — The four conservatively dressed, slightly swarthy men descended the Atlanta Pullman at the Broad St. station here, and followed the luggage-laden Red Caps into the towering rotunda upstairs. With other Pullman passengers, they entered the station dining room and seated themselves around the lunch counter.

"Ted should be down on the 7:50 from New York," one remarked as they studied the menus. "He should be here before we finish breakfast."

"At that rate we should be down to the conference at Capahosic long before noon," another replied, "so we can watch the World Series before we get down to business."

Two young Negro waitresses had been watching the four intently from the moment they entered.

They conferred briefly then quietly summoned an elderly Negro from the kitchen. The elderly woman surveyed the quartet closely, and then shrugged before returning to the kitchen. Finally, a white woman — the lunchroom manager — emerged from the kitchen and scrutinized the four closely.

Eventually, she nodded to the waitresses who came over smiling and courteously took the four breakfast orders.

A short time later, a tall dark man — obviously a Negro — entered and joined the four at the lunch counter. The waitresses threw him a couple of inscrutable glances as he stood chatting with his friends, and then finished serving the quartet.

The newcomer seated himself at the counter and studied the menu, but the girls were suddenly busy on the other side of the counter. One white passenger, who was talking softly, in a Southern drawl to a companion across the counter, nodded and smiled in recognition of the newcomer. They had adjoining roomettes coming down on the New York train.

One of the waitresses seemed mildly distracted as the newcomer asked to give his order:

"In a minute, sir," she said, and promptly disappeared.

There was another short conference between the two waitresses, and finally the younger one came over for the order. Both disappeared into the kitchen and finally one returned with pencil and paper.

"Could you give me that order again, sir?" she said with a blank face, but twinkling eyes. "I want to write it down and get it straight."

The manager came back near the counter and studied the five customers for several minutes. Then with some hesitation, she walked around the counter, and sat on the stool next to the swarthiest of the original four.

"You will pardon me, sir," she spoke with trepidation, "but are all you gentlemen together?"

"Yes," he answered.

"Him, too?" she asked nodding toward the tall dark man with the small beard.

"Why yes."

"Pardon me again, sir," she murmured conversationally, "but what nationality are you all?"

"We are Americans," he replied.

"But what kind of Americans? What race are you?"

"We are Negro Americans," he said, drinking the last of his coffee.

The manager flushed and stuttered. Lowering her voice, she muttered, "I'm sorry, sir, but I thought [illegible] four were Filipinos."

"Oh, that's all right," was the reply, "but we're not. We're Americans."

The manager blushed even deeper. [. . .]

"We've made a mistake," she said, glancing around at the plates of the four who had already finished their breakfasts.

"You see," her voice trailed off as she got to her feet.

She came around between the counters and leaned toward the tall dark Negro on the end.

"I'm sorry, sir," she whispered, "but we've made a mistake. Until you came in, we thought your four friends were Filipinos."

"Really?" inquired the tall Negro politely.

She stammered and started over again: "You see we've got a law here in Richmond. We've got a colored dining room over there, and we can't serve you in here."

The Negro smiled and looked down the counter at his friends, three of whom, like the half dozen white customers, were unaware of what was going on.

Noticing the glance, she stammered, "we served them, but by mistake. I thought they were Filipinos —"

The Negro regarded her smilingly, but silently, and she went on whispering:

"It's embarrassing, sir, I know, to me as well as you, but how was I to know they weren't Filipinos? How could anybody know. That's what's the matter with things like this. It's embarrassing all around."

The Negro still smiled, but said nothing.

"I can't let the girls serve you here," she whispered almost desperately, "but I can have her take it around to the colored dining room. I'm sorry, sir, but we have this law and — and — and I didn't know they weren't Filipinos, and nobody here would know if you just went —"

"Don't bother," said the Negro, "just cancel the order."

"I'm glad you see it like a gentleman," she said, twisting her apron in her hand, "and I'd be glad to see you got good service over there, because this whole thing is embarrassing all around, but how could I know —"

"Don't take it so hard," said the Negro, not unkindly. "You don't make the laws nor own the railroads."

She was still stammering apologies when he got up and signaled to his friends he was ready to leave with them.

"But what about your order?" asked one of the unknowing ones.

"Oh, I can't eat in here with the Filipinos," the tall Negro observed smilingly, and the others laughingly joined in what they thought was a joke.

Apprised of the situation outside, the four "Filipinos" were indignant, and inclined to return and make an issue of it. But the tall Negro demurred.

"What can she do about it?" he asked.

The first of the four, Dr. Albert W. Dent, president of Dillard University of New Orleans, La., asked indignantly, "you mean to say that she thought we were Filipinos, and, as such, had rights that were to be denied us as American citizens?"

Dr. Rufus E. Clement, president of Atlanta University and an elected member of the Atlanta School Board[,] said:

"The significant thing about the whole incident is that not one white patron in that lunchroom cared one way or the other whether we ate there or who or what we were."

William J. Trent, executive director of the United Negro College Fund, said:

"I thought you were kidding. How could anybody mistake us for anything but what we are — American Negroes. The waitresses knew from the beginning."

Dr. F. D. Patterson, executive director of the Phelps Stokes fund in New York City, said:

"I know what we can do right away. We can each of us write the President of every railroad which runs into Richmond and tell them what we think of this. Then we can all go to Byrd Airport and make our reservations to leave here this week-end by air. And each of us should point out in our letters that five of us arrived here by railroad, but all five are leaving by air."

The tall Negro said: "If you well-fed 'Filipinos' have concluded your discussion can we get on to the airport where I can get some breakfast and telegraph the New York Post how I came to Ol' Virginny—first class?"

OVERCOMING HATE

Poston recalls here his 1928 arrival in New York. White reporters did the research on this series, to put the black New York experience in a context, and Poston, as writer on the series, tied it together. The second article's Aunt Dinah shows the lengths to which some whites will go to make excuses for their refusal to relate to Negroes, and the third article examines how blacks entered New York politics to gain a niche in the city's decision making.

"Prejudice and Progress: The Negro in New York I"
Ted Poston, Henry Beckett, Peter J. McElroy, Marcy Elias, Joseph Kahn, Irving Lieberman, and Edward Katcher
New York Post 16 April 1956: 4, 37

Your editor suggests:

"Why don't you start the series by describing how it feels to be a Negro in New York? How does it differ now from 28 years ago when you first came up from the South?"

And you say, jokingly:

"How do I know? I haven't been a Negro for so long that I've forgotten how it feels."

But suddenly you realize you are only half joking.

It is one of the glories of New York that here—more than anywhere else in America—a Negro can, at times, forget that he is a Negro. It is one of the tragedies of New York—and America—that no Negro, at all times, can forget completely.

You have Negro friends, of course, who insist that they have never suffered a single incident of discrimination in their whole lives in this city; who say they have never been reminded even once that they are different from anyone else.

But the very vehemence with which they advance the argument and their insistence on bringing up the subject cast doubts on the validity of their claims.

You consider the editor's proposal seriously and realize that your 28 years here could not be typical. But what individual's experience — no matter how lucky or how unfortunate — is typical of the whole?

You try to recreate the gangling youth who came to Harlem more than a quarter of a century ago from the limited freedom of Hopkinsville, Ky., and other points South.

What happened to him — say from 1928 — that couldn't happen to him now? What bitter path did he travel in reaching his decision that he would be better off here than down there? When did he discover that freedom is a relative thing; that there is no real Mason-Dixon Line to American race prejudice?

You search your memory for some experience which may have colored your outlook on race relations. But you find specific incidents hard to recall. It could be that you have forced yourself to forget unconsciously.

But two early incidents — one which would be impossible and the other improbable now — do stand out.

It is June, 1928, and you've been two days in New York, and you have a secret desire which you will not confess, even to your brother and his wife with whom you are living.

You have never seen a movie in your life from an orchestra seat. The Rex and Princess Theaters in Hopkinsville and movie houses in other Southern cities have always sent you upstairs to the peanut gallery.

So you go alone to the Victoria on West 125th St. in the heart of Harlem and buy an orchestra seat. You start into the almost empty theater and a young white girl takes your ticket in the lobby, but murmurs:

"You'll have to go upstairs."

You say you bought an orchestra ticket, but two husky white ushers show up one on each side of you and tell you:

"Do what the lady says."

You didn't know then — as so many Negroes don't know even now — that New York State had passed a Civil Rights law way back in 1909, and that the first successful test of that law had been over a theater's refusal to permit a Negro woman to occupy an orchestra seat.

So you slink from the Victoria, accept a refund from a contemptuous white cashier, and don't even tell your brother and sister-in-law what happened.

(*A week later, though, you are occupying your first orchestra seat. Your sister-in-law has taken you to your first Broadway musical, a "Little Show" starring Libby Holman and Clifton Webb, and you're right down there in the sixth row center.*

(*You don't even notice that the middle-aged white woman next to you is fidgeting in her seat or that her escort snorts and goes to the back of the theater. You hardly listen as he whispers audibly on his return: "The manager doesn't know how they got down here; he said they wouldn't have sold them tickets if they knew."*

(*But your sister-in-law is amused. "I got Sophie, a white friend in my office, to get these tickets," she whispers to you. "If I'd gone to the box office, they would have said they had only balcony seats."*)

The other incident took place at Far Rockaway Beach in July of 1928.

It was the first integrated beach you'd ever seen and no one seemed to notice that whites and Negroes were romping uproariously together in the rather clean sand and the [dirtier?] water.

You are luxuriating near one of the bulkheads when a scream for help comes from the deeper water. You are no Johnny Weissmuller, but you swim as fast as you can toward the screaming woman.

A stronger swimmer, a husky, swarthy white youth, spurts past you and has the drowning woman in his arms as you paddle up. You reach out to give him assistance, and he snarls:

"Get your goddam black hands off this white woman; she don't need no help from you."

Before you can make a shocked reply, a foam-crested wave dashes the couple into the end of the bulkhead. The man is knocked unconscious; you push the woman to the bulkhead where she clings precariously.

For a moment, you contemplate murder — "Let the bastard drown" — but you pull him to the bulkhead and safety and hold him there until the lifeguard arrives.

"This is one white man," you tell yourself wearily as you climb unaided back to the beach, "that you'll hate as long as you live."

But you don't. A half hour later, after he's been revived, he comes over and apologizes to you for what he said. And how can you hate the first white man who has apologized to you for anything in 19 years of life?

[. . . T]wo years later [. . .] you had gotten even with at least one white man. [. . . .]

You'd gone to visit a white acquaintance at an apartment house in the East 70s, and the white operator had stepped out of the elevator to inform you emphatically that:

"I won't take a nigger up in this elevator."

"Pay it no mind," you'd snapped, stepping quickly into the empty elevator. "I'll take myself up; I'm an old elevator man."

And you'd chuckled for days afterwards, remembering how the operator had to climb 13 flights of stairs to reclaim his empty car.

(It was an interracial party there that night and you and a very imposing deep-voiced guest seemed to be the only Negroes present. You were puzzled by a beautiful young blonde who always happened to be on the other side of the room no matter where you wandered.

(You were more impressed by the white tie and tails of the other Negro guest — he was going to the opera later — but you lost your awe when he finally agreed to sing. For he cupped his hands before him in a dignified pose and then rang out with "Mammy's little baby loves shortnin', shortnin'; Mammy's little baby loves shortnin' bread."

(You glanced accidentally across the room and saw the cute little blonde blushing. You recognized her then. You had met her a year before in Mike's Bar and Grill up on Harlem's Seventh Av. She was "passing" for white at the party. The one direct glance she gave you seemed to promise an explanation later. But you never saw her again after that.)

Henry Lee Moon, an old friend who now directs public relations for the NAACP, reminds you of another incident. It was then 1934 and you both were "old" New Yorkers and reporters on The Amsterdam News.

The two of you were having dinner in a second class Greenwich Village hashery after a stimulating evening in the home of a white acquaintance in the neighborhood.

For a while you were unconscious of the muttered grumbling of an elderly white woman at a table behind you. But suddenly she yelled:

"Why don't the damned niggers stay up in Harlem where they belong? Why do they have to come down here dirtying up our places?"

You look up suddenly and see the Greek owner of the place descending menacingly on your table. You brace yourself to defend your rights, but he keeps on past to the woman's table.

"You get the hell out of here and stay out," he roars at her angrily, "and if I catch you in here again disturbing my customers, I'll call the cops right away."

She got.

Moon and another friend, Thurston Lewis, were with you that year when you made your first test of the Civil Rights Law which had been amended to make possible the arrest as well as civil action against any person who discriminated because of race, creed or color.

You order the arrest — much to the indignation of an Irish desk-lieutenant — of a Negro elevator operator at a Claremont Av. apartment house near Columbia University for refusing to take you up to visit two friends.

"We don't allow Nigras in this house," said the Negro elevator man, speaking for the insurance company which owned the building. (The girls you wished to visit, summer students at Columbia, were both colored, but apparently their fair complexions had fooled the management. Thurston, who was fair also, had visited them earlier with no difficulty.)

Anyway, after the offender had been booked and jailed, you triumphantly call an NAACP lawyer and boast that you have forced an arrest under the amended law. The lawyer listens closely to the details and then reluctantly informs you:

"Ted, the amended law covers apartment hotels, but not apartment houses. You've locked that man up illegally. He's got a good case of false arrest against you if he ever finds out."

Fortunately, the elevator operator never did find out. He was arraigned the next morning before Magistrate Benjamin Greenspan who apparently wasn't aware of the extent of the law, and defended by insurance company lawyers who also didn't know that apartment house elevators were not covered. (They are now.)

In fact when Greenspan recognized you and Moon as star reporters on The Amsterdam News, he called all three of you behind the bench for a whispered consultation.

"Look," he said, motioning at the disheveled defendant, "that poor guy didn't know the law. He was only carrying out orders from the insurance company which hires him. So, since he's already spent a night in jail, I'm going to give him a real lecture on tolerance and civil rights, and let him off with a suspended sentence."

Thurston, to whom you have not confided the facts of life, starts to protest, but Moon stomps him on his instep, and graciously seconds Greenspan's proposal.

So you magnanimously accept the now-repentant elevator operator's apology in open court, and make a dignified exit under the benign smile of the magistrate.

But once outside, you make a sudden dash for the quickest transportation back to Harlem.

Your Claremont Av. friends finished summer school and left for Nashville, Tenn., the next day. So you never saw the elevator operator again.

And anyway, the statute of limitations has now run out.

"Prejudice and Progress: The Negro in New York II"
Ted Poston, Henry Beckett, Peter J. McElroy, Marcy Elias,
Joseph Kahn, Irving Lieberman, and Edward Katcher
New York Post 17 April 1956: 4, 40

How does one go about preparing a series of articles on segregation and discrimination against Negroes in the largest — and reputedly most liberal — city in the nation?

You and your co-workers search out the race relations experts, the Negro and white leaders, and examine all the data available in public and private agencies throughout the city.

You visit the slums, talk to the people in their homes, churches, barber shops, gin mills and other places of public assembly.

You also visit other sections of the city less frequented by Negro New Yorkers and watch the reactions of people there to this stranger in their midst.

And you ponder the query of one of your staff co-workers who had been examining the bulging files in The Post morgue.

"What more can The Post say on the subject that it hasn't been saying daily over the years?" he asked. "We could probably do the series from our own clips."

You keep digging. But even as you assemble new facts and get into recent developments, you can't tear your mind from the string of reminiscences started by your editor with his query:

"How does it feel to be a Negro in New York?"

So you try to recall when it was that you started feeling like a New Yorker first and a Negro second, after your youthful arrival here in 1928 from Hopkinsville, Ky.

You are about to settle for the first 10 years, and then recall an incident which happened around 1938.

You were a newspaperman and active trade unionist by then and you'd joined fellow Guildsmen on a picket line in front of the old Brooklyn Eagle. (You'd already led a successful strike on The Amsterdam News and had almost as many white friends as colored.)

So you are sophisticated enough to be amused when your wife [Miriam Rivers, Poston's first wife] finds an ad for a new Brooklyn restaurant called "Aunt Dinah's Kitchen," and suggests that you dine there when your picket stint is over.

It was a quaint but immaculate little tearoom down in a side street basement, but "Aunt Dinah" appears to be a buxom blond German and she gets flustered when the Negro couple enters her place.

"You're early," she says, although it is past 6 P.M. "We won't start serving dinner for a long time now." And she blocks your approach to a table.

You notice two white patrons quietly eating at other tables and murmur:

"Oh, that's all right. Just give us the same as those people have. We're not choosy."

The hostess blushed, but fixed her face in stern lines.

"I won't serve you in my dining room," she snapped. "If you want to go back there in the kitchen, maybe the chef will give you something. But not out here."

And she gestured toward a swinging service door through which a Negro chef (maybe he was "Aunt Dinah") was peeking apprehensively.

You are an old New Yorker now and sure of your rights. So you explain to her, patiently, that she can be locked up under the amended Civil Rights Law for refusing a Negro service because of his race or color.

She laughed scornfully and jeered:

"Go on and sue me. See if I care. I know all about that so-called law. You'll have to wait three years at least before your suit comes up. And even if I lose, it'll be worth $500 to keep your kind out of here."

"Oh, we'll sue you eventually, Madame," you assure her genially, "but right now we're talking about having you locked up."

"You can't do that," she insisted. And she was still insisting two hours later at the station house when the desk lieutenant interrupted her long and bitter tirade to ask plaintively:

"Madame, can I do something for you?"

"And what can *you* do for *me?*," she inquired haughtily.

"Well, I could get you some cigarets or a toothbrush or something like that," the lieutenant replied. "Because if you don't have $500 cash on your person for a desk bond, you're going to spend tonight in jail."

She didn't have the $500 and she still seemed unable to believe it when the arresting officer led her off to a cell. But she was freed by a Brooklyn magistrate the next morning, so you recalled her jeering challenge and promptly sued her for $1,000 damages.

The civil suit came up in Municipal Court the day after Hitler invaded Austria, and the presiding justice, finding that the late Heywood Broun, Charles Grutzner and other prominent fellow pickets were to be witnesses on your side, decided to make the most of it.

After listening to the testimony with constantly arching eyebrows, he called a brief recess and retired to his chambers to write out his charge to the six-man jury. (Copies of which were later distributed to each of the newspapermen witnesses.)

You listen to the charge (which even to you seemed a bit weighted against the defendant) and watch her as she fidgets nervously.

The justice holds up a copy of that morning's paper and points to a picture of elderly Jewish generals in full uniform being forced to scrub the streets of Vienna. He denounced the rise of intolerance all over the world, and concluded:

"This virus must be halted and it will be halted.

"There is no place in the sovereign State of New York for intolerance. Jury, retire and return your verdict."

The lawyer for "Aunt Dinah's Kitchen" was so perturbed that he tried to settle the case on the spot for $750 damages. But the jury returned too quickly for his offer to be accepted.

"And how do you find?" the beaming justice asked, leaning over the bench to see that each of the newspapermen had a copy of his charge.

"We find for the defendant," said the foreman.

"The defendant?" roared the judge in indignation. "Do you know who the defendant is in this case?"

"Sure," rejoined the foreman of the all-white jury, "that white lady over there is the defendant."

Memory will not let you forget one footnote to the incident.

You storm from the courtroom determined not to drop your 10-year-fight for your civil rights. You pick the most exclusive-looking tearoom on lower Fifth Av. and enter it belligerently for lunch.

You half hope you'll be denied service but you're not. Indeed the service and the food are excellent. Only one thing goes wrong. When you reach for your wallet to pay the bill, you find you had left it at home. And you feel no better when the head waiter waves aside your promise to return with the money immediately.

"Oh, don't bother," he said. "Just drop it by next time you're in the neighborhood. We're always glad to have you."

So maybe 1938 wasn't the year of maturity either.

But what of 1940? You'd spent three years on a metropolitan daily, had gotten some exclusive interviews with elusive public figures, and had found there were advantages as well as disadvantages to being a Negro in New York City.

A ranking city official with whom you later became friendly [Mayor William O'Dwyer] explained why he had opened up so fully on your first interview with him.

"Well, I figured like this," he told you. "If a Negro is good enough to hold a first-string job on a major daily, then he must be a helluva newspaperman. So I decided to get you in my corner from the beginning, so you wouldn't start looking for something to beat my brains out with."

Yes, maybe by 1940, you were beginning to feel like a New Yorker. But then a war broke out somewhere and you were given a three-month leave to help Sidney Hillman and Bob Weaver get the defense effort moving down in Washington.

The three months stretched out into five years, and you're doing all right in the Fair Deal government.

But one night you come back home and tell your Philadelphia-born wife [Marie Byrd Tancil] that you're going back to New York.

"I can't take it anymore," you say, recalling a near-fist fight with a white bus driver that morning and a donnybrook that night with a Negro cab driver who preferred white customers in Washington.

"Maybe New York spoiled me," you admit, "but I'm tired of Jim Crow theaters, Jim Crow restaurants, Jim Crow hotels and this whole Jim Crow town." (That was wartime Washington.)

"But aren't you thinking of making your White House work official?"

your wife protests. "Wouldn't that make you the first Negro to serve officially as an Administrative Assistant to the President of the United States?"

"Sure," you concede bitterly. "But suppose I took the job. And suppose
President Truman passed on [NAACP head] Walter White or [the Urban
League's] Lester Granger or some other Negro leader and asked me to take
him to lunch? What could I do? Grab a cab and take them two miles up
to 14th and U St. Northwest? There's no nearer place to the White House
that a Negro can eat in dignity, if at all."

You win the argument, and a few days later you are back in New York
and at The Post.

But the New York freedom you'd envisioned eludes you at first.
Washington — and the deep South through which you had traveled on
your ever-changing government duties — have done something to you.

For the first time in years (even before Aunt Dinah's Kitchen) you feel
unsure of yourself in New York. You hesitate about entering certain restaurants and other public places, with an almost unconscious fear of how you
might be received.

You realize that you have begun to equate mere stares of curiosity from
white New Yorkers with the glares of unmasked hostility encountered in
official offices in some Southern areas.

So you take yourself in hand and consciously snap out of it.

One rather searing incident, which even now you recall reluctantly,
helps restore your equilibrium if only because it shows how the South can
condition a Negro.

The Negro in point is your father, a man who had spent most of his then
90-odd years fighting all forms of discrimination in Kentucky. [. . .] Ephraim Poston [. . .] had sued every Jim Crow agency in the state where he
had been a respected educator.

You visit him in Paducah, Ky., and he flies back to New York with you
for a second view of the big town. His trip is an unrivaled success until the
night before he is due to return home.

You've taken him to a Broadway show and are forced to ride the subway
home when most cabs seem unavailable. You dash into the car to save a
seat for him and he sinks into it with audible relief.

You are startled a minute later when he leaps suddenly to his feet and
takes the strap beside you.

He'd only realized then that the seat you had saved for him was next to
a white woman.

You look at each other and look away ashamed. You both remain silent for the long ride to Brooklyn.

How can one say to a father who has fought all his life for equality that: "The crackers got you anyway."

You realize that this never could have happened to a Negro who had spent his life in New York. Nor even to you who had been here not too many years. So you know New York is your town from then on.

And it is so much your town later that the question is no longer uppermost in your mind when the city desk sends you to cover a luncheon of the National Conference of Christians and Jews at the Waldorf.

It is a deadline story with no advance text. So you go directly to Elmo Roper [an early polling expert] and get his speech notes and hurry to the hallway outside to call the office for the 1:30 P.M. edition.

The hall telephone is on a little round table in the corridor and you take the phone behind some adjoining drapes to escape the noise of the luncheon. The clinking of the silverware seems unusually loud from that distance, but you finish dictating your story.

And you step from behind the drapes to find the small telephone table completely transformed. A spotless white cloth and shining silverware have been placed upon it, and a cherry-centered grapefruit is resting in a bowl of ice.

"The man in charge," said a hovering waiter, gesturing toward the Southern-born white press agent for the National Conference of Christians and Jews, "told me to set this up out here for you.

"He said you might be uncomfortable at the press table, for several of the papers have sent young white ladies to cover the luncheon."

You almost blow your top, but you don't. You take the apologetic press agent aside and tell him that this is New York, and this is a tolerance outfit he's working for. You turn down his pleas to go to the press table anyway — because you really do have a legitimate assignment elsewhere.

And when your paper inadvertently hears of the incident later and determines to get the offender fired, you intercede in his behalf and quote your longtime friend, Henry Lee Moon, now an NAACP official, to the effect that:

"Those things happen here, but there's a difference.

"For unlike the South, prejudice up here is often a reflection of individual bias and ignorance. And it has neither the backing of the State nor the power of public opinion behind it."

You console yourself with that thought for a while. But you are a little shaken the next year when the National Conference of Christians and Jews gave its tolerance award in the entertainment industry to the man who had owned the National Theater in Washington, and who had closed it down rather than admit Negro patrons at the demand of Actor's Equity.

Today, however, one Negro can recall these incidents with wry amusement. But only because experience has shown that few, if any, could be repeated today.

There have been later incidents, and there will be others, of course. But even these cannot shake the belief that New York has become more adult in race relations even as other parts of the country were becoming more juvenile.

The laws have helped, of course, and New York has enacted the most comprehensive body of civil rights legislation of any state and city in the country.

But it is more than just laws, or a more rigid enforcement of existing statutes. There is an atmosphere of tolerance (in the better sense of the word) on both sides of the fence that didn't exist in 1928, or 1948 for that matter.

You may never be able to determine when you became a New Yorker first and a Negro second — if indeed, you ever did.

But a once-gangling Negro immigrant from Kentucky will have to admit that he and New York City have both come a long way since 1928. [. . .]

"Prejudice and Progress: Jim Crow in New York III"
Ted Poston, Henry Beckett, Peter J. McElroy, Marcy Elias,
Joseph Kahn, Irving Lieberman, and Edward Katcher
New York Post 18 April 1956: 4, 60

Let's stop kidding ourselves about Jim Crow in New York. He lives here, too.

We have herded most of our 850,000 Negro citizens into ghettoes which would shame even some Southern towns.

We send thousands of Negro children to segregated schools under the very conditions which the Supreme Court said "generate a feeling of inferiority . . . that may affect their hearts and minds in a way unlikely ever to be undone."

We confine some Negroes to the lowest-paid jobs in some industries, bar them from some others and hold them back in still others.

Beyond that, a Negro here is a little more likely to get pushed around by a cop than is his white fellow citizen, and there aren't many adult Negroes who at some time or another have not suffered humiliation, deprivation, inconvenience or discourtesy solely because of the color of their skin.

But don't let Alabama and the rest of the South fool themselves either. New York City is still the best place in America for a Negro to live.

John Gunther recognized this a decade ago in "Inside U.S.A.":

"By and large, the Negroes (of New York City) have greater opportunities in more fields than in any comparable city; they have better chances in education, jobs, social evolution and civil service; they are nearest to full citizenship of any (Negroes) in the nation."

And since that was written, the Negroes of New York have made the most monumental strides in their unparalleled drive toward full citizenship.

One prominent Negro New Yorker and race relations expert — and what Negro in America isn't a bit of an expert on that question — went even further.

"It's more than just a question of 'education, jobs, social evolution, civil service' or the statistics you might muster to support the contention," he said.

"Negroes are better off in New York, well, because it is New York. Because it has the most stimulating environment, the greatest cultural advantages; because it offers more to more groups of people — Negroes included — than any other city in the country.

"You might say it is the greatest city for Negroes because it is the least American of all the American cities. Somehow, despite the existing prejudices, there are not the sharp divisions, the provincialism, the daily interracial tensions which mark most other American cities, especially those in the South."

Roy Wilkins, who has been singed by residential segregation here even though he is executive secretary of the NAACP and thus one of the most influential Negroes in America, will tell you:

"Of course, there is discrimination in New York. But nobody here dares brag about it. If Negroes have accomplished anything in this city they have made the term 'discrimination' a dirty word. Even the worst bigot who tries to practice it will seek some other excuse to justify his action."

And Dr. Robert C. Weaver, State Rent Administrator and outstanding authority on Negro labor and housing, says this:

"Yes, 'discrimination' is not a dirty word in most other cities, including Chicago where I worked several years. Here, in New York, Negroes have some stature, hold public office, have position in the community. They also have voice and background, and their opponents are reluctant to admit that they are anti-integration."

Julius A. Thomas, director of industrial relations for the National Urban League, a man who has done much to open up new areas of employment for Negroes during the last decade, puts it this way.

"New York may not be a utopia for the Negro worker but here we've made tremendous strides in every direction. Today, you can find a Negro employed in every kind of job.

"Of course there is segregation and discrimination in some fields still—air, bus and railroad transportation; the waterfront, banking, television, newspapers and some branches of the trucking industry.

"But by and large in New York City, if you have the qualifications, we'll get you the job. That's something that couldn't happen, say, in Montgomery, Ala.

"And if you don't get the job you're qualified for, well, there are people in New York who are paid just to listen to your squawk. And these people are paid to do something about it."

And William H. Butler, director of the Travelguide Agency, which stresses "Recreation without Discrimination" for Negro travelers in the U.S. and abroad, will tell you:

"In New York, every entertainment and recreation media is wide open to Negroes. Ice skating at Radio City, golf courses, beaches, just about everything you can think of.

"You can get a first-class hotel room practically anywhere you seek it; you are welcome in the supper clubs and places like that—but I still can't say what might happen at the Stork Club.

"I remember not so many years ago when there was a bitter situation in one of the chain restaurants. They were horrible about service to Negroes. You'd go in, sit down and you just waited and waited. They wouldn't tell you couldn't eat there—they simply just didn't serve you.

"Well, pressure was put on that outfit—a series of law suits. And today they not only serve you, they welcome Negroes."

But these are all successful men talking. A psychiatrist we talked to observed that such well educated, self-assured and articulate Negroes can take care of themselves in any society and might have no idea of the broad discrimination suffered by Negroes who are not so highly placed.

So The Post reporters went into the rotten slum homes, the churches, the barber shops and the bars of the less fortunately situated Negroes.

To talk to us, Mrs. Hannah Simpson, 67, and a grandmother, had to take time out from her daily battle against the vermin and rats in her third floor walkup on W. 141st St. in a block once called the most densely populated in the world.

Mrs. Simpson came here 13 years ago "as soon as my son could scuffle up enough to send for me" — from a rural area near Biloxi, Miss.

She can never remember a moment "when times weren't tight" here but she'll never go back to Mississippi, nor anywhere else in the South.

Why?

"Well, maybe it's hard to say. It's the little things as well as the big ones. But I know I ain't never going back.

"Now me, I'm a church woman. I don't hold with dancing and shows and movies and things like that. But my grandchildren do, and they can go right down there to that Roxy and set on the ground floor with everybody else. Nobody tells them to go up to the buzzard's roost.

"And when our landlord here who don't ever fix nothing tried to jack our rent up $3 for nothing just the other month or so, my Jennie looked him right in the eye and said:

"'You want us to take you to the Rent Commissioner?'"

"And you know what? That white man didn't say a word. And next week he fixed that hole in the ceiling, and we didn't pay him no $3 extra neither.

"Naw, I ain't never going back South."

To Simeon Bowlin, 43, a cab driver who was born not far from Pendleton, S.C., it is quite simple.

"It's the law; that's the difference," he said. "I don't mean the law up here about it's wrong to deny somebody this or that; I mean the night-stick law.

"Oh, I know some cop can get frisky and bust a Negro over the head for nothing — here or anywhere else. But he can't get away with it here like he might somewhere else. If it happened in Harlem, the folks would be on him.

"Could you imagine any one of us suing a cop down in Carolina? The difference is, up here, the law's on anybody's side who is right."

But if you want to start a real argument, go to Harlem and suggest that there's not much difference between life for a Negro here or anywhere else, especially the South.

A Negro patron did just that the other night in a bar and grill at the corner of 154th St. and Eighth Av. and 15 fellow drinkers looked at him in astonishment.

"I'd rather be a lamp post in Harlem than mayor of Brunswick, Ga., where I came from," a truck driver spoke up. "I wouldn't take no part of Georgia if you gave it to me — and that goes for Mississippi, Arkansas, Alabama or any other part of 'Bam'."

In the two-hour discussion which followed, no one seriously suggested trading New York with all its problems for a return ticket home.

"I've got a brother in Savannah," one man said, "and he's doing all right. Got his own business and is building himself a house out on Victory Drive. He's always asking me to come back. Says I can make twice the money there that I make up here. And I say, 'All right, I can make the money, but what could I do with it in Savannah, Georgia?'

"And he knows as well as I do that he can have all the money in the world down there but as soon as those rebs decide they don't like him, he's up the well-known creek — business, new home and all."

But let's not be smug about the reputed freedom of the Negro citizens of Our Town. To them it is more than a question of whether it is better here or back down home. They're quite aware of the day-to-day limitations of being a Negro in New York City.

Take housing, for example, and listen to Dr. Weaver:

"Residential segregation is much more general in cities of the North than in the South . . . Manhattan has more racial segregation than Atlanta."

But leave the experts again and talk to the people in the slums and you will find bitterness and hatred — diffused and disorganized perhaps but deep-rooted and vocal nevertheless.

Ralph Ellison was dealing more with fact than fiction in "Invisible Man" when he described how Negro slum dwellers used the first Harlem riot as a cover to burn down their rotting tenement.

This fictional scene was recalled the other day when a Negro skilled worker, whose income has doubled in the last 10 years, said:

"We missed two wonderful opportunities in those two Harlem riots. We should have burned the whole damned place down to the ground then. Then they'd have had to let us live somewhere else. There would have been no Harlem in which to keep us cooped.

"Yes, I know there might have been a great loss of life if such a thing had happened. But would we have lost more lives then than we've lost in the 20 years since the first riot through tuberculosis, pestilence, rat bites, tenement fires and our other slow killers?"

On a more lofty level, we found a Negro educator bitter at a white colleague.

"He was the first to circulate a local petition in our set on the Emmett

Till case," the educator recalled. "He raised the first collection last December for the Montgomery bus strikers.

"Yet last summer, when he knew I was fighting with real estate agents all over town to try to find a decent place to move away from the ghetto — he never once told me of three vacancies in his own apartment house on the East Side.

"You know, that's what is wrong with so many of our liberal white friends up here. They'll fight like hell for your rights as long as they don't inconvenience their own."

Or listen to Mrs. Esther R. Barr, a highly trained Negro woman who for six years has been case-work supervisor in charge of the Social Service Division of Montefiore Hospital. Turned down on living accommodations in Jackson Heights, Elmhurst, Astoria, the Upper Bronx and all parts of Manhattan outside Harlem. Mrs. Barr says bitterly:

"I have decided to return to my home in Indianapolis and seek employment there or elsewhere. . . . In Indianapolis, I know what the restrictions are and where to look for a home.

"I've been in the South only once. But there is one advantage down there. You know exactly how you stand and what you can't do. Here, you never know when you will be shocked and humiliated."

That is the heart of the problem, according to Dr. Fredric Wertham, the psychiatrist who directs the Lafargue Clinic in the heart of Harlem.

"Prejudice is more cruel in the South," Dr. Wertham says, "but there is a distinction. If a man is prepared for it, he can be hit in the stomach and it may not hurt him. If he is not prepared and does not expect it, he may be knocked out.

"Well, in the South, a Negro expects the worst and is prepared for it. Up here, he thinks everything is all right, but then when he tries to live in a decent place, he finds that he is excluded, and that knocks him out."

"Prejudice and Progress in New York: The Negro in Politics IX"
Ted Poston, Henry Beckett, Peter J. McElroy, Marcy Elias,
Joseph Kahn, Irving Lieberman, and Edward Katcher
New York Post 25 April 1956: 4, 73

One sultry night back in 1930, a Pennsylvania red cap called Big Ed Stephens dropped by the Cayuga Democratic club in Harlem's old 19th A[ssembly]. D[istrict]. to try to collect a $2 debt from a district captain.

The captain was out and the club was almost deserted but Stephens was surprised at the warm reception he got from Martin J. Healy, the white Tammany District Leader.

"Big Ed," said Healy, "how would you like to run for the Assembly from the 19th?"

"Are you kidding?" the red cap replied. "You know we could never beat the Republicans and that kid Myles Paige they're running in this district."

"Maybe not," Healy conceded, "but I've been busy with other matters. We've got to file our petitions tonight, and we've got to put up somebody. It may as well be you."

(The "other matters" with which Healy was busy included his impending indictment and trial for allegedly selling a magistrateship [outside his district][2] *for $10,000, and other charges that he had plundered the public till for some $2,400 a year on a school book deal.)*

Big Ed said he'd run — and there the matter ended as far as he was concerned. He made no speeches; he conducted no campaign. He tended to his business at Penn Station.

So no one was more surprised than James Edward Stephens — unless it was Martin J. Healy and Myles A. Paige, now a Special Sessions Court Justice — when the November returns showed that the red cap would be the only Negro in the New York State Legislature the next year, having defeated Paige by 428 votes.

It was less surprising to most Negroes who knew the quality of red caps in those depression days that Stephens went on to make an excellent Assemblyman. For he was a graduate both of Howard University and the Brooklyn Law School.

And before Healy finally dumped him after five years in the Assembly, Stephens was responsible for several important pieces of legislation, including a law which forbade insurance companies from selling inferior policies to Negroes.

It is a long jump from Big Ed Stephens, the first Negro Democrat to sit in the Assembly, to Hulan Jack, the Negro ex-Assemblyman who is now Manhattan Borough President. But New Yorker Negroes have made it, hitting all the stops in between.

For if Negroes have reaped one benefit from the city's greatest anti-Negro evil — its residential segregation — it has been this: Negroes have become one of the most potent factors in the political life of the city and the state. [. . .]

BUS BOYCOTT

After Poston chronicled the situation of Negroes in New York, his editors sent him to Montgomery, Alabama, where Martin Luther King Jr. was leading a bus boycott and gaining the world's attention.

"Ted Poston in Alabama: The Negroes of Montgomery I"
New York Post 11 June 1956: 4, 42

You fly South. Your long dormant memory outraces the plane which bears you through the night.

You're heading back to Alabama for the second time in your newspaper career. And 22 years fall away as you recall that first trip.

You'd arrived that time at night, too, but stealthily and by bus. For the Klansmen of Decatur, Ala., had sent written notices to the Amsterdam News and other Negro papers warning that they would "take care of any nigger reporters who stick their nose in our business here again."

(The "business" at hand then was the third trial for [the] lives of nine illiterate Negro youths who had been hauled from a train at Paint Rock, Ala., and unjustly accused of the rape of two white girl hoboes near a place called Scottsboro.

(So you'd descended the Decatur bus in overalls with your rickety portable typewriter wrapped in brown paper to resemble a bundle of clothes. You'd carried out your role of a curious country boy from Morgan County for two weeks, while the late Tom Cassidy of the New York Daily News *visited the Morgan County Circuit Courthouse "White Men's Room" twice daily to pick up your dispatches from the partition by the "Colored" room and file them to the* Amsterdam News.

(You'd mailed your typewritten copy nightly in the mail car of the midnight express at the Decatur railroad station. And one night a dozen suspicious white youths cornered you there and knocked out two of your front teeth before you convinced them — with carefully pre-arranged credentials — that you were a Negro minister.

(And the loss of the two teeth hurt less than the loss of your dignity when one of the youths sent you on your way with a kick in the pants and the observation that "Nigger preachers is all right; they wouldn't be mailing no stuff on how we treat our niggers.")

You smile in recalling the incident, but not at the incident itself. You smile at your cleverness in concealing the forgotten occurrence from your New York Post editor.

For the editor, like many New York friends, had been apprehensive when you agreed to go to Montgomery, Ala., to complete the series of articles begun with the Post survey on "Jim Crow in New York."

"Have you ever been to Alabama on a story before?" he'd asked one day, after too carelessly closing the door of his private office.

"Oh, sure," you'd replied, hoping he'd forgotten the Editor and Publisher account of your difficulties on the original Scottsboro Case.

"Where'll you be staying in Montgomery?"

"At the Ben Moore Hotel, a Negro hotel there. I've already got reservations."

"Does the city desk know where to reach you at all times? Have you left the names and phone numbers of other people there who can contact you at any moment?"

"Yes," you'd replied, but added: "Look, I don't know what the situation is down in Montgomery. But this I do know. The crackers there have made too many boners already to take any chance on making an even bigger boner with me. They can't afford to let anything happen to me with the whole world watching the Montgomery bus boycott story."

You remembered a little uneasily that the words you'd just uttered were almost identical to the argument you had made to the city editor back in 1949 persuading him to let you go to Tavares, Fla., to cover the "Little Scottsboro" rape case. That assignment had some unpleasant moments, ending with a 90-mile-an-hour chase by a lynch mob before you got back to the safety of New York.

But this time you really didn't visualize any personal difficulty or danger and your hunch proved to be right. In almost three weeks in the cradle of the Confederacy you never encountered any real trouble.

But, like most New Yorkers who have followed the progress of the then six-month struggle over the bus boycott, you would expect to find an armed camp atmosphere as the issue dragged on towards a showdown.

Well, you didn't find that, either.

You'd mentioned your editor's fears to a comely but highly intelligent young Negro writer who had just spent her three-week vacation in the supposedly embattled southern city.

She laughed softly as you discussed it just a few hours before your plane was due to leave LaGuardia Field.

"If you've got to go South, Ted," she'd said, "where else could you be safer than in the one town in America where 50,000 Negroes are sticking together?

[. . .] "You have really to see them to believe it. Nothing like this has ever happened to Negroes anywhere before. [But] believe me, it's going to happen somewhere else and soon."

And she didn't predict Tallahassee, Fla., either.

But both Tallahassee and Montgomery were in your future when the Eastern Air Lines Constellation touched down at the Atlanta, Ga., airport at 4:07 A.M. and you found you had a three-hour wait before taking off for Birmingham and Montgomery.

You looked around the terminal and reflected that you might as well be at LaGuardia or Idlewild. There were about a dozen Negro passengers among the two score persons nodding in the large waiting room and no two were sitting together.

You browsed through your morning papers and kept that impression until a few minutes later when you headed for the large sign marked "MEN."

You were almost through the door when, from the corner of your eye, you saw another sign reading "Colored Men." But your momentum — or perversity — was so great by then that you kept on through the door marked "MEN."

The spacious and well-equipped room seemed deserted, and you thought to yourself that it was just as well. Just then, however, a cubicle opened and a large red-faced white man stepped out and looked at you expressionlessly.

Well, here we go again, you murmur, as he walks wordlessly and deliberately toward you. Finally he speaks:

"Got a match?" he asks courteously and in a deep Southern drawl.

"Sure," you say quickly, handing him one as you both light up.

"Come down from New York?" and when you nod yes, "Rough trip?"

"Not bad," you say, and he cuts in "Rough as hell out of Detroit. Was raining when we left there. I'll be glad to get home to Birmingham on Flight 575."

When he finds that you are taking the same flight to Montgomery, he suggests a cup of coffee, and when you both obtain one at the coffee counter, he says, "Let's go over into the lounge to drink it. It's better sleeping there."

He flips a half dollar to a drowsy Negro skycap as you enter the lounge (there was already one Negro passenger nodding there) and says:

"Boy, we're both taking that flight that leaves here at 8:30. If we doze off and don't hear the call, be sure to wake us up."

You don't doze, however. You discuss the weather, the Dodgers, Vice President Nixon, and finally the school desegregation business.

He's against desegregation, doesn't believe either of us will see it in our lifetime, but he's also opposed to the White Citizens Councils who are claiming the headlines in his native Birmingham.

"We got a screwball named Ace Carter who organized something he calls the North Alabama Citizens Councils. He's out to bar the Jews and I guess he'll go after the Catholics next. That kind of business—and I guess you read about the King Cole thing³ too—that does nobody no good."

And, then with a wry smile: "But you got to admit that your NAACP or whatever you call it helped to bring a lot of this on."

You continue the conversation on Flight 575, but in a more desultory manner, as you sit together in the short flight to Birmingham. When you deplane there to stretch your legs, he bids you a courteous but quick good-by and joins friends or associates who are awaiting him.

So you walk around the terminal to investigate a certain situation. And there it is: "MEN," and "Colored Men," right around the corner.

There is only one drinking fountain in the Birmingham terminal, however, and you go there.

You don't realize then that you are having your last unsegregated drink in Birmingham.

But you are. For when you go back through the airport for an overnight Atlanta trip eight days later, something new has been added.

(It is a much smaller and shorter drinking fountain placed six feet from the main one. And the battered tin signs above each read "WHITE" and "Colored." So you contained your thirst until you got to Atlanta. And although you were really thirsty on your return trip the next day, you again staved it off until you got back to Montgomery.)

For one of the first things you had noticed on your original arrival at Montgomery's small Dannelly Field was that there was only one "MEN" and one drinking fountain, and you'd availed yourself of both freely.

(Your joy was short-lived however. For by the time you left Montgomery almost three weeks later, the citizens had approved a $420,000 item in a

$5,675,000 *bond issue which would permit Montgomery to use local tax-payers' money [Negro as well as white]*[4] *to establish segregated toilet, drinking and eating facilities at an enlarged Dannelly Field — and to hell with the C[ivil] A[eronautics] A[uthority] and its denial of federal funds for this purpose.*

(Negro voters had cast an estimated 2,000 of the 2,544 votes against the measure in a total vote of 8,234.)

But that was in the future, too. The first person to greet you at Dannelly Field was a Negro youth in his early teens who asked if he could get your baggage for you. As he walked away with the checks, a large white man approached you and asked courteously:

"Would you like to take the airlines limousine into town, sir?"

Since you'd actually arrived two hours earlier than the Montgomery Improvement Assn. expected you, you said yes.

You looked up as the Negro youth went past you carrying your folded valpac bag in his arms. He walked over to the Eastern ticket counter and dumped the bag on the scales.

"You've broken both handles off the gentleman's bag," he told the airline clerk. "You'll have to pay him for it."

"How do I know you didn't break them, bringing it from the field?" the clerk inquired.

"Ask the baggage man out there," the youth responded courteously but firmly. "It's the airline's fault. You've got to pay the gentleman for his bag."

The clerk looks from the youth to you and then quietly apologizes for the accident.

"If you'll take the bag by the Jefferson Davis Hotel after you empty it, sir," he said, "they'll be glad to repair it and settle any damages."

The youth, satisfied, picked up the bag in his arms and strolled with you to the airlines limousine.

"You have to catch these things when they happen," he remarked conversationally, "or else you might not get your rights. I've seen it before."

And he gravely accepted his 50 cents tip and returned to the terminal.

You are still pondering the youth's adult demeanor when the limousine halts in front of a Trailways Bus Terminal in the center of Montgomery to discharge a Negro woman who is taking a bus to Selma, Ala. The driver also removes your bag from the trunk and places it on the sidewalk.

You point out that you are a stranger in town and plan on going to the

Ben Moore Hotel. He suggests politely that you can get a cab from here and hails a Negro bellhop who is crossing the street towards you.

"He'll call you one," he says.

You hand the bellhop a coin and ask if he can call you a cab.

"Sure," he said, "but wait a minute."

The bellhop walks past you to the white limousine driver and asks quietly:

"Why don't you take the gentleman to his hotel? Why should he have to call a cab?"

"I can't," said the driver. "It's against the regulations."

"What regulations?" persisted the bellhop, firmly but not truculently. "You carry the other passengers to their hotels. Wasn't this gentleman an airlines passenger?"

The white driver flushed and said nothing as the bellhop persisted: "Wasn't he an airline passenger?"

Just then a passing Negro-driven cab slowed in inquiry and the white driver hastily gathered the broken-handled bag up in his arms and rushed it to the cab.

"I'm sorry, sir," he said, as you climbed in. "I don't make the regulations."

The Negro bellhop was standing right behind him smiling. He flipped back the half dollar you'd originally given him.

"No charge, sir," he said with a sardonic grin. "Always glad to accommodate a gentleman."

Later—after a Mother's Day visit to the Dexter Avenue Baptist Church, where you'd heard Rev. Martin Luther King's learned sermon on "The Role of the Negro Mother in Preparing Youth for Integration"—you are sitting on the M[ontgomery] I[mprovement] A[ssociation] leader's front porch prepared to begin your assignment.

One pillar of the rambling white house is still slightly shattered and a hole in the concrete porch still marks the spot where a clumsy dynamite bomb landed early in the bus boycott.

You are chuckling at the valpac and limousine incidents when a large-boned middle-aged Negro woman lumbers across the street and walks up the steps in houseshoes.

"Which one of you gentlemen is Rev. King?" she asks.

You gesture toward the minister who is just going inside to take a phone call.

"I'd like to give him a big hug," she confides, "but he's such a little bitty sweet thing that I'm afraid I'd break him in two."

On King's return, she wrings his hand and explains:

"I'm from down in Watumpka (Ala.)," she said, "and I couldn't go back there to meet my Shepherd if I had to tell him I'd been in Montgomery without shaking the hand of Rev. Martin Luther King.

"You know, even the white folks way down there are watching you all up here. My sister's Missus asked her: 'What's they doing up there and who's this King preacher you hear so much about!'

"And my sister said: 'I told her all I knew was what I read in Jet Magazine —'

"And I told my sister: 'Don't tell 'em nothing. Talk with your mouth shut!' "

You are in Montgomery, Alabama.

"Ted Poston in Alabama: The Negroes of Montgomery IV"
New York Post 14 June 1956: 4, 49

It was 2:30 in the morning and your final party of 12 was breaking up on the spacious tree-shaded patio of the Citizens Club, a Negro night club on the outskirts of West Montgomery.

Since early evening, with your guest list constantly changing, you had been discussing how it feels to be a Negro in Montgomery — the benefits, the drawbacks, the day-by-day irritations which were crystallized by the spontaneous bus boycott.

You had come to the club earlier with Rufus Lewis, former college football coach, political leader and owner of the membership club. On entering the club proper you had walked under a bright blue neon sign proclaiming

"Every Member a Registered Voter."

The Citizens Club had been the original headquarters of the hastily established Montgomery Improvement Assn. before pressure had been exerted to have it moved. It went then to the basement of Rev. Ralph D. Abernathy's First Baptist Church, and finally to its present compact quarters in the Bricklayers' Union Building at 530 C S. Union St.

But Lewis, founder and leader of the city's most influential Democratic club, has not only remained active in the movement, but will head its important next drive — a sustained campaign to get at least 10,000 Negroes registered in Montgomery.

And he chuckled as he told you:

"Despite all the pressure being exerted right now on all white candidates for office to reject Negro votes, individual candidates still sneak out here at night to seek support and insist they don't mean what the Citizens Council makes them say."

But not much of the discussion had been political that night as long time residents of Montgomery from various walks of life tried to explain — many for the first time — what it meant to them to be a Negro in the Cradle of the Confederacy.

"There is really nothing too wrong about Montgomery that a little desegregation wouldn't have cured," one professional man had opened the early discussion. "But the white people couldn't see it.

"There was probably no town in the South where Negroes were so willing to accept separate and unequal treatment as here — if only they had been allowed to keep their humanity in the little things."

An insurance man who spends his vacations either in New York or on the West Coast, agreed:

"It's the little things, all right, but they are not so little when you have to live with them daily.

"There's not a first-class restaurant in Montgomery where a Negro can go out for a decent meal or an evening of relaxation. I was embarrassed last night when you insisted that you would not have dinner at our home again until we let you take us out somewhere.

"Oh, we have some few places of our own — the Citizens Club here, the Raven Drive-In further out, and the food is good at Dean's Drug Store counter and a few other places. But you're barred by custom and by law from any first-class place in Montgomery."

(*Mention of the law brought to mind the Montgomery City Code which you'd spent the previous night reading. For Section 14: Article 5 specifies that:*

("It shall be unlawful to conduct a restaurant or other place for the serving of food in the city, at which white and colored people are served in the same room, unless such white and colored people are effectually separated by a solid partition extending from the floor upward to a distance of seven feet or higher, and unless a separate entrance from the street is provided for each compartment.") [. . .]

A neatly dressed Negro factory worker laughingly recalled an incident at his work place which taught him a section of the Montgomery City Code he'd never known before.

"There are only a few pecks [peckerwoods, or white people] out to our place," he recalled, "the foreman and straw bosses who walk around while we do the work, but we all get along pretty good. And every pay day, a few of our boys like to gamble a bit on the lunch hour.

"These pecks always imagine themselves helluva gamblers and they're always horning in on the game. One day one of the pecks got broke quick and when the foreman wouldn't lend him any money, he cussed him out and walked away.

"Well, pretty soon the law came driving up and locked up everybody in the game, the foreman and two other white boys included. The peck who had lost had blown the whistle.

"They thought they'd been grabbed for gambling, but it turned out that they were nabbed for violating the Jim Crow laws."

(Section 28 of the Montgomery City Code specifies that: "It shall be unlawful for a Negro and a white person to play together or in company with each other in the city in any game of cards, dice, dominoes or checkers.")

"Well, we weren't playing dominoes," the fellow concluded.

But there was little levity in the recitals of other denials and inconveniences which continued on through the night.

A Negro doctor said:

"I had to drive over a hundred miles last Sunday — to Birmingham — to get in just one game of golf. It meant I had to rush through one round and practically head back home again.

"Of course, I could have driven the 40 miles to Tuskegee and tried to play on the Veterans Administration course there. But the course is restricted and it's not so good either."

An educator recalled:

"My wife was downtown shopping last summer for some things for herself and our little three-year-old whom she's taken along with her. We've had a fairly large account there for years.

"Well, the baby wanted to go to the toilet and my wife asked the salesgirl where she could find it. The girl looked flustered and then mumbled something about they didn't have a toilet in the store. This is a big store, mind you.

"My wife didn't argue with her. She just handed back the purchases she had made, and then went over to the credit office and asked them to close out her account.

"The manager got word of what was happening and rushed over. He apologized for the salesgirl and personally directed my wife and baby to the restroom. So we decided to keep the account. But we finally closed it out anyway when they kept billing my wife by her first name and ignoring her signature as 'Mrs.'"

You've already learned that several of the downtown stores—who are as dependent on Negro patronage as the now almost defunct Montgomery City Lines—installed Jim Crow toilet facilities for their Negro patrons.

Others got around the "seven-foot-tall" eating partition regulation by installing small lunch counters for Negroes in their basements with separate entrances as required by law.

And "before the bus protest brought things to a head," one of your guests admitted frankly that night, "there were no widespread objections to even those inadequate arrangements.

"Fact is, it was better than nothing. And when you got to go, you got to go. And even Jim Crow beats nothing under those circumstances."

But another put in:

"Since they've really been feeling the loss of Negro patronage through the protest movement, things are beginning to change in several places.

"I just walked through several of the stores recently and I noticed that the 'White' and 'Colored' signs have been taken down off some of the drinking fountains, and drinking cups made available for everybody.

"I also noticed that in at least one store the same signs have been painted out on the doors of the toilets." [. . .]

It was now 3:15 A.M. and the orchestra had long since departed. Even the juke box had been silent for hours.

The last of your guests depart reluctantly and a college professor sums up the problem for all:

"Sorry to pull out even now," he said, "but most of us have got to be on our pick-up routes before 6 A.M. this morning to get our regular customers for our car pools.

"We don't want to inconvenience the good white folks in Cloverdale, Normandale, and other sections who would be completely lost without their domestics.

"Who said we were trying to wreck our Southern Way of Life?"

"Ted Poston in Alabama: The Negroes of Montgomery V"
New York Post 15 June 1956: 4, 48

She was an unlettered woman of about 45, and she had been working as a domestic since her early teens. But she displayed an amazing grasp of economics which should have shamed Mayor W. A. (Tacky) Gayle and Montgomery's other two City Commissioners.

She was the only Negro to whom you had talked who had actually been fired for refusing to ride the Montgomery City Lines buses during the protracted boycotts.

"But they hired me back that same night they fired me," she explained. "They had to.

"Because I'm helping them buy that new house they got out in the Mount Meigs section. Because, without me, they couldn't keep that 1955 Buick the Mister insisted on turning the old car in for."

The other six women in the bright red station wagon, which was taking them to their domestic jobs at 6 A.M., chuckled appreciatively. But you found the answer a bit complicated, so you asked her to start at the beginning.

"Well," she said, adjusting her plump body to a more comfortable position, "the Mister ain't such a bad man as white folks go. And until this White Citizens Council thing come along, all of my dealings was with the Missus.

"But after Tacky Gayle, Clyde Sellers and that other Commissioner, Frank W. Parks, got mad at us for not riding them buses, and put it on the television that all three of them had joined the White Citizens Councils, the Mister felt he had to join, too.

"So he comes back home from one of them meetings where they had made him a sergeant or usher or something the night before. And he walks into my kitchen just as I'm getting ready to put dinner on the table.

"'Sarah,' he said to me (that is not her name). 'Sarah,' he said, 'you ain't one of them fools that have stopped riding the buses, is you?' And I said, 'Yessuh, I is.'

"And he say: 'I ain't gonna have none of this Communist foolishness in my house, Sarah. Now you're coming to work on that bus tomorrow morning.' And I say: 'No, sir. I don't think so.'

"And he say: 'Now don't talk back to me like that, even if you is been here three years.' And before I could say anything else, the Missus calls him in the dining room, and he says to me: 'You just wait a minute, we'll settle this when I come back.'

"I could hear them arguing out there while I put the stuff on the stove to keep it warm, and I could hear him tell the Missus: 'She'll do what I say or get out—'

"So I got my bag together and walked on out the back door while they still was arguing. In a few minutes, Mrs. Alberta James (driver of the Hutchinson Street Baptist Church station wagon) came whizzing by, and I got in and went on about my business."

She paused in her long recital, and one of the other women murmured: "Tell him about what happened that night."

"Well," she took up again, "I'm setting home about 10 that night and getting ready to go to bed and there came this knock on the door. I guessed who it was right away, and I went there, and sure enough it was the Mister.

"And before I could even open the screen, he says: 'Sarah, you coming to work tomorrow morning ain't you?' And I said: 'No, sir, I don't guess so; you fired me.'

"And he say: 'Look, ain't no need us losing our heads like this; you come on back to work now.' And I said: 'No, sir; you fired me, and another lady wants me to come to her tomorrow. She said she'd pay me $15 instead of the $12 the Missus pays me.'

"Well, that sort of hit him and he don't say nothing for a minute and I don't say nothing neither. And finally he say: 'If it don't be for the children liking you so much, I wouldn't do it. But you come on back and I'll give you the $15 if I got to.'

"And I say: 'Well, I promised this other lady—' and he said: 'Sarah, you know the children like you; now you come on back to work tomorrow morning.' I don't say nothing and he keeps on talking. He wants to apologize but he can't make himself do it.

"So finally I say: 'I got to ride the bus?' And he say: 'I don't give a damn; you just get there the best way you can. But get there, Sarah; you hear me?'"

The other women couldn't contain their bubbling laughter any longer.

But you ask: "But what is this about you paying for their house and car?"

The laughter subsides as she answers rather caustically:

"It's just this. I get there at 6:30 every morning. I dress and feed the children and get all three of them off to school while the Mister and Missus both rush out to their work.

"I clean up the upstairs and fix the lunch for the children when they come home for lunch. Then I clean the rest of the house and fix the dinner for the children and the Missus and the Mister. They come home and ain't got nothing to do but set down and eat.

"I admit that she washes up the dinner dishes, for I go home after I serve it, but that is all she does do."

She paused and then continued in a soft, bitter voice:

"Now if I wasn't there to do it, she'd have to do all that herself. And she couldn't do it and go to business too.

"Well, she pays me $12 a week so she can go out and make $52 a week in her job. I know that's what she make, for I seen her payroll stub.

"Now if it wasn't for that $40 a week she makes on me, they couldn't meet the mortgage or the payments on that new car neither. They couldn't make it on his check alone."

"It's the God's truth," one of the other women seconded from the jump seat in the station wagon. "And they ain't the only ones. Practically every one of them young couples and plenty old ones, too, in these new subdivisions can't make it if the women don't work too."

"And if we all was to quit work," another put in, "and the womens had to stay at home, there'd be more dispossessing than you could shake a stick at. The installment people would be taking back everything they owned."

But the original narrator was not through. She was smiling when she concluded her story.

"You know," she said, "I hadn't promised no other lady nothing. And nobody offered me no $15, although I probably could get it somewhere else if I tried.

"But I heard the Missus tell the Mister just that week before that she was getting a $6 raise. And I felt some of that raise belonged to me."

And the general laughter was unrestrained.

You had wanted to recite this little lesson in economics to Mayor Gayle, but he had refused to see you despite the importunings of Grover C. Hall Jr., editor-in-chief of the Montgomery Advertiser.

For it was Mayor Gayle, during the "get-tough-with-the-Negroes" early stage of the boycott, who had publicly appealed to white housewives not to drive their Negro domestics to work as a means of breaking the back of the protest.

"Don't accommodate them," he'd told the white women, "They're laughing at you behind your backs."

The women in the station wagon did indeed laugh uproariously when you mentioned this, and one said:

"He also said on the television that he heard a lot of us was being fired 'cause we wouldn't ride them buses. Who did Tacky think he was kidding?"

But if Mayor Gayle and the other two City Commissioners are unaware of the impact of the six-month-old boycott on the economy of Montgomery as a whole, many other whites are not.

Surely the question was in the mind of a prominent white merchant who went through elaborate negotiations with a Negro business man to have you brought to his home late one night "for a completely off-the-record talk on this mess."

When he first approached the Negro intermediary, he had insisted that you not even be told his name. But he was finally persuaded that the name was unimportant if he couldn't trust a newspaperman anyway.

His original purpose, of course, was to enlist your aid in trying to persuade Rev. Martin King, Jr., Rev. Ralph D. Abernathy, Dr. Moses W. Jones, E. D. Nixon and other Negro leaders to call off the bus boycott.

"This thing has already cost Montgomery more than $2,000,000 in money losses alone," he had said. "It's not helping anyone, and surely it won't help the Negroes either if they force half the city into bankruptcy."

You tried to tell him—but he didn't believe you—that neither King nor any of the Negro leaders could really call off the bus boycott.

"They didn't really start it, you know," as he hardly listens. "And they can't end it either. The people, the plain, ordinary Negro people here started this thing and only they can stop it."

Then you tell him of the lesson in economics you'd learned in the station wagon that morning. He seemed impressed, but he was more worried over the mercantile problem.

"Do you realize that we all had the worst Christmas business in the history of Montgomery?" he asked aggrievedly as if you were somehow partly responsible for it.

"I know of at least three credit stores which would have been forced to close down completely if they hadn't had a little pickup at Easter.

"Don't King and that bunch realize that people are losing their jobs over this foolishness? What're they trying to do? Make a ghost town out of Montgomery?"

He mentioned a supermarket which had been forced to let 15 employes out because of a loss of Negro patronage.

"Somebody put out a tale that the owner had contributed to the White Citizens Councils. Well, that's a damned lie and I know it. I asked the man personally. In fact, you won't find any of us business men joining the White Citizens Councils and I hope you let your people know that."

You ask tactfully how many of the fired supermarket salespeople were Negroes and he flushes at your impertinence.

"That's not the point," he said, adding: "I know what you're talking about. I know they've been beefing about having Negroes hired in sales jobs. But if they wreck the stores, then there won't be no jobs for anybody. Can't you tell them that?"

You try to tell him that as far as you have been able to learn there is no organized Negro boycott against the white stores, although many individual Negroes resent the segregated facilities and small discourtesies in some establishments.

"But the main thing," you say, "seems to be that the Negroes don't ride the buses anymore, and the new transportation routes of the car pool operation just don't run through the City Square (which is really a circle).

"If they changed their routes to run through there," you venture, "the police would probably harass their drivers more than they are doing now."

It was not a satisfactory conference on either side and you saw no reason to tell the merchant that things are going to get worse for him in Montgomery before they get better.

For the boycott movement which has spread in all directions from the bus situation has given the biggest boost yet to Negro business in Montgomery.

You remember the first of the twice-weekly mass meetings you had attended at St. John AME Church, and the quiet, conversational speech by which Rev. King had stirred the crowded auditorium to near bedlam.

Among other things, King had said:

"Until we as a race learn to develop our power, we will get nowhere. We've got to get political power and economic power for our race. For there's never been a moment when the dollar was segregated.

"Let us learn in this struggle that we must patronize Negro business. We've felt too long that if the white man touches something, it is just a little better.

"Let nobody fool themselves. We know at times our own business men fall short, but keep on trading with them anyway until they are strong enough to do better.

"We've got Negro doctors in Montgomery, and they are just as good as the white doctors. I don't see how we can go down to these white Jim-Crow dungeons they set aside for us and keep on being called Mary and Sam or any other first name.

"We've got two Negro lawyers; let's use them. When they arrested me, they said 'You'd better get you a good white lawyer to get you out of trouble,' and I said: 'Brother, you're talking to the wrong man.'

"We've got Dr. (Richard) Harris down there at Dean's Drug Store. We ought to buy him out and make him have to open a whole chain of drug stores.

"But two things we must gain as a race. We've got to get political power. And we've got to get economic power. So let's get both together."

Later, a manager of one of the five large Negro insurance companies which maintain branch or home offices in Montgomery told you:

"I know it's a terrible thing to say. But sometimes I find myself giving thanks for the White Citizens Councils."

He then produced a mimeographed copy of a handbill which was handed out at a White Citizens Council meeting at the State Coliseum last Feb. 10. Titled "A Preview of the Declaration of Segregation," the handbill said, in part:

"When in the course of human events, it becomes necessary to abolish the Negro race, proper methods should be used. Among these are guns, bows and arrows, sling shots and knives.

"We hold these truths to be self-evident that all whites are created equal with certain rights; among these are life, liberty and the pursuit of dead niggers."

The handbill, after assailing the bus boycott, ended with:

"My friends, it is time we wised up to these black devils. I tell you they are a group of two-legged agitators who persist in walking up and down our streets protruding their black lips. If we don't stop these African flesh eaters, we will soon wake up and find Rev. King in the White House.

"LET'S GET ON THE BALL WHITE CITIZENS."

The insurance agent said: "Soon after that meeting, the head of one of the white insurance companies here which had been selling inferior policies to Negroes for years announced that he had joined the White Citizens Council.

"So I just mimeographed his statement and made up a few hundred copies of this and the Negro handbill and gave my agents a copy of each to show their Negro prospects.

"And, man, we've been so rushed with Negroes transferring their old policies to us that we haven't been able to write up new business. The good thing is that many of these Negroes who switched are probably getting an honest insurance policy for the first time in their lives.

"I tell you, these White Citizens Councils are a very educational group — in more ways than one."

SCHOOL INTEGRATION

In September 1957, three years after the Brown v. Board of Education *decision, several Little Rock, Arkansas, teenagers tried to put into action the Supreme Court's directive to accomplish integration "with all deliberate speed." Daisy Bates, president of the Little Rock* NAACP, *who, with her husband, L. C. Bates, published the* Arkansas State Press, *worked with the nine young people who entered Central High School. Poston, Carl Rowan, and other reporters from around the world witnessed that endeavor.*

At first, President Eisenhower ignored the drama in Little Rock, but when international press reports cast American "democracy" in a negative light as a result of the ruckus, he sent in troops to maintain order. Because Poston was black and was staying in the Bates home — in the room Daisy Bates called "Ted's Post" — he had unique access.

The following academic year, 1958–59, Governor Orval Faubus closed the Little Rock high schools rather than allow integration to continue. When the schools reopened in the fall of 1959, Poston and Rowan were standing outside the Bates home when a car full of whites came whizzing around the corner, spraying bullets. Neither reporter was hit, but bullets narrowly missed some white children watching television in their home next door (see Poston, "Little Rock High Schools Reopening"; Bates 184).

"Nine Kids Who Dared . . . the Human Drama in Little Rock"
New York Post 24 October 1957, sec. M: 2

Little Rock, Oct. 24 — Mrs. L. S. Green, a soft-spoken widow and first-grade teacher at the all-Negro Stephens Elementary School here, is a woman of inner calm and independence.

Since the death of her husband, a Post Office employe, in 1953, she has sought to instill her own feelings of independent thought and action into her two sons, Ernest, now 16, and Scott, 14.

So she was neither surprised nor disturbed last May when Ernest came home from the Horace Mann High School and told her that he was considering transferring for his senior year to the all-white Central High School under the city's gradual integration program.

"He and I talked it out as we talk out most things here," she recalled in her shrub-shrouded white bungalow home here.

"He said he wanted to go and I said it was up to him since he had to put up with whatever might happen there. I didn't let myself get too worried. I prayed about it, of course, but I have an inner peace which does not let me worry unduly."

She had never had to worry much about Ernest, one of the most popular students at Horace Mann. From early childhood and especially since the death of his father, he had been able to look out for himself.

Although there was no pressing economic necessity, the tall, well-built youngster had worked summers and some winters since he was about 11. He had started out as a newsboy for the Chicago Defender. At 13 he wanted to earn more money so he hired out to a neighbor and became a brick-mason's helper. And the next summer and winter he took a job as stockboy and cleaner in a white downtown shoe store.

"On Saturdays," Ernest says, "the manager used me as a salesman. I was racking up some good commissions, until some of the older white people complained and made him stop me."

But by last summer, Scott, who at 14 seems huskier than Ernest, was big enough to take over the shoe store job and Ernest got a locker room job at the Westridge Country Club, a predominantly Jewish social establishment here.

"It was probably the easiest job I've ever had," he said. "I passed out towels for the swimming pool, helped the members with their kids and did things like that.

"I only worked from 11 in the morning to 5:30, and got two good meals each day. But most of the time I just sat looking at television or reading. It was a cinch."

But in another way, it was the most important job that Ernest ever held. For not only were two of his fellow white workers students at Central, but also several sons of the country club members went to school there.

"We sort of hung around together out there and got pretty friendly," Ernest recalled, "and it turned out to be a good thing later."

This meant, of course, that when the nine Negro kids finally enrolled at

Central, Ernest was the only one who had several acquaintances, if not close friends, among the nearly 2,000 white students in the school.

"They greeted me pretty friendly-like," he said. "We weren't real tight, but at least they indicated that they were glad to see me there.

"And on that first day when I was sitting alone in the cafeteria, it was one of the club members who came over and invited me to have lunch with him and his girl. It surprised me and I was glad to sit down with them. It was a good gesture and it made me feel a little more at home."

But that was also the day when the segregationists rioted outside the school and when the Negro children were rushed home amid false reports that they had been beaten up and bloodied.

"It was to be some time before we got back in school again," he said, "but one of the fellows kept in touch with me. He'd call and tell me what was going on, how most of the students felt, what the hotheads were planning and things like that. He even told me what they were studying, so I could keep up."

His acquaintanceship with several students may also be a factor in that the easy-going Ernest is the only one of the three Negro boys who has not been molested during his brief tenure at Central.

"They've roughed up both Jefferson (Thomas) and Terrance (Roberts) who are only 15 and smaller than I am," he said, "and even the girls have had pencils, screws and other objects thrown at them.

"But so far they haven't done anything to me. I only got one bad telephone call. Somebody called here one night and said, 'Nigger, go on back to Horace Mann,' but even that hasn't been repeated."

Ernest thinks his immunity may be because all of his classmates are seniors "and those fellows don't want to get into trouble in their senior year." Others think that his wit and demeanor are factors, too.

They recall that turbulent day when a bunch of the "hotheads," urged on by the segregationist Mothers League, tried to lead a mass walkout of white students from the school.

Several of the leaders were scurrying through the halls buttonholing students and trying to get them to walk out, too. Two of the ringleaders approached two white boys standing on each side of Ernest and urged them to go out.

"No," each one replied smilingly, "I'm not going out. I'm chicken."

The frustrated leaders turned and glared at Ernest who smiled and murmured:

"Don't look at me, man. I'm not going out. I'm chicken, too."

Two of the would-be strikers grudgingly joined in the spontaneous laughter which followed and didn't walk out with the handful who staged the unsuccessful demonstration.

Ernest said that the segregationist leaders among the students not only jostle, push and aggravate the Negro students whenever a member of the 101st Airborne Division is not present, but that they also rough up any white boys who appear friendly to the Negroes.

"But in spite of that, some of the fellows still stop us in the halls to talk, and to show you that they accept you in spite of the bunch of thugs who threaten to rough them up.

"I guess that is one reason why the white girls are more friendly to us than the boys. They can't rough the girls up. One girl in my class lent me her notebooks for three or four nights so I could catch up on the lessons I missed during the three weeks out."

The natural leader of the Negro students at Central, Ernest has not let the tensions there or outside affect his normal teen-age life. [. . .]

A tenor sax man himself, he jams regularly with other members of the jazz club they organized unofficially at Horace Mann, although three of the boys are now playing professionally.

He looks forward to the week-end "socials" with the crowd but he also carries out his duties as an Eagle Scout (which he became last December) and as an usher at Bethel AME Church. [. . .]

The Little Rock dispute, if anything, has drawn a close-knit family even closer. When riot pictures showed a Negro editor being kicked outside Central, the older sister, Treopia Green, 21, telephoned from Baltimore where she teaches kindergarten to ask if Ernest was all right.

A widowed schoolteacher aunt, Mrs. Treopia Gravelley, is at the house twice daily, and the family continues the custom of reciting a blessing in unison at each meal.

Mrs. Green insisted that both boys give up their part-time jobs to concentrate on their studies and both mother and aunt look forward to Ernest's graduation as the first Negro to finish Central. He will then choose the college at which he will study electrical engineering.

There is little discussion of the present situation in the home, although Ernest is well aware of possible problems in the future.

"We may as well face it," he said the day after the 101st Airborne Division slashed its guard force by 50 per cent.

"They've got to take those guards out of Central some day. And it is possible that it may be tough there again.

"But if that happens, it's just the price we've got to pay. And for what is involved, I think it is cheap at the price."

"A Woman Who Dared: Mrs. Daisy Bates"

New York Post 3 November 1957, sec. M: 2

Little Rock, Nov. 2 — Both sides in this embattled Southern town are agreed on one thing: if there had been no Daisy Bates there would have been no 101st Airborne Division patrolling the halls at Central HS.

And no nine Negro children in the once all-white high school.

And Daisy Bates agrees to one thing. If there had been no Lucius Christopher Bates behind her, she might have been run out of Little Rock years ago.

Mrs. L. C. Bates is president of the Arkansas Conference of NAACP Branches. Technically, she is co-editor, with her angular, hard-bitten husband, of the Arkansas State-Press, the state's largest and most influential Negro weekly.

Between them, they've turned this once racially complacent town of 125,000 persons upside down since the first issue of the State-Press hit the streets May 9, 1941.

Little Rock was a "good" town back in 1941, but the "goodness" was based on Negro acceptance of segregation and second-class citizenship. The Bateses set out to change that overnight. There is still segregation and second-class citizenship in Little Rock. But not as much as when Daisy and L. C. decided to challenge it.

Even their worst enemies in Little Rock — and these are not all white segregationists — will admit that neither has ever wavered in a 16-year campaign for full civil rights, not even when both were clamped in jail.

They began in 1941 on white police brutality, after a reputable Negro insurance man was knocked down and kicked by a white policeman who challenged the insurance man's version of an automobile accident involving a white man.

"At that time," one observer remarked, "if a white cop didn't break a Negro's head when he arrested him, everybody agreed that he was a pretty good white man who just happened to be on the police force."

The Bateses were also incensed at the common Southern practice of going easy on any Negro who happened to cut up or shoot another Negro so long as he didn't challenge a white man.

But before they were through Negroes had been appointed to the local police force, and Negro offenders were getting as stiff sentences for molesting their own kind as they were sure to get if they challenged a white man.

Then Arkansas became one of the first states to pass a "right-to-work" law. The State-Press denounced it as a "right-to-scab" law and urged Negro workers to join labor unions.

And when the Negro union leaders at one of the local oil companies were arrested — after a scab had killed a picket at the struck plant — the State-Press came out with flaming headlines:

"FTA Strikers Sentenced to Pen by a 'Hand-Picked Jury' — State Law Used to Intimidate Negro Labor."

"I had just promoted Daisy to city editor that morning," L. C. recalls, "and we wound up in a jail cell that night."

The charge was contempt of court. The Bateses managed to make bail quickly, and eventually won vindication in Arkansas Supreme Court.

The State-Press then spearheaded a successful fight to end the "white primary" in the Arkansas Democratic Party.

"We won that one too," L. C. recalls. "But one of the troubles which ensued was this: too many Negroes immediately regarded the granting of the franchise to them as a new industry coming to Arkansas. They started selling their votes for $1 each.

"That's how Gov. Faubus got elected the first time. Most of the Negroes who elected him didn't vote for him because he was a so-called liberal; they voted for him at a dollar a head. We supported former Gov. Cherry, his opponent.

"Well, if he tries for a third term — and that's what everybody thinks he's out for — he'll have to raise the ante. Not even the least self-respecting Negro will buy what Faubus did at Central HS for a lousy dollar."

Daisy Bates had always been active in the NAACP, but she didn't take over leadership until certain conservative members in the branch let it be known unofficially that the Bateses got just what was coming to them when they went to jail in the labor case.

She was a popular and good leader. But not until May 4, 1956, did she endear herself to every Negro woman in Little Rock and others through-

out the South. On that day she had been on the witness stand giving a dep-
osition on the NAACP's suit for school integration here.

She had been badgered all morning by Leon B. Catlett, one of four
school board attorneys, although she had set him back at one point by mur-
muring: "The word is pronounced 'Negro,' Mr. Catlett, not 'Nigrah.'"

But as the afternoon session opened, Mrs. Bates said she wished to make
a statement. Leaning forward in the witness chair, she told Catlett:

"You addressed me several times this morning by my first name. That is
something that is reserved for my intimate friends and my husband. You
will refrain from calling me Daisy again."

Rocked back on his heels, Catlett could only stammer: "Well, I won't
call you anything then."

Daisy Bates was born some 35 years ago ("give or take a couple of years,"
mutters the caustic L. C.) in Huttig, Ark. (pop. 500), and has been fighting
discrimination since that early day when a white neighborhood butcher
called her a "little nigger."

Educated in Memphis and at the all-Negro Philander Smith and
Shorter Colleges here, she has always been just about a step ahead of her
contemporaries.

During World War II, for instance, she received national fame as the first
(and then only) woman pilot in the Arkansas Civil Air Patrol. But mention
it, and she'll tell you:

"Don't take that too seriously. I was handling publicity for Philander
Smith, where the pilot training course was being given, so I enrolled to give
the program a shot in the arm. I don't think I racked up more than 25 hours
of solo flight. And when I found myself landing at the Jackson, Miss., Airport one evening when I thought I was over Little Rock—well, I just gave
the whole thing up."

Among the 300-odd newspapermen who hurried here at the height of
the Little Rock drama, Daisy Bates stirred up considerable wonderment.

Most of them, apparently, had expected to find an elderly, umbrella-
shaking, retired schoolmarm with the passions of fading years. Instead,
they found a svelte, sophisticated young matron who could trade witticisms
with them, but who was implacable in her protection of the nine Negro
students against exploitation.

The reporters drank her whisky, stared in amazement around her
$35,000 split-level ranch house [. . .] and tried to reconcile what they were
seeing with their preconceived picture of an oppressed Negro family in the

South. Especially a newspaper family which had lost $10,000 in annual advertising because of the State-Press stand on segregation.

One awed Chicago reporter wrote rapturously of the Bates home in a predominantly white neighborhood. [. . .]

The Chicago man also learned that the Bates residence is guarded every night by off-duty policemen — paid for by Daisy and L. C. — against the vandals who have burned crosses on their lawn, thrown effigies there and hurled a pop bottle through the large picture window in the front.

A piece of cardboard covers the hole now. And when will they fix it?

"Oh, when this mess is over," says Daisy. "Why put in a new window now so they can break it out again?"

On the night after the rioting took place outside Central HS, a bug-eyed policeman rang the Bateses' bell to tell them that they had just intercepted a 100-car caravan of white segregationists only one block from their house.

"There was enough dynamite in the first car to blow you all to kingdom come," he said.

Daisy and L. C. took it in their stride, as they have been taking it for years. Just as they take the daily insulting telephone calls asking for "that black bitch Daisy Bates," and the pile of daily letters. One received last week said:

"Mrs. L. C. Bates, if you have any business to tend to you better get done for your days is short."

But bigoted whites are not the only enemies of the Bateses in Little Rock. There are many Negroes who loved the status quo, who resent the nationwide publicity Daisy has elicited, and who feel she is conducting a "one-woman show" on integration at Central HS.

And then there is C. H. Jones, the publisher of the only other Negro weekly in Little Rock, and the bully boy of the Capital White Citizens Council — not to mention the Mothers League of Central HS.

When Faubus made his nationwide TV broadcast, he held a copy of Jones' Southern Mediator-Journal before the cameras to buoy his argument that Negroes as well as whites had planned violence in front of Central HS if the Governor hadn't called out the National Guard.

Last week, Jones said:

"I don't know why the Governor picked my newspaper. I try to be fair and write the news like everybody else. But I want integration just as much as Bates and his crowd."

But just last week, Jones brought out a new issue of the Southern

Mediator-Journal. And the lead story charged that a local Negro editor, "not the editor of the Mediator-Journal," had joined forces with a Negro Communist newspaper reporter to try to precipitate a race riot in Little Rock despite the acceptance of the Negro children at Central.

L. C. Bates was so incensed at the article that he went downtown and consulted with a prominent city official to see if libel charges could be filed against Jones.

"Why take the trouble of suing him?" the official asked. "Why don't you just go back out there and use your pistol to whip him up the side of his head. I'll see that you are not prosecuted."

That was a dangerous suggestion to make to L. C. Bates. It took Daisy most of the night to talk him out of it.

L. C. gets mad. But all this amuses Daisy Bates. Anyway, she's too busy every day calming the fears of nine sets of parents, bolstering the nine students' determination and fascinating visiting newspapermen.

BROOKLYN CLERGYMAN

Thirty-five years after Poston wrote this profile of his Brooklyn pastor, the Reverend Gardner C. Taylor gave the sermon at the ecumenical religious service for President Bill Clinton's January 1993 inauguration.

"The Mississippi Still Flows Downstream": Close-up of Gardner C. Taylor
New York Post 16 February 1958, sec. M: 2

It may well be said that life began for Gardner Calvin Taylor at 19 . . . on a lonely country road in Louisiana where a white man's life ended violently.

The militant young minister, who last week at 39 became the first Negro and the first Baptist to head the powerful Protestant Council here, was then a student at Leland College, a backwoods all-Negro institution at Baker, La., 13 miles from Baton Rouge.

Son of a minister, he had scorned the ministry as a calling. He wanted to be a lawyer to fight for civil rights and had already been accepted as a next-year law student at the University of Michigan.

He was working his way through Leland as chauffeur for Dr. J. A. Bacoats, the college president. But he and another Negro student were not on official business as they sped down the lonely country road on their way back to school.

Suddenly another car, containing two white men, cut in front of them. There was a crash. Dr. Bacoats' car was demolished. Neither Taylor nor his companion was hurt.

But in the road beside them lay one white man dead, and another unconscious and bleeding profusely. The only two witnesses to the accident were two poor whites — an itinerant lay Baptist preacher who also worked for Standard Oil, and an impoverished sharecropper who happened to be passing by.

"Things were pretty tough racially down in that section of Louisiana in those days," Taylor recalled the other day in the beautiful 10-room, three-story house at 1337 President St., Brooklyn, in which his family now lives.

"They are still tough there even today, but not like they were then. So the best I expected was probably years in prison; the worst could have been a lynching.

"But the next morning at the inquest these two poor white men got up and testified in my behalf. They said the accident was not my fault. They said I was driving within the speed limits. (I'm not sure I was.) And I walked out of court a free man."

Free, but "shook up."

"I think I began a reassessment of my life at that moment. For the first time I was ashamed of myself for having kidded the guys on the campus who were planning to become preachers; for telling them I thought them awfully simple.

"So I went to Dr. Bacoats, who was pastoring Mt. Zion Baptist Church in Baton Rouge (which my father had headed until his death in 1931), and asked him if he could get me into Oberlin College in Ohio, where he had graduated. Leland was not an accredited college, but he succeeded in getting me accepted for Oberlin conditionally."

And 13 years after the death of his father, the Rev. W. M. Taylor, Gardner C. Taylor was pastor of Mt. Zion.

Much had happened in the intervening years, during which he was helped by his widowed mother, Mrs. Selma Taylor, who went back to teaching school at $57 a month in order to allow him to go to college.

He had met and married an Oberlin undergraduate Phi Beta Kappa student named Laura Scott.

"I had seen her picture in the Pittsburgh Courier when she made Phi Beta and impressed her by telling her this when I first saw her at a little Baptist church (also named Mt. Zion) in Oberlin. I didn't tell her I'd boasted to a friend the year before that 'I'm going to go around with that girl when I get up to Oberlin.'"

He had pastored his first church (Bethany Baptist) in nearby Elmira, Ohio, as a student minister, for $3 a week.

"They asked me how much I wanted and I was afraid to ask for too much. They finally raised me to $40 a month and I promptly bought a Plymouth coupe with a rumble seat. The motor fell out of it when Laura and I were driving back from getting our marriage license . . ."

He had been called to Beulah Baptist in New Orleans "whose congregation was small in numbers but progressive in its desire for civil rights.

"I became one of five 'Young Turks' in New Orleans," Taylor recalls. "Every Sunday we would take our American flag to Shakespeare Park (Negro) and speak on our rights. We coined an expression you hear a lot of now: 'A voteless people is a hopeless people.'"

He had continued the fight when he left New Orleans for Baton Rouge and his father's old Mt. Zion; and the battle for the ballot was not always bloodless. A Negro professor and Taylor associate from Southern University was beaten to death at Opelousas, La., when he went there as a "Young Turk" to spur the Negro registration campaign.

"But he didn't die in vain," Taylor said the other day. "Opelousas now has more Negroes registered proportionately than any other parish in Louisiana. And recently they elected a Negro doctor to the town's governing body."

Back home at Mt. Zion in Baton Rouge, Taylor became head of the Louisiana State Citizens Committee for Equalization of Teachers' Salaries and School Facilities. "The word 'integration' wasn't used much then.

"They told us it would be a freezing day in July before Negro teachers got equal salaries and that the Mississippi River would flow upstream before Negroes got the ballot in Louisiana.

"Well, both things happened, and I don't recall any freezing July days in Louisiana, and the Mississippi is still flowing downstream."

Taylor came to Brooklyn's 10,200-member Concord Baptist Church of Christ, 833 Marcy Av., in April, 1948. It happened through a series of coincidences.

The former pastor, Dr. James Adams, had met him at a Baptist convention in Atlanta and invited him to address Concord's centennial celebration in 1947. He accepted, but Dr. Adams died three weeks later without imparting his wishes to the church's officials.

The church then invited the Rev. Marshall Shepherd, prominent Philadelphia Baptist minister and political leader, to make the address, but, because of a previous engagement, Shepherd suggested young Gardner C. Taylor of Baton Rouge.

Taylor accepted this second invitation, and his centennial address became a stepping stone to a career which was to see him become vice president of the board of directors of the Urban League of Greater New York, member of the General Council of the American Baptist Convention and a member of the City Commission on Intergroup Relations.

He also became president of the Brooklyn Division of the Protestant Council of the City of New York, and last week the first Negro to head the citywide organization of 1,700 churches of 31 denominations here. The next step may be appointment to the Board of Education to succeed the retiring Rev. John M. Coleman of Brooklyn's St. Philip's P. E. Church.

The itinerant preacher and the impoverished farmer on that lonely Louisiana road were the first white men to come to the aid of Gardner C. Taylor in the time of emergency. But they were by no means the last.

When Concord Church burned down in October, 1952, with a $750,000 loss (only $310,000 covered by insurance), the Rev. Arthur A. Bouton, pastor of Union Methodist Church a half mile away, was the first of two dozen white ministers to invite Taylor's congregation to share his church with his own parishioners the next Sunday.

And in his sermon from Union's pulpit, Taylor said frankly:

"Before the fire, each of our groups stuck pretty closely to itself. Let's admit it, there has been enmity among many of us in this area. Fortunately it never flared into the open. But this fire has relieved a great deal of the latent tension. There's a new feeling of common humanity around here now."

And in the short space of two years and nine months, a new $1,413,000 Concord Baptist Church was completed on the ruins of the old gutted structure — thanks to the aid of a Catholic layman, Richard Brennan, president of Brooklyn's Brevoort Savings Bank.

"He arranged a loan of $375,000 for us at a low rate of interest," Taylor recalls, "and he even arranged to make those terms more elastic if the necessity arose. Banks are usually reluctant to make loans to churches. If something happens, what can they do with the building?"

Even before he came to Concord, Gardner Taylor had become rather famed as an orator. "I was a pretty good debater in college and I always loved to talk. That is probably one reason I wanted to be a lawyer, at first."

In 1947, he addressed the World Baptist Alliance in Copenhagen, Denmark, and in 1950 he addressed the same group in the Municipal Auditorium in Cleveland. The next year he gave the commencement address at Colgate-Rochester Divinity School, and in 1955 spoke before the Golden Jubilee of the World Baptist Alliance in Westminster Hall, London.

A large dark man who is proud of his color, Taylor now lives on President St. with his retired schoolteacher-mother, now 71, his wife and 5-year-old daughter, Martha. [. . .]

He is not sorry that he gave up a probably lucrative career as a lawyer, but he understands why he wanted to be one during his youth.

"I was a voracious reader of The Crisis (official NAACP organ), the Chicago Defender and Pittsburgh Courier (militant Negro weeklies), George Schuyler (a Negro author and editor), Oswald Garrison Villard and Heywood Broun.

"I thought I'd become a lawyer and devote my life to the whole area of civil rights.

"I realize, now, of course, that there is a great opportunity for ministers to make their contribution to this field alone. You have only to look at Martin Luther King and Ralph Abernathy down in Montgomery to realize this."

He'll get another look at both of them next April 20 when he returns to Montgomery to preach the rededication sermon at Abernathy's First Baptist Church, which was destroyed by white dynamiters during the Montgomery bus boycott crusade.

For Gardner C. Taylor is at home with the doctrine of the brotherhood of all men so often preached by the two young Montgomery ministers.

It was taught him by an itinerant white preacher and an impoverished white sharecropper who once held his life in their hands on a lonely Louisiana country road.

UPGRADING SCHOOLS

Profile of a contemporary civil rights activist who knew the legendary, near-mythical Harriet Tubman.

"She Prepared for Norfolk—for a Lifetime"
New York Post 5 February 1959

Norfolk, Feb. 5—Many people here refer to Mrs. Vivian Carter Mason, the greying matron who prepared 17 Negro children for their successful assault on Virginia's "massive resistance" program, as "the Harriet Tubman of Norfolk."

But few understand the half smile with which she greets the compliment.

For little Vivian Carter, a native of Auburn, N.Y., knew the real Harriet Tubman and heard from her own lips the stories of the fantastic exploits of the Union Army spy who led hundreds of Negroes to freedom during the Civil War.

And even fewer residents here, either Negro or white, know that Mrs. Mason shared Miss Tubman's accounts of her exploits with a brother who is not unknown in the field of civil rights.

He is Elmer A. Carter, newly appointed chairman of the New York State Commission Against Discrimination (SCAD).

But Vivian Carter Mason needed neither an historical acquaintance nor a famous brother to carve her niche in Norfolk. She's been at it since she returned here in 1944, after educating her son, W. T. Mason Jr., in New York City, New Rochelle and then Howard University Law School in Washington.

The wife of a real estate and insurance man who formerly was supervisor of the Norfolk Community Hospital, Mrs. Mason had been active in civic affairs long before 151 Negro children applied for admission to Norfolk's all-white secondary schools.

In 1945 she organized the Women's Council for Interracial Cooperation, whose 18 original members have now grown to more than 400.

"As one of our first projects," she recalls, "I took 80 women, Negro and white, on a tour of our rat-infested slums. They were horrified.

"I think the best measure of our success in that field is this: There is nothing now left in Norfolk as bad as what they saw that day."

And so it has been in other areas here.

She led the fight for slum clearance, for increased Negro voting, and, as chairman of the NAACP's State Education Committee, she was in the forefront of the fight for integration.

But she was in North Africa last fall when she read that the federal courts had ordered Negroes admitted to local schools, and that Gov. Almond had closed down the schools rather than admit them.

"I immediately got in touch with Robert D. Robertson (local NAACP president) and asked what I could do," she recalls. "He told me to rush on back and see about setting up a school for the kids while we continued to fight in the courts."

She came home and organized a school which even the local white school officials admit was superior to the private tutoring classes set up by the Tidewater Educational Assn. and other pro-segregation groups.

Operating the tutoring classes for the 17 Negro children cost more than $1,000 a month, but neither Mrs. Mason nor Robertson was daunted.

"He rallied the whole Negro community behind the project," Mrs. Mason says of Robertson, who heads the Seafood Workers Union here. "Clubs and church groups contributed freely. Business men pledged $25 and more a week. Some social groups gave up their annual dances and donated the money to our school."

Mrs. Mason was unimpressed when visiting newspapermen remarked on the poise of the Negro children who went alone and in small groups to the six integrated schools Monday.

"These kids are no different from hundreds of Negro kids we have here," she said. "There has just been no occasion to bring it out. Even we might not have noticed their dignity, their seriousness and their dedication if a situation like this hadn't brought it out."

On school reopening day last Monday, reporters, scurrying from school to school, were surprised to find the president emeritus of the National Council of Negro Women emerging from each institution as they arrived.

Each time they besieged her with questions. Finally one of them asked:

"Mrs. Mason, how long had you been planning for this integration?"

And the woman who first learned of race pride at the knee of a great abolitionist answered simply:

"All my life."

NAACP HISTORY

For "research" on this history of the National Association for the Advancement of Colored People, Poston had only to recall people he had long known. Langston Hughes was working on a book-length history of the NAACP, Fight for Freedom, *that would be published in 1961. He told Poston, "You should have been the author to write this* NAACP *book I'm doing . . . as I'm sure you'd have the whole story at your finger tips. Me, I had to research."* [5]

Poston's Post *colleagues have pointed out the paper's close association with the* NAACP *simply because Poston's friend Moon served as the organization's public relations director and as editor of its monthly organ, the* Crisis. *Poston used to watch the wire service teletype, then telephone Moon whenever there was breaking news on the racial front.*

"Two Score and Ten Years Ago . . ."
New York Post 8 February 1959, sec. M: 4

Fifty years ago next Thursday, on the centennial of the birth of the Great Emancipator, 53 white and Negro clergymen, social workers, publicists, educators and philanthropists issued a call to "all believers in democracy to join in a national conference for the discussion of present evils, the voicing of protests, and the renewal of the struggle for civil and political liberty."

The Lincoln Day Call, which brought nearly 300 leaders of both races to New York City on May 31 and June 1, 1909, had been penned in vitriol by Oswald Garrison Villard, publisher of the New York Evening Post and grandson of William Lloyd Garrison, the famed abolitionist. It said, among other things:

"If Mr. Lincoln could revisit this country in the flesh, he would be disheartened and discouraged. He would learn that on Jan. 1, 1909, Georgia had rounded out a new Confederacy by disfranchising the Negro, after the manner of all the other Southern States. [. . .]

"He would learn that the Supreme Court . . . has laid down the principle that if an individual State chooses, it may 'make it a crime for white and colored persons to frequent the same market place at the same time, or appear in an assemblage of citizens convened to consider questions of a public or political nature in which all citizens, without regard to race, are equally interested' . . ."

The Call and the conference—from which grew the National Assn. for the Advancement of Colored People—were the brainchild of Mary White Ovington, a young white social worker in New York. Miss Ovington had been horrified by the bloody race riots in Springfield, Ill., Lincoln's hometown, the previous August. And she had responded to the challenge of William English Walling, a Kentucky-born white journalist who had concluded a searing account of the Springfield massacre by asking, "What large and powerful body of citizens is ready to come to their (the Negroes') aid?"

Today, only two of the original 53 signers of the Call survive—Dr. W. E. B. DuBois, the revered Negro writer and historian, and the Rev. John Haynes Holmes, pastor emeritus of the Community Church here.

But next Thursday afternoon, when commemorative services on the NAACP's 50th anniversary are held at the Community Church, William English Walling's widow will read Villard's "Lincoln Day Call" in full.

Thursday's speakers will also include another descendant of abolitionist Garrison, New York lawyer Lloyd Garrison, and Arthur B. Spingarn, NAACP president since 1940 and vice president and chairman of its National Legal Committee from 1911 to 1940.

Arthur Spingarn, unlike his late brother, Col. Joel Spingarn (who established the annual Spingarn Medal for outstanding Negro achievement in 1914 and who headed the NAACP until his death in 1939), was not one of the original signers of the Call.

But no living person has enjoyed a longer, livelier, more effective association with the organization than this energetic, chubby little lawyer whose twinkling eyes and erect carriage belie the 81st birthday which he will share next March 28 with another fighter for the liberal cause—Herbert H. Lehman.

Arthur Spingarn can recite the unparalleled progress made by Negroes—and America—since Lincoln's Birthday, 1909. He can tell how the NAACP proposed—and couldn't raise—a tiny budget of $6,500 in its first year of operation—and how last year, for the first time, it raised more than $1,000,000.

He can point out that lynching has—largely as a result of NAACP efforts—become an obsolete crime; how the same Supreme Court so roundly castigated by Oswald Villard has now outlawed segregation and discrimination in voting, travel, public institutions and facilities, some areas of housing and, finally, public school education.

He can, and does, boast with justifiable pride that fair employment practice statutes have been enacted in 15 states and 26 cities; that New York City and Pittsburgh have outlawed discrimination in private housing; that a Civil Rights Act was passed by Congress last year for the first time in 82 years.

Arthur Spingarn, looking lovingly back over the years the other day at NAACP headquarters, 20 W. 40th St., recalled not only the progress but the personalities who contributed so much to the Negro's steady march up Freedom Road.

Looking back to those first days in 1909, he said:

"All we had then and for the next year or so was a Continuation and Advisory Committee which grew out of that conference. Incidentally, Jacob H. Schiff, grandfather of the present publisher of The New York Post, was a working member of that Committee."

As for the earlier publisher of The Post, Oswald Villard, Spingarn says:

"I don't know what we would have done without Ozzie. He not only wrote the Call, but served as the first disbursing treasurer after our second conference in May, 1910.

"We had only one paid employe, and a very poorly paid one, even then—Miss Richetta Randolph, a stenographer. (She retired as NAACP office manager in 1946.) And we had nowhere to go, we couldn't afford office rent, until Ozzie gave us two rooms free in the old New York Evening Post building down at 20 Vesey St.

"And then, after we persuaded young DuBois to leave a good teaching job in Atlanta to be our director of publicity and research and to found The Crisis as our official organ, we found we didn't even have money to pay him the pittance we'd promised him. I recall that Ozzie reached down in his pocket once and lent us $300 to carry us for a month."

Spingarn recalls vividly how DuBois quickly made The Crisis self-supporting and pushed its circulation beyond 100,000 during World War I.

"Of course," he said, "there was no real established Negro press then; no Ebony, Jet or similar publication. And if a Negro wanted to know what was happening to Negroes, he had to read The Crisis. DuBois demonstrated that they really wanted to know."

He also recalls John R. Shillady, the towering, flamboyant, Dublin-educated Irishman who became the NAACP's first "fully paid" executive secretary in 1918, after Frances Blascoer, Miss Ovington, May Childs Nernery and Roy Nash had all held the post for love and little or no money from 1911.

"We agreed to pay John $6,000 a year," he said, "and he was worth every penny of it. But his association with us led to the great tragedy of his life."

Around 1920, it appears, Texas (setting a precedent which would be unsuccessfully tried again in 1958) tried to tax the NAACP out of business.

After a brilliant — and successful — defense in the courtroom at Austin, Shillady emerged from the courthouse to find a blood-thirsty mob, led by the local sheriff, intent upon lynching him. He escaped death — but barely — by fleeing.

"But because he ran to save his life, he blamed himself for losing his nerve," Spingarn recalled. "And it preyed on him so much that he finally suffered a nervous breakdown. Truth was, he had done the only wise thing. There never was any question of dishonor."

The ailing Shillady was succeeded in 1921 by a Negro scholar who also was a talented composer, educator and diplomat — James Weldon Johnson. And Johnson's appointment as the first Negro executive secretary is a bright spot in Spingarn's memory.

"Jim was already on the staff as field secretary," he said, "and was getting about $1,800 a year. He agreed to accept the bigger post but only on one condition — that he be paid the $6,000 Shillady had been getting.

"He said it was not a question of money; it was the principle. He insisted that no Negro should ever be asked to accept less money than a white man for doing the same job. Joel and I could both have kissed him. For wasn't this exactly what all of us had been fighting for?"

Johnson got the $6,000.

It was Johnson, incidentally, who was responsible for recruiting his own successor — a man who was to become synonymous with the NAACP for many years. On one of his field trips, Johnson had run across a very energetic, imaginative young insurance agent in Atlanta, and persuaded him to come to New York to work for the NAACP.

That young man was Walter White, who succeeded Johnson as executive secretary in 1930 and remained in the post until his death in 1955.

Spingarn is so full of stories and anecdotes about Walter White (who in turn recruited his own capable successor, Roy Wilkins, from the Kansas City [Mo.][6] Call, a Negro weekly) that he can't possibly choose among them. But he regards as White's greatest personal achievement the NAACP defeat in 1930—not long after White took office—of Senate confirmation for the late Judge John J. Parker (an anti-Negro jurist who later became more liberal) as a U.S. Supreme Court Justice.

"That fight marked the political coming of age of the American Negro," he says, "the first example of the Negro's potential political influence. And none of us wanted to tackle Parker, despite his anti-Negro record. President Hoover was determined that he was going to be confirmed, and we dreaded the public defeat.

"But Walter said we could lick him, and we only let him go ahead because we loved Walter so much. Well, history records what he did."

Spingarn and Walter White once found themselves vilified not only by their Negro followers but by white liberals as well, all over the country. That was in 1937, when both stood alone in urging Senate confirmation for the Supreme Court of Alabama Sen. Hugo Black—a one-time member of the Ku Klux Klan.

The NAACP president the other day gave the first public explanation.

"The year before President Roosevelt nominated Black," he said, "Walter and I had sent him 36 suggested amendments to the education bill Black had introduced in the Senate. We expected at best to get a curt letter of rejection from the gentleman from Alabama, but instead we got an invitation to his office.

"The first thing he told us when we walked in was: 'I'm accepting 35 of your 36 amendments to my bill, but you don't really want the 36th one; it would hurt your cause more than help it.' We talked it over and he convinced us he was right.

"And when we walked out, Walter said if a man like that can come out of Alabama, then there's hope for all we are fighting for. And the best proof that Walter was right is that the *liberal* Supreme Court which has voided most of Ozzie's justified protests of 1909 dates from the day that Hugo Black took his seat on our highest tribunal."

In recalling his own most thrilling personal moment in his nearly 50 active years with the NAACP, Spingarn skips over the 11 Supreme Court civil rights victories which he won almost single-handedly between 1911 and 1930 (when the NAACP Legal and Educational Fund Inc. was set up by the late Charles Houston and his brilliant protege, Thurgood Marshall).

"My great moment," he recalls, "was that day in 1917 when I marched down Fifth Av. with 15,000 persons, predominantly Negro, in a silent parade of protest against lynching and against the whole massacre of Negro men, women and children in the infamous East St. Louis (Ill.) riots.

"The papers had poked fun at the idea. Everybody had looked for just 'a nigger parade.' But the whole silent protest was such a fine, serious, dignified performance that even the people who had laughed at the idea or had opposed it were deeply impressed."

The successful lawyer, author and noted bibliophile (who in 1947 presented the Howard University Library in Washington with the world's most extensive collection of books and pamphlets by Negroes) treasures one observation made by a London interviewer on a recent trip to Europe.

"Mr. Spingarn got mad about it 50 years ago," the interviewer wrote, "and he's mad still."

"That's about the nicest thing ever said about me and the NAACP," Spingarn concluded. "True, we've won a hell of a lot of battles, but the war isn't over. And until it is, I hope none of us loses our sense of indignation."

1960s

Poston's career peaked by the 1960s. His reputation established, he was considered dean of black journalists. In failing health from arteriosclerosis, he no longer spent much time on the road. Instead, he was based at the rewrite desk: other reporters did the legwork and called in their information, and he put the story together. Here he compares two white politicians' receptions in Spanish Harlem.

"The Kennedys and the Lodges Pay a Visit to East Harlem"
New York Post 13 October 1960: 3

It would have been a tough act to follow anywhere—but especially at the corner of E. 116th St. and Lexington Av. in East Harlem.

There was petite and pretty Jackie Kennedy—eyes sparkling and hands clasped in front of her like a small child reciting for her elders in the parlor—bringing greetings in both Spanish and Italian.

And the block-long crowd—"About 10,000 I'd say," said Police Inspector McKeon—"Maybe 7,500" said veteran reporters—loved it.

Not that the Henry Cabot Lodges didn't try to top it four hours later on the same corner.

Following her husband through the crowd—"Five thousand," said a Chief Inspector; "3,500" said McKeon; "a couple of thousand at the outside" said reporters—the tall and charming Mrs. Lodge started shaking hands.

She continued shaking every available hand after she mounted the platform, ignoring two large pictures of Jack Kennedy smiling down behind her from the windows of the Freedom Club of the Independent Democrats at 151 116th St.

And as her husband rose to speak in English to a predominantly Spanish-speaking crowd, she sank to the platform floor, curled her shapely legs under her and continued shaking hands with hundreds of Puerto Rican youths who crowded around and jostled each other for the privilege.

Had the election been held last night in East Harlem, the Kennedys would have defeated the Lodges hands down.

The result might have been different, however, had the Republican standard bearers penetrated further into Harlem yesterday.

For in front of the Hotel Theresa at 125th St. and 7th Av., where Jack and Jackie Kennedy went after their East Harlem triumph, some rather puzzling things happened as the Democratic candidate and other party bigwigs addressed the crowd.

Because, on a corner and in a community which is noted for the exuberance of its crowds, Sen. Kennedy was greeted by one of the most polite but restrained audiences in his current campaign.

Not even the redoubtable Rep. Adam Clayton Powell, Jr. seemed able to stir the large assemblage as he denounced Vice President Nixon for signing a restrictive covenant on a Washington house from which he moved four years ago, or for his failure to renounce the announced support of the Grand Kleagle of the Georgia Ku Klux Klan.

And there were some scarcely concealed smiles as Powell introduced Kennedy as "my friend of 14 years," and Kennedy arose to praise "my friend and colleague for 14 years."

"Is this the same Kennedy," one defeated Powell opponent asked audibly, "that Adam called a weak candidate just a couple of months ago and predicted couldn't carry Harlem?"

But Kennedy, with Jackie still looking on adoringly, did almost approach the old enthusiasm at a couple of points.

Once was when he said that President Eisenhower should speak out on foreign and domestic issues affecting civil rights, and again when he reminded the audience that:

"One fourth of all the votes in the UN General Assembly will be African in 1962."

Some GOP adherents later expressed sorrow that Lodge hadn't ventured further into Harlem yesterday.

For the speech he gave in East Harlem to an audience that was 90 per cent Spanish-speaking might better have been designed for an audience in front of the Theresa, that one-time abode of Fidel Castro.

In his 116th St. speech, Lodge promised that Nixon would appoint a Negro to his Cabinet; place Negroes in the diplomatic service from the rank of Ambassador on down; desegregate the schools and eating places. [. . .]

But the Kennedy-Nixon contest was held in Spanish Harlem. And little Jackie won it with her schoolgirl Spanish — and without shaking a single hand.

CLASS

Poston was feeling touchy and out of sorts due to ill health. Trying to gauge the attitudes of his middle-aged generation of Negroes during a decade of upstart black militants, he sensed that his group would not be flattered by dissection of its social life for a readership of whites.

Memo to Paul Sann on Negro Society, 3 July 1962
James Wechsler Papers, State Historical Society of Wisconsin

Since you suggested the possibility of such a series [on Negro Society] I have spent most of my off-time since then being more "social" than is my wont and trying to provoke informal discussions on the subject. [. . .]

[. . .] I reluctantly gave up my weekend blue-fishing [. . .] to be a weekend house guest of a rather stuffy couple because I knew that other guests at their Connecticut summer estate would be people who would commonly be thought of as members of "Negro Society."

The results of this informal research of one week [. . .] has convinced me that the only loser in a venture of this kind would be The New York Post itself. [. . .]

Here are a few reasons why the mere mention of the subject seemed to arouse indignation and resentment among the discussants:

1. Most of them contend quite seriously [. . .] that there is no such thing as "Negro Society," if we use the commonly accepted Webster definition that it is "that part of the community which marks itself apart as a leisured class, with much time given to formal social affairs, fashionable sports, etc."

This does not mean, of course, that there is a dearth of "formal social affairs" in the community, but they are the very antithesis of what one would regard as the offerings of a group "which marks itself apart as a leisured class." There is nothing of the "exclusiveness" which would be expected to dominate such affairs, and guests might range from members of the oldest Negro families in the area to the wealthy and well-behaved numbers bankers whose profession is no secret to anyone present.

[. . .] My wife [Ersa Hines Clinton] and I both belong to about a half dozen social and fraternal clubs whose formal bids are widely sought after. And guests at our last affair — at my tables — included a Federal Circuit Judge, a General Sessions jurist, an Appellate Division Justice along with at least one Pullman porter, two numbers bankers and three liquor salesmen.

And no one was ill at ease or seemed to feel out of place.

Now, lest you think that this frank discussion so far is very interesting to you and therefore might be even more interesting to your readers, mainly white, let me warn you that publication of even these bare facts in The Post would bring down universal condemnation on this newspaper and an even further loss of esteem (and possibly circulation) in the Negro community.

Why? Well, Point II might help explain it.

2. Most of my discussants contended [. . .] that the very term "Negro Society" is anathema in the community. [. . .]

[. . . T]here is undoubtedly a new pride in race [. . .] that resents any effort to break up Negroes into stratified groups.

This is a development which I have watched carefully [. . .] during my 35 years in the Harlem community. The old lines of color — the high yellows against the blacks — of nativity — the American Negroes against the West Indians — of professional status — the doctors and lawyers against the untutored — have broken down.

As a result, the social affairs are no less elaborate but the focus and participation is far, far different.

Unlike the old Coachman's Club, the Debutantes, the original Comus Club, the Gay Northeasterners and the original bastions of exclusivity in the Negro community, the present social organizations (and they include some of the names of the older ones) now seek social purposes with their affairs which include all well-behaved segments of the community.

Most of these present clubs now devote their efforts to taking out $500 life memberships in the NAACP. Its members form such auxiliary groups as the National Urban League Guild, the Friends of the YMCA, the Friends Committee of the Northside Center and direct their efforts toward supporting their own community projects. And after they have made that contribution, then they may give a formal affair — and each gives at least one such affair annually. Guests at these affairs are usually the persons who gave financial support to their community efforts.

Well, I can see you thinking that even this might be a second piece of a series and that it might be quite interesting to Post readers.

To which I might add that Negroes are goddam tired of being "interesting" to white people. [. . .]

And a number of my discussants over the weekend made it quite plain when I was finally forced to admit that I was considering doing a series on "Negro Society." A few quotes, not written down then, but clearly remembered, may be enlightening: [. . .]

"Why does The Post insist on setting the Negro aside as something *outside* the rest of the community? Did they ever consider a series on Jewish High Society, or colorful Little Italy, or Lace Curtain Irish vs. Shantytown Irish? No, but let's write about the Negroes. Don't you know: they even have a SOCIETY!"

"Look, we made a pretense of having a 'Negro Society' when we had nothing else left us. We've passed that stage a long time ago and we don't need The Post to remind us of it."

[. . . M]ost of those people had at one time, if not now to hear them tell it, a deep regard for The Post. But, as one put it:

"Not even the Daily News and the Mirror go out of their way to single out Negroes for so much special treatment. Why is The Post so determined to show that something is different from everything else if it happens to be Negro?"

There was, of course, lots more of this but some of it might be understandable in a history I have been privileged to observe myself over my 35 years in this big city. [. . .]

But in the pre-Depression days when I first came to Harlem there was a studied attempt on the part of certain segments to live up to the fiction of Van Vechten's "Nigger Heaven."

Color was indeed a factor in "Negro Society," and many of the "exclusive" organizations then prided themselves on their lack of pigmentation of their members, or the fact that no West Indians, no matter how prosperous or cultured, were admitted.

There were exceptions of course. [. . .] My sister-in-law was a member of a very old Brooklyn family and also for a short time a Broadway actress

in "Lula Belle" with Lenore Ulric. And this was a period when Negro entertainers were accepted in most groups "because they know so many white
people."

It does not take hindsight to see that such a society was a reflection of
the denials of the whole society to Negroes in the 1920s. [. . .] At the time
I often thought of a story which my father used to tell of a man who found
a brand new hat in a muddy street in a Southern town and picked it up to
find a man mired under it up to his neck in mud. The pedestrian expressed
sorrow at the white man's plight but he cut him short by saying: "Oh, don't
bother about it, I've got a mule under me."

The point of the story was white-Negro relations, but it was quite appli-
cable at that time to the pathetic efforts of some few Negroes to establish a
"Negro Society" which would set them aside from the mules under them.

[. . . A] few [other] recollections of those days may show the differences
of today.

The most "exclusive" club I recall from that period was "The Coachmen's Club," and it was exactly that. It was founded by Negroes who drove
the coaches of New York's 400 [the wealthiest and most exclusive social set]
and therefore were arbitrars of manners in the Negro community. Their affairs were really the epitome of elegance — I know, because I had not been
accepted at the time and I often worked for the Negro caterer who serviced
their affairs. The Coachmen went out of business when FDR came in.

(Interesting? I wonder how many Irish Post readers would like to be reminded that their forebears were hodcarriers, or Italian readers that their
parents were push cart peddlers or Jewish readers that their family rise
came from a second-hand store?)

The leading young people's "exclusive" group was the Gay Northeasterners, a group of daughters of Negro doctors, lawyers and an occasional
real estate man. I recall once that a young Negro doctor was barred from
one of their dances because he brought a girl whom they called "unacceptable." (He was really barred because he had declined to escort the Gay's
president to the dance.)

The Gays are still in existence, but the current president is married to a
leading numbers banker whose 6 months term and other difficulties were
outlined in our series on the Pad. His wife stopped speaking to me for a
while but we're good friends now.

The most exclusive of exclusive groups at that time was the Debutantes.
They were 18 young girls which the late A'Lelia Walker, heiress to the Ma-

dame C. J. Walker hair-straightening millions (and the only authentic millionaire in Harlem at that time), selected for the debut of her daughter — an affair which cost about $50,000 in those days.

The girls organized themselves into a club called the Debutantes and they kept the club and the name until the youngest member was in her 40s. The club still exists but community jeers finally forced them several years ago to call it the Gothamettes.

I mentioned these two latter clubs in some detail because I made it a point to talk to at least one of the original members during the last week and at least one is quoted in the earlier observations. The other, a volunteer community director for the United Negro College Fund, was even more indignant at the possibility that "The Post is planning to single out Negroes again" as something bizarre and interesting.

You may gather from the above that I don't think we should try to do the series on Negro Society. If you think my reasoning faulty and decide to do it anyway, I would like to raise a couple of personal points:

1. If such a series is done I'd rather not have anything to do with it. This is personal, but also in connection with my job. [. . .] I feel that one of my most valuable assets to The Post has been my entre to, and acceptance by, practically every group and strata of the Negro community. [. . .]

If I participated in such a series as proposed, I think I would lose this value. [. . .] In short, I wouldn't like to contribute to something which I feel might well affect The Post adversely and thereby my own bread and butter.

The second reason is more simple. [. . .] I don't believe in the existence of a specified, well-defined Negro Society. And I'm sure you wouldn't want me to try to create something which I feel sure doesn't exist.

I might close by saying that this is the first time that I have written a series *against* a series.

TED

CIRCULATION

Executive editor Paul Sann wanted to know why the New York Post *was losing black readers, and Poston analyzed the reasons. Both this memo and the previous document reflect Poston's contention that black readers are not a monolith. African Americans come from diverse backgrounds and have var-*

ied tastes. They want coverage in the mainstream press, but not in a condescending or mythic way.

Memo to Paul Sann on Negro Readership,
17 July 1962

James Wechsler Papers, State Historical Society of Wisconsin

[. . .] The Post no longer has the esteem and prestige in the Negro community that it once enjoyed. This has been too painfully impressed upon me on too many occasions — none of my own seeking.

But as I did with the suggested series, I think I should offer some background against which we can measure what I believe to be our present position.

It is my belief — both as a longtime reader and also as City Editor for many years of The Amsterdam News — that no daily paper outside the old New York World ever enjoyed the esteem in the Negro community here that The Post held for years. And I think this esteem became even higher with the demise of The World.

One reason for this was the feeling among Negroes that The Post was the only daily paper with a sincere and continuing interest in the Negro as citizen and in his fight for full citizenship.

This is nothing for which any of us here can take credit in the early days, because it pre-dated both the present management and staff of this newspaper.

If you can forgive some more personal recollections, I can recall, for instance, how the first Harlem riots (in 1935, I believe) occurred the day before our press run at The Amsterdam News, and although our own reporters were in the thick of it, we held up our press run the next day until we could read — and rewrite — The Post for our weekly edition. We were not disappointed by the delay and overtime. Because I recall that The Post that day was the first, and almost only, daily paper which stressed the economic and social factors which had precipitated the Harlem explosion and we unashamedly stole whole gobs of its stuff as thinly-veiled rewrite.

I think that it was around this time that most of the major Negro weeklies in the country began to subscribe to The Post by mail for the same reason.

I can remember the late Robert L. Vann, founder and publisher of The

Pittsburgh Courier saying to me at the 1940 Democratic convention in Chicago: "You can say what you want about the dailies, but we swear by The New York Post. It's the only way we can be sure of what is happening to our people in New York."

But I can also recall running into John H. Johnson, publisher of Ebony and Jet and owner of the largest Negro magazine empire in history, saying — only half-jokingly — in Washington last December:

"We have subscribed to The Post from the first week that we started printing The Negro Digest. But sometimes now I wonder if it's worth it. What's wrong? Have you all lost interest in The Brother?"

I don't know what our mail subscription is now among the Negro publications, but Johnson is by no means the only Negro editor or publisher who has chided me about the same thing.

There were other factors in those days too. The Post, for instance, was the first of the dailies to drop the use of "Negro" tags in crime stories except where such identification might be necessary for the apprehension of an unarrested felon.

The NAACP, in its long drive against this practice, cited The Post's position on this to other dailies. One by one, they all came around to pretty much the same thing. I think this was widely appreciated among Negro readers, especially the intellectuals who sort of regarded The Post as their Bible.

(Ironically, our pioneering in this field was not always appreciated by Negro publications. For Ralph Matthews, national editor for the Afro-American Newspapers, once told me: "The Post is carrying this equality thing too far. How can I tell which stories to clip and rewrite if they keep on failing to say whether a club member is involved or not?")

But the NAACP gave The Post a lot of well-deserved credit for pioneering in what they regarded as an important step towards the acceptance of Negroes as just some other Americans.

Yet, today, the same NAACP contends that The Post was the first of the local dailies to revive the practice of identifying Negroes in crime stories in which race played no vital part. And I have had my ears bent about this more times than I care to recall.

There is a human factor which I think illustrates my own feeling about our former and present prestige, and this involves my years of work here. But it is not altogether a personal thing.

Jimmy Graham and I once seriously considered doing a book—or a magazine article at least—on the stories The Post *didn't* publish but about which The Post often did something as a service to its readers.

This involved the hundreds of individuals—at least 90 per cent of them Negroes—who brought their own personal problems to The Post merely because they thought we were interested in them and their problems. In many cases, we could do nothing, but they seemed to feel better for just having talked to us. (Every now and then we hit the jackpot as we did the time we dug up a truck driver alibi-witness way out in Colorado that saved a Negro from the electric chair in a Brooklyn trial; you may recall the case).

But it was Graham's feeling, which I fully shared, that those people, especially the Negroes, felt that if anybody wanted to help them, if anyone understood what they were up against, that it was The New York Post.

Much of this social service or "bleeding heart" work, as it was jeeringly called, fell to me. I bitched like hell at the time but not seriously because I knew what word of mouth appreciation could do in our community. And, occasionally, we did come up with something good.

There was never a week without a half dozen or so of such in-person visits and sometimes there were almost that many in a single day.

There are not that many such visitors in a month now. My interpretation may be wrong, but I still feel rather nostalgic about them.

And I feel that this trust and personal identification with The Post came not only from the occasional sob stories which occasionally brought some sort of rough justice to otherwise hopeless people, but also from the broad spectrum of Post interest in the struggles of a minority group—in this case, Negroes.

I think it was almost a decade before the 1954 Supreme Court decision on public school segregation (and almost two decades before the current interest in de facto segregation in the North) that Fern [Marja Eckman] did a swell series on the Jim Crow educational setup at, I think, Hillburn, N.Y. I probably recall this forcefully since I got at least two letters praising *me* for Fern's stories.

But this was quite a routine thing that Negro readers seemed to expect of The Post. You probably recall Bob Williams' series on Bilbo, Opotowsky's Mississippi and Louisiana stuff, and Kempton's unforgettable Southern pieces over the years. I did a few of these things myself.

But the sum total of it all was that Negroes had come to believe that no matter where other Negroes were in trouble — Mississippi, Florida, Little Rock, Montgomery, New Orleans, Clinton, Tenn., Cicero, Ill., or New Rochelle, N.Y. — anywhere Negroes were up against it, they had only to buy The Post and find out what was really going on. Because The Post usually had somebody there to tell them about it.

It could be argued that The Post overplayed the issue on some of these cases, although I don't think we did. But I do feel that we not only attracted and kept many Negro readers but that we reached a lot of white liberals and just good-hearted whites who did have an interest in such situations and were glad to be able to do something about it. (I'm sure that at least 75 per cent of the tens of thousands of dollars raised in money and kind for the victims of the economic squeeze in Haywood and Fayette Counties in Tennessee were raised by white people — and you may recall that The Post was practically the only paper here which exposed that situation.)

There has been a growing feeling in the Negro community, if I can accept the unsolicited comments that I receive almost daily, that The Post, somewhere, has, in the words of Ebony's Johnson "lost interest in The Brother."

And I think others than me might have had some indication of this possible belief. I recall listening to the radio one night last year when [James] Wechsler was on some program and hearing one Henry Lee Moon (he didn't identify himself on the air as Director of Public Relations for the NAACP) chiding Wechsler for The Post's failure to carry many really vital stories about Negroes or to extend the coverage to situations which it once did freely.

(I didn't know until several weeks later that Moon, at Wechsler's request, had written an itemized list of such items. But when he showed me a copy of his letter, it provided only a compilation of complaints I had received from many other sources before that.

(Most of the complaints added up to this: No one had done a better job on covering the Freedom Riders than The Post, yet when the most important development came — the ICC [Interstate Commerce Commission] ban on segregation — there was nothing in the early editions of The Post despite front page coverage in the Times and Herald-Tribune; ditto the desegregation of some 100-odd eating places in Atlanta, Ga., and several similar stories.) [. . .]

But I do think there was a period in recent months — and it still exists in some areas—when many old Post readers decided that the paper, indeed, had given up or "lost interest in The Brother."

I can recall quite a number of occasions when I have called some Negro leader for comment or background on some running story only to be greeted with: "Don't tell me The Post is interested again in what happens to Negroes." There was usually an accompanying smile or joke, but there was some sincerity behind the crack.

Frankly, I think we have exhibited more interest in very recent months on the real big stories on the question, but I do think we have suffered a loss of esteem during the period that—rightly or wrongly—many Negroes felt that Post policy had changed on the subject.

I have been told more than once that the *new* Herald-Tribune devotes more space and special coverage than we do to stories that once were regarded as The Post's specialty.

(And both the Tribune and the Times have special Negro promotion men to push their home delivery and other services in every major middle class, luxury and even public housing development in Harlem. I suggested at one time that we do the same thing and even recommended several young men—including a couple of guys from the Ebony-Jet empire. But apparently none of them came up to our qualifications. Anyway, most of them got interviews but no job.)

This whole thing has gone too long, but I think I might mention one other question. That is the matter of our previous series on Harlem. If we have lost some esteem—and I think we have—some credit must be given to these series.

I remember the barbs I got when we really built up the first one in which we promised to "tell the truth about Harlem." I don't recall much new in that series and I seem to recall that we wound up with at least one big libel suit.

I didn't find the response to our Negro Middle Class one too enthusiastic either. [. . . T]he majority of people [. . .] seemed to feel that it showed little insight, said nothing about the problems of Negroes who "escape" to the suburbs and was generally inadequate.

But one reason I recommended against the High Society series was a conviction that there is growing resentment in the community against The Post for what many regard as a patronizing attitude towards the Negro and an effort to segregate him from the rest of the larger community as something different and bizarre.

May I offer my apologies? It seems that I find it hard to stop when I discuss something about which I have some deep feelings also.

TED

PRESIDENT KENNEDY

When President John F. Kennedy was assassinated on 22 November 1963, all media shifted into high gear. Poston appraised what Kennedy had attempted on the civil rights front.

"JFK and the Negro"
New York Post 24 November 1963

The identical telegram was delivered Friday night to 1,119 branch offices in 49 states of the Union. It read:

"The tragic assassination of President John F. Kennedy can be ascribed in great part to his strong civil rights program and racial attitude. The NAACP calls for nationwide observances Sunday or the following Sunday to mourn the loss of our great President."

The wire was signed by Roy Wilkins, executive secretary of the NAACP. But it easily might have borne the signature of every major Negro leader in America—with the possible exceptions of Elijah Mohammad, Malcolm X and some insignificant leader of some off-shoot Muslim sect.

The wire also might have been superfluous. For Black America was already mourning "the loss of our great President." Not since the early days of Franklin D. Roosevelt had the country's most oppressed minority placed so much hope in one man.

It was not always that way.

When Sen. John Fitzgerald Kennedy began his major drive for the Presidency in 1959, he was by no means the main choice of Negro Americans. Despite his years in the House and the Senate, he had no discernible record in support of civil rights.

And this made him unacceptable to millions of dark Americans who had moved toward freedom under the adroit and suave FDR and the brusque but uncompromising Harry Truman of 1948—only to be slowed to a crawl under the euphoria of Eisenhower.

So many other Democrats were more acceptable in the early days of

1960: Humphrey of Minnesota, who had led the civil rights rebellion at the 1948 convention; Kefauver of Tennessee, who might have reflected the New South. Even Adlai Stevenson of Illinois, who many Negroes thought had learned the hard way that "moderation" is not a pretty word in all circles.

Kennedy won the nomination. But he was by no means far ahead — if ahead at all — of Richard Nixon in most populous Negro districts when election day was less than one month away.

Then a fairly well-known young Negro minister named Martin Luther King was jailed by racists in Georgia. Kennedy acted, but Nixon, by his own later admission, decided to play it cagey — and silent.

John Fitzgerald Kennedy became the 35th and youngest elected President in history.

There were other — and probably more decisive — factors, of course. But try to tell most Negroes that!

But he was still a question mark in that beginning. How did he come to be so beloved — if bedeviled — in the end?

Well, there were big and little things in the three-year interval. And all wove the picture of the man mourned today. One might illustrate it with two cases:

He began, on Inauguration Day, by observing quite audibly that there were no Negro officers in the Coast Guard contingent which marched before him as he stood to take the oath. (A small thing, perhaps, to some 160,000,000 Americans. A hope and harbinger of the future to 18,000,000 who still didn't know the man.)

He ended, on a dusty street in Dallas, as the hope for the first meaningful civil rights legislation since Reconstruction and — to many Negro Americans — the best and last bulwark against a Republican hopeful who would leave their fate to the tender mercies of those who had oppressed them.

He might not have known this at the end (although he probably did) for he was picketed by civil rights advocates Thursday and Friday in Texas as he was on his last visit to New York.

Although his acquaintanceship in Negro circles was limited before he became President, he knew personally more Negroes at the time of his death than any other man who ever had occupied the White House. And it was not only that he integrated most social affairs there and invited more Negroes in a month than his predecessors had done in years.

One man who was no stranger to those environs under Roosevelt and Eisenhower told The New York Post last year:

"I guess the difference is his attitude, his man-to-man approach. I know it sounds corny, but I think you somehow feel that you are discussing your problem on a basis of equality with the President of the U.S. for the first time, because the President himself has made it obvious that he regards you as an equal."

A civil rights leader had this observation on the man's personality on many non-social occasions:

"When you brought the facts down front, he didn't get his back up on his dignity like Truman, nor look hurt and mad like Ike. Neither did he try to charm the pants off you like FDR.

"He'd listen to your facts — and probably add some even worse from that phenomenal memory of his — and then he'd say:

"'You may be right, but I just can't do it that way. Now why don't we try it like this . . .' You might have to disagree with him, but always on tactics, seldom on goals."

Notwithstanding, few Negro leaders were uncritical of President Kennedy and — tactics or not — much of the criticism was deserved.

He made a big campaign issue of a Presidential "stroke of the pen" to ban discrimination in housing, but waited over two years to take his own pen in hand. And even then his executive order was far more limited than it could have been.

He promised that civil rights legislation would be the first order of business if he were elected President, but it took three years and the hoses and hounds of Birmingham to blast the first fairly comprehensive civil rights bill from the White House to Capitol Hill.

But even when they assailed him publicly, many Negro leaders would admit privately—when no rival was present to brand them an Uncle Tom—that without John Fitzgerald Kennedy, there might not have been a Birmingham, an Albany, Ga., or a Jackson, Miss.—in the context of those names and places today.

This isn't to say that JFK nor his Attorney General brother Robert were architects of the Negro revolution which brought hundreds of thousands of disadvantaged Americans into the streets and another 200,000 to Washington's Monument and the Lincoln Memorial.

But without the Kennedys it is possible to debate whether such a revolution would have been possible. For the 35th President of the U.S., most leaders will admit, gave a once deadly discouraged mass the things upon which revolutions feed — hope and dignity.

One nationally known leader who consistently demanded that the President "speak out" on the indignities confronting Negro Americans said privately after James Meredith went to the University of Mississippi and Vivian Malone to Alabama:

"He doesn't do it often enough, but when he does he lays it on the line. And it sure sounds good when those federalized troops are there to sing out the chorus."

Not that the troops were there as often as demanded — and there were few weeks during his Administration that such demands were not being raised — especially when American citizens of color like the NAACP's Medgar Evers continued to be hounded, shot down or beaten merely for trying to exercise their Constitutional right to vote.

Those who persisted and registered were extremely limited — although Robert Kennedy instituted thrice more voting suits than any other Attorney General in the history of the U.S.

John F. Kennedy's name won't be on the ballot in 1964, but his greatest tribute yet may be the fact that more Negro Americans will go to the polls in the South in the next Presidential election than have ever made that march before.

To the average Negro American, the President might have succeeded most in the field of his most apparent failure — Negro employment. As one observer in this field admitted privately:

"Our jobless rate is still twice as high as theirs despite everything he's tried. One thing you've got to say: he might not have got us the jobs yet, but he's sure helped create the atmosphere which might get more of us the jobs someday."

Most leaders will admit that he not only appointed more qualified Negroes to high-ranking and responsible "non-racial" jobs than any predecessor, but that more Negro career employes were upgraded and more new government jobs opened to them in the last three years than in the last three Administrations combined.

And although the President's Committee on Equal Employment Opportunity and its "Plans for Progress" have not been able to break down all anti-Negro barriers in either industry or labor, it has compiled a record unequaled by Roosevelt's original wartime FEPC or the Truman and Eisenhower committees which followed it.

"He did with industry and labor what Time magazine said that the NAACP had done with the whole problem," one commentator said: "He made 'discrimination' a dirty word. They might practice it but they don't proclaim it."

Negro leaders, and their never-so-united followers, while maintaining pressure on the President for more rapid progress up until the day of his death, were not unaware of the price he might have had to pay—had destiny so decreed. And neither was he.

No one was more aware than John Fitzgerald Kennedy that it was quite possible that enough anti-Negro resentment might have been aroused in many white quarters—especially in the "Oh-not-next-door" Northern suburbs—to endanger his own reelection next year.

He admitted as much in one of his recent press conferences and he was even more outspoken in one of his last group meetings with Negro leaders.

"I know this whole thing could well cost me the election," one participant quoted him as saying, "but I have no intention of turning back—now, or ever." [. . .]

MINIMAL RACIAL PROGRESS

What did the writing of these articles on the racial situation take out of the reporter? Change in the South was Poston's passion—his only "children" were rising journalists, especially black. Poston had tried to do in journalism what other blacks were doing in other venues. In this book review, however, his normally upbeat tone gave way to a serious reflection on how much harm is done even to the majority race by systemic racism. Poston acknowledged the truth of Silberman's thesis that militant blacks' patience might finally be at an end.

"Plain Talk for Both Sides" [review of *Crisis in Black and White*, by Charles E. Silberman]
   New York Post 17 May 1964: 47

Let's face it. We never have, so this is the crux of our tragedy: The reality of race relations in this country is so terrible that none of us dares face it, or even admit the truth.

No one dares to face the obvious fact, for instance, that white America has no intention of granting the Negro his full and equal rights, and that all the Negro can hope to get is what he is willing and powerful enough to take.

On the other hand, no responsible Negro leader can afford to admit publicly that if all discriminatory practices were abruptly halted, say, at 11 A.M. tomorrow, the Negro's position in this country would remain fundamentally unchanged. For an inferior cannot compete on terms of equality, and America — not without deliberation — has made the Negro an inferior.

So all of us have fearfully rejected reality and created illusions which mask our dread of what we will not admit. We've spoken in partial truths, shrouded the inadmissible facts, and made a shibboleth of regarding the Negro problem, in the words of Gunnar Myrdal, as "An American Dilemma."

But not Charles E. Silberman, the Fortune editor and Columbia economist whose "Crisis in Black and White" is by far the most important of the spate of volumes on the subject interminably rolling off the presses in anticipation of the coming "long hot summer."

Like a surgeon, Silberman uses a scalpel to uncover the cancer before seeking the cure.

"The United States," he states bluntly, "— all of it, North as well as South, West as well as East — is a racist society in a sense and to a degree that we have refused so far to admit, much less face . . ."

And, flatly: "Myrdal was wrong. The tragedy of race relations in the U.S. is that there is no American Dilemma. White Americans are not torn and tortured by the conflict between their devotion to the American creed and their actual behavior.

"They are upset by the current state of race relations, to be sure. But what troubles them is not that justice is being denied but that their peace is being shattered and their business interrupted. It will take more than an appeal to the American conscience to solve 'the Negro problem.'"

Step by step, as he explores each of the areas of inequality which are the real American way of life — in schools, jobs, housing and, most of all, identification and self-esteem — this acute author tells why he feels that "nothing less than a radical reconstruction of American society is required if the Negro is to be able to take his rightful place in American life."

Silberman believes this reconstruction is inevitable, that it must take place if America is to survive as a nation. And he says that one of the most potent forces in this reconstruction will be the American Negro.

For the solution to the problem is the acquisition of power: political, social, economic. Negroes constitute a large and rapidly growing proportion of the population of large cities. And this will provide an opportunity for the acquisition of political power no other ethnic group has ever had:

"Negroes are well aware of this fact, and they are determined to make the most of it."

But the political front is only one of the areas in which bitter — and possibly bloody — confrontation must come unless Negroes and whites both face the realities, Silberman contends, documenting his case in each specific area.

It is not surprising that Malcolm X endorses this book, for even he has never so bluntly exposed white America's crimes against itself and its black brothers. It is more important that Malcolm's enthusiasm is shared by Harvard's Jerome Bruner, the Urban League's Whitney Young and the National Council of Churches' Eugene Carson Blake.

Silberman hopes his book will offend and anger all Americans, black and white.

"The truth must be faced — now," he says, "while there is still time. It is never too soon for a nation to save itself; it can be too late."

HARLEM RIOTS THROUGH THE YEARS

In this history of twentieth-century America's black mecca, which provides background for the summer 1964 riot as well as the riots of 1935 and 1943, Poston pleads for the city to hear the violence's message. A despairing attitude has replaced Poston's typical jaunty style, which had formerly highlighted the positive in situations whenever possible.

"Harlem"
New York Post 26 July 1964

It has been many things to many people over the years — none of them necessarily true.

To the early Negro migrants who filtered into a predominantly Irish and German community after the turn of the century, it was a land of expectation, later to be symbolized by the Tree of Hope before the long-gone Lafayette Theater on Seventh Av.

To the thrill-seeking whites of the Roaring Twenties, it was the place to go — the home of happy feet, Connie's Inn, the Cotton Club and other late hour oases where gangster owners saw to it that the high-stepping entertainment was all Negro and the paying customers all white. I lived there then; I know.

To struggling Negro artists and writers, accepting the patronage of such diverse wealthy Negroes as cosmetics heiress A'Lelia Walker and numbers baron Caspar Holstein, it was (in the words of liberal white novelist Carl Van Vechten) "Nigger Heaven," birth place of the Negro Renaissance.

Hundreds of thousands jammed into the three-and-a-half square mile area bounded roughly by 110th St. on the south, the old Polo Grounds on the north, Third Av. on the east, and St. Nicholas, Morningside and Manhattan Avs. on the west. Harlem was — and is — something else again. And it always was to the hundreds of thousands of Negroes who preceded them there.

Last week, for the third time in as many decades, they tried, in the words of an expression indigenous to Harlem, "to tell it like it is."

But how did [the] Harlem [riot] happen? In a way, it is more intriguing — and more chilling — than the myths which have grown up around it.

Believe it or not, New York at the turn of the century, was the "open city" which the Commission on Human Rights is now trying to re-achieve.

Dr. Robert C. Weaver, Administrator of the U.S. Home and Housing Agency and one of the nation's outstanding authorities on ghetto living, has pointed out that "Residential segregation is a relatively new phenomenon in New York City. Harlem has really developed only since 1905. Before that the early Negro population was in Brooklyn largely [. . .] and many were homeowners, well distributed throughout the city."

And Charles Abrams, the international housing authority, told in "Forbidden Neighbors" how in 1901, the city's 60,000 Negroes were scattered all over Our Town, although most of them were centered in the San Juan Hill district around West 53d St.

What happened? Well, around the end of World War I, when the early Negro migrations were swelling the city's non-white population, two Negro real estate men — Philip A. Payton Jr. and Barbados-born Solomon Riley — got a bright idea.

They found out that scores of flats and walk-up apartments in the West 120s uptown were going begging, as economically-improving Irish and German families were moving out of that community. Payton persuaded the owners to rent a few apartments to home-hungry Negroes by saying "they'll pay twice what you're getting for them now."

The experiment succeeded far beyond Payton's dreams. And Riley, a belligerent, bull-chested man who looked more white than Negro, refined Payton's discovery. He not only spurred the Harlem gold rush; he became one of the earliest of the "block busters"—using his white wife and step-daughter to purchase houses in wealthy all-white communities and then threatening to move banjo-playing Negroes in if the houses were not re-purchased by other whites at Riley's inflated prices.

But Payton and Riley were pikers, even if both made and lost millions. They only proved that segregated housing—then as now—was good business, and the bankers took it up from there.

This started back in 1934 when the influx had already turned Harlem into a teeming, predominantly Negro ghetto, although a few streets in the east and west 130s still remained integrated, and the Negro upper middle class basked in Striver's Row, the elaborate town houses designed by architect Stanford White for the city's wealthy whites on 138th St. between Seventh and Eighth Avs.

On the heels of the stock market crash and the depression, several of the banks started foreclosing on loans and mortgages made on properties often bought with a shoestring in Harlem during the easy-money days of the early migrations. And they were astounded at the exorbitant rents being paid. Of course, they knew little and cared less about the house rent parties, the doubled and tripled up families which made payment of the high rents possible.

So, 37 banks and lending corporations formed the Mortgage Conference of N.Y. in 1934. Ostensibly the conference was to fix mortgage interest rates and prevent new construction which might reduce income from the holdings of participating members. But, as the Justice Dept. was to prove in a federal suit in 1946, the Mortgage Conference did something else. It decided to confine the Negroes and "Spanish-speaking persons" to the Harlem they now had overflowed and to perpetuate the profits from prejudice in the minority rental market.

The firms went about it like this: they prepared and kept current maps showing every block in the city in which a Negro or Puerto Rican lived. They refused to make mortgages on any such block. In the words of the Justice Dept. civil suit which forced the Mortgage Conference to dissolve in 1946 under a Federal Court consent decree:

They "induced the owners of real estate in certain sections of New York City to refuse to permit Negroes or Spanish-speaking persons to move into such sections" in order to "restrict Negroes and Spanish-speaking persons to residence in certain sections of the city . . ." The 37 banks and financial institutions also conspired, the Justice Dept. proved, "to deny the owners of property occupied by Negroes and Spanish-speaking persons the mortgage financing required to maintain the real estate in habitable condition and to operate it successfully at reasonable rent levels."

It is small wonder then that between the formation of the Mortgage Conference in 1934, and its court-ordered dissolution in 1946, Harlem erupted with two major property-oriented riots. For in that period, the community had become, as novelist Ralph Ellison says in the August issue of Harper's magazine:

". . . a ruin — many of its ordinary aspects (its crimes, its casual violence, its crumbling buildings with littered areaways, ill-smelling halls, and vermin-invaded rooms) are indistinguishable from the distorted images that appear in dreams, and which, like muggers haunting a lonely hall, quiver in the waking mind with hidden and threatening significance.

"Yet this is no dream but the reality for well over 400,000 Americans, a reality which for many defines and colors the world. Overcrowded and exploited politically and economically, Harlem is the scene and symbol of the Negro's perpetual alienation in the land of his birth."

Ellison, author of "The Invisible Man," is a novelist and he actually wrote that now published essay in 1948. But New York had a more updated and factual warning about what Harlem is like today in the release a few months ago of the penetrating study by Harlem Youth Opportunities Unlimited, Inc. entitled: "Youth in the Ghetto: A Study of the Consequences of Powerlessness."

This study, and its "Blueprint for Change," hit squarely at the conditions which brought only band-aid palliatives after the major Harlem outbreaks of 1935 and 1943 — not to mention last week's inevitable outburst. For HARYOU, of all the groups which have studied that over-studied community, for once tried to "tell it as it is." And no reader of that report — from Mayor Wagner down — should have been surprised that Harlem erupted again.

But will the city listen to HARYOU — or anyone else — where Harlem is concerned? No one listened after the riot of March 19, 1935. That one was touched off when a false rumor swept through Harlem that a Negro boy had been caught stealing in a five-and-dime store on 125th St. and that store employes had taken him to the basement and had savagely beaten him up.

Another rumor had the boy dead — and in 12 hours, three men, one of them white, were dead. More than 100 others, Negro and white, had been shot, stabbed, stoned and stomped. Another 121 persons had been arrested for inciting to riot, looting, disorderly conduct and carrying concealed weapons. And the business thoroughfare of West 125th St., as well as most of Lenox, Seventh and Eighth Aves., was a shambles.

Mayor LaGuardia, who had ridden a loudspeaker truck during the height of the disorders and who had appealed to the love and loyalty Harlem had always extended to him, appointed a Commission to study the causes of the outbreak.

That study group, and another, the New York State Commission on the Condition of the Urban Colored Population, made detailed reports. But in a nutshell, they only reported what everybody knew: the people were poor; they were exploited by merchants and landlords alike; they were desperate, and they just broke loose.

But what happened afterwards? Harlem remained the same Harlem.

And nothing fundamental had been changed up to the night of Aug. 1, 1943, when still another false rumor swept through Harlem — one saying a cop had killed a Negro soldier. Within the next eight hours, six men were dead and 320 persons had been treated for gunshot and stab wounds, broken skulls and fractured limbs. Forty-four cops were wounded and three lay in Harlem Hospital in critical condition.

And the damage wreaked on stores in 1935 paled into insignificance. The Uptown Chamber of Commerce estimated that its members and property owners alone suffered losses estimated at $5,000,000. Over 800 claims, totaling $6,500,000, were filed against the city.

The city and the state again appointed commissions. Some observers said that each could have saved money by reprinting the 1935 reports, although there were a few hopeful developments. The state soon passed its first major anti-bias law and set up the State Commission Against Discrimination. The city, with an unintended assist from the Metropolitan Life Insurance Co., which publicly announced that Negroes would not be permitted to live in its tax-aided Stuyvesant Town development, passed the first of its fair housing laws.

But each advance had its drawbacks, especially on the housing side. Robert Moses, who had publicly defended Metropolitan's right to bar Negroes from Stuyvesant Town, became head of the city's Commission on Slum Clearance, which became almost synonymous with "Negro clearance" as the program developed. For, strangely enough, most of the high rent Title I projects which sprang up in the city were built in areas — outside of Harlem — where Negroes had lived peacefully for generations.

So cleared out of their old, even traditional, neighborhoods on the Upper West Side, in Hell's Kitchen and San Juan Hill, on the Lower East Side where they had lived since runaway slaves established the notorious Five Points sanctuary which shocked the visiting Charles Dickens, where could most of the Negroes go?

Where else but Harlem?

Then, on Thursday, July 16 [1964], ominous news swept through Harlem again — only this time it was not a false rumor. An off-duty police lieutenant named Thomas Gilligan had shot and killed a Negro schoolboy named Jimmy Powell. The Police Dept. insisted that the killing was justified, saying the boy had come at the officer with a knife.[1]

Harlem waited two days this time. But then it took five days to end the rioting and looting which spread to its sister community in Brooklyn's Bedford-Stuyvesant and could well have found echoes in the other Harlems in the South Bronx and Jamaica.

But is anybody really listening even now? Will the city learn belatedly that the civil rights revolution of 1964 is no longer confined to Mississippi? Will anybody get the message?

VOTING RIGHTS

Some southern blacks had yearned a lifetime for a say in the nation's business, if only through voting.

"Ted Poston from Alabama: A First-Time Voter at Seventy-seven: 'Good, So Good'"
New York Post 4 May 1966: 5, 74

Montgomery, May 4—Jeff Hamilton, gaunt, gangly and a little feeble, stepped proudly out of the Hamner Hall polling place in Precinct 2 North, a happy smile on his thin and sunken lips.

"It's good," he muttered to no one in particular as he stepped gingerly down the two steps, a cane assisting him. "It's good. So good. God, it's good."

Jeff Hamilton had just voted for the first time in his 77 years of life.

And he was not only willing but anxious to discuss this major event with a total stranger.

"Why did I turn out today?" he echoed the question, his forehead wrinkling under a leather hunting cap. "Why, I had to go with the majority of my people. And it looks like that's where my people are going today."

But why in 77 years in Alabama — 25 of them in Montgomery — the stranger persisted, had he never voted or tried to vote before?

"It's a long story, son. A long, long story, and I'll tell you like it was."

But feeling into the pockets of his shabby but immaculate faded overalls jumper for his pipe, he waved a greeting, "Lo, Miss Bess," to a truly feeble little lady in her 90s who was being assisted up the steps by friends and Negro campaign workers.

The stranger had ridden in the pool car which had brought "Miss Bess" and three other contemporaries to Hamner Hall and it had taken her over five minutes to negotiate the short distance from the car to the polling place steps. And apparently she was still muttering the prayer she had intoned insistently in the car: "Just once in this life, Lawd, just one little time in this life."

Rufus A. Lewis, the now powerful leader of local and statewide Negro Democrats, had been pressed into pool car chauffeur service when demands of the elderly exceeded 500 calls before the polls had even opened. He answered indulgently the others' queries of:

"We just voting for one man, ain't we, Mr. Lewis? No? Well, where are our four Negro men? I can't take time for them other 31 white mens, except Mr. Flowers you got on here." (A marked ballot clutched by all.)

Or: "You know I can't read, Mr. Lewis, but my little grandboy has drawed circles around each one of them 35. Maybe I can find them that way."

And: "I been setting on my front porch since 5:30 waiting for you all. But it's worth it."

And, in a way, it was. For Miss Bess, the Jeff Hamiltons and the even more ancient and infirm were the catalysts of the revolution which sent tens of thousands of Negroes to jammed polling places all over this state. There was no accent on youth. The anxious elders dominated every precinct.

Jeff Hamilton was asked why.

"Well," he said, leaning one thin shoulder on one of the few shade trees around the sweltering polling place, "they don't know as well as we do.

They ain't discovered yet what they been missing and they ain't been missing it as long as us."

A studied pause and: "But don't bad mouth all them youngsters. How else would Miss Bess and the others have got here today. Some of them ain't going to gee and ain't gonna haw, but most of them gonna appreciate sometime what this all means."

Then Jeff Hamilton went back to the beginning — his birth in 1889 in Butler County, on an impoverished farm outside Greenvale.

"They told us then that voting was white man's business. Said us coloreds had never voted. But I remember my Pa told me he had heard that some Negroes had voted in Alabama, though he had never seen one." (There were 104,418 Negro voters in Alabama in 1867, although the figure had been driven down to 6,108 by 1947.)

"They wouldn't have let us off to vote anyhow then. They were working us from king to can't."

World War I rescued Jeff Hamilton — temporarily — from Butler County, and sent him to France with the [American Expeditionary Force's] Company C, 548th Labor Battalion.

"Yes, we talked about what we was going to do when we got back. But that was mostly the boys from up north. It was worse than ever when I got back down here. You know they was lynching us right and left. It was worth your life to be even caught in the courthouse."

But Jeff Hamilton, whose $120-a-month World War I Army pension is the mainstay of his withering years (he and his wife, Anita, only get $66 from Social Security) is an honest man, so he chuckled apologetically as he admitted:

"I can't say that's why I didn't try to register then. I was wild as a rabbit and I just didn't think about nothing like that round that time. Maybe that's why I can't be too hard on these kids today."

Then, reflectively: "Well, maybe there was more than that. Everything was so cut and dried against us then. We knew we had nowhere to go. But these youngsters down here today got things working for them. They got more reason than we ever had . . ."

So when did he finally decide to register?

"I tell you when it first cross my mind serious. That man [John] [2] Patterson got elected Governor. He was a bad man for us — 'Nigger this, nigger that' all the time.

"I said to myself and to Anita [Mrs. Hamilton, 69],[3] I said I sure wish I was registered. That man's got to go."

Did he try to register then?

"Well, no. I didn't. But two of my cousins did. They went down three or four times and the white folks there smiled as sweet as sugar. They told them: 'You'll hear from us,' but they never did."

What finally made up his mind decisively?

"That man [George] Wallace. You know he came in right after Patterson and he's the worst of all. You can be sure I didn't vote for Sister [Lurleen] Wallace, as the Rev. Martin Luther King calls her."

Did he vote for all the 35 candidates marked on the sample ballot he still fondled in his gnarled fingers?

"Well, no. But I did vote for Mr. Flowers. I did that first of all. And then I voted for Rev. [Jesse L.][4] Douglas like Martin Luther King asked us when he spoke at Rev. Douglas' First CME Church last Thursday night. I voted for three or four others. I don't know who they was — but I hope some of them was colored."

What single force had contributed most to the revolutionary change he detected in some conditions in Alabama?

Forcefully: "You ever hear of Mr. L. B. J. Johnson? That man's something else again. To my way, he sure is."

Then Jeff Hamilton set off on the mile-and-a-half walk to his home at 2330 Chappell St. spurning car pool offers with "Let the old folks ride."

He apologized to the stranger.

"I got to get back so Anita can come up here and cast her vote. She's setting home with the afflicted child of my sister while my sister is voting over at the Cleveland Av. station.

"It's the first vote for all of us. And it's good. God, it's good!"

HARLEM POLITICIAN

Poston knew Adam Clayton Powell beginning in 1928. The two men were friends, but both of them understood that Poston's obligation was to report the news objectively. This article captures Powell's flavor in a tone of critical affection.

"For Powell, the Campus Pays Better Than Congress"
New York Post 15 January 1968: 3, 17

San Francisco — Adam Clayton Powell expects to more than double his former $30,000 Congressional salary this year by addressing white college students across the country on the virtues of Black Power, the excluded Representative told the New York Post here today.

"I picked up $5,000 out here on my first four days," Powell said, lounging in a silk bathrobe in his 8th floor double suite in the Jack Tar Hotel, "and I turned down $1,000 today from the University of Oregon and another grand from another school because sheer exhaustion is threatening to bring me down with the flu."

A bit wan under his deep Bimini tan, Powell discussed the new career opening before him with a seeming awe.

"I've never seen anything like it," he said softly, "and this is only the beginning. I've been flooded with invitations from all over the country. I've got to get myself organized if I'm to accept even half of them.

"With this flu about to bed me, I'm flying back to Bimini tomorrow to get my health straight, and then I'm going to open my cross-country tour by accepting invitations from the student bodies of four white colleges and universities in Florida.

"Then I'll open my North Carolina tour at Duke University, after another short rest in Bimini. Then the student bodies of six Eastern colleges — Amherst, Williams, Wellesley, Holyoke and Smith will sponsor me at the University of Massachusetts —."

The adjoining door of the other suite opened and in walked Ardie Ivie, assistant to UCLA's dean of student activities. He told Powell that the Student Council of the University of Oklahoma was on the wire and offering him $1,500 "plus full expenses for you and your staff" for any date he would set.

"Put them down at the end of the Florida tour," Powell said wearily, then "No, hold it, Maybe we can hit them when we go to Indiana and Michigan State. Then we can go from there to Oregon and Washington State and pick up those cancelled dates. It should be warm enough up there by then."

As the tall, gangling Ivie went to the other suite to take care of the University of Oklahoma, a trim young man emerged from the bathroom, naked to the waist, muscles rippling.

"That's my other bodyguard — Ed Brown," Powell chuckled. "He's earned his Black Belt in karate. He can disable any human with a single blow."

Brown, as unsmiling as Ivie, gazed at the visitor steadily from behind the large dark glasses which both wear until Powell told him: "Oh, he's an old friend, but he'll probably try to beat my brains out on 'Face the Nation' when we get over to the CBS studio." [. . .]

But mention of the upcoming CBS program aired yesterday brought Powell back to the matter of this year's income.

"I'm doing this CBS thing for free," he said. "It's good national exposure. But TV is opening up too. I met a young TV producer the other day on one of my walks through Watts and he's giving me $1,000 for a 30-minute radio-TV thing which he is going to package for independent stations across the country."

He concentrated on reaming out his pipe, and said softly:

"What really impresses me is the amount of money these student organizations have in their treasuries. Why, they've got some $6,000,000 out there at UCLA — over $3,000,000 of it in cash — and don't forget that it is the students and not the college administrations who are bringing me to the campuses."

The disarming Powell grin again, and: "You know, it's rather ironic that I haven't been invited to a single Negro college. Of course the United Negro College Fund is the factor there. Without all that money they get from people like the Rockefellers, any one of those Negro colleges would go down in a minute. But I think I just might drop in on Florida A. & M. while I'm doing Florida. Yep, I think the students would welcome me at Tallahassee."

But commercial TV and campus treasuries are not the only things keeping the wolf away from Adam's Bimini door. He delivered a fiery sermon on "What's in Your Head?" yesterday to an overflow congregation at the prominent Third Baptist Church here, and received "a very fine honorarium and expenses."

Powell modestly terms his California foray "sensational" and, in fact, has been wildly hailed by at least 20,000 students, 99 per cent of them white (he claims 35,000, and accuses the press of underestimating his appeal on four campuses). He has derided established figures like Roy Wilkins and Whitney Young, and exhorted the white students to pay homage to and follow the very men who pushed most whites out of the civil rights movement — Stokely Carmichael, H. Rap Brown and Floyd McKissick.

The white students applauded.

His press conferences, daily, are wall-to-wall affairs. (Here in San Francisco yesterday, a town without newspapers because of a strike, he probably drew more radio, TV and out-of-town newsmen than Los Angeles' Mayor Yorty could have mustered.)

Occasionally, however, questions arose which would have embarrassed another man.

Yesterday, one reporter asked about charges by the UCLA student group that their illustrious guest had skipped out, leaving them with a $500 tab at the Bel Air Sands Motel in Los Angeles — after the Associated Students Inc. had paid him $1,250 for his appearance.

"It was a misunderstanding," Powell said equably. "I thought the $1,250 was exclusive of expenses. But I didn't pick that hotel with its plush sitting room and kitchenette. My name is not on the registry. It was five members of their group who rushed in and ordered all those steak dinners and drinks."

"The bill has been paid by the university," said Ardie Ivie from behind his black glasses, while Ed Brown scowled through his at the impertinent questioner.

Undaunted, another reporter reminded Powell that he had told the press in Los Angeles that the Rev. Martin Luther King had come down to Bimini 10 days ago to tell the Congressman-elect that King's own non-violent program had failed and that Adam Clayton Powell represented the only hope for the Negro people. The reporter said that King had denied this in New York Saturday and said he hadn't even conferred with Powell during his three days of rest on Bimini.

Powell replied: "I don't want to call anybody a liar, so I won't say anything."

He added: "He [King][5] conferred with me personally on each and every one of those three days; he not only begged me to come to Atlanta at any price I wanted ($1,500 and expenses), but I have five witnesses who heard him say to me:

"'Adam, despite my own position, posture and image, you are the only man who can save the situation facing the black man in the U.S.'"

At one press conference in Los Angeles, Powell looked out and saw his former wife, jazz pianist Hazel Scott, in the audience. He rushed over and embraced her.

"She looked great," he said later, "real great. She had just closed an engagement in one of the big night clubs. She told me that Skipper [his son, Adam Clayton Powell III][6] was coming down to visit me next week."

Powell was less effusive when CBS's Morton Dean mentioned his third — and estranged — wife on "Face the Nation," and recalled that Mrs. Yvette Powell had claimed that her husband had once told her that he was not a Negro at all, but the illegitimate descendant of a white slave owner.

Said Powell: "Anyone who has an estranged wife has automatically inherited a liar."

MEDGAR EVERS'S BROTHER

Coming home on the night of 12 June 1963, Mississippi's NAACP *leader, Medgar Evers, was shot in his driveway. Keenly interested, the* Post *sent Poston to cover the first trial of Evers's killer (who was not brought to justice until 1994). In 1968 Poston profiled Evers's brother, Charles, who seemed to have taken up where Medgar left off. Although Charles Evers did not win election to the U.S. Congress, he became Mississippi's first black mayor since Reconstruction when he was elected to lead the city of Fayette, and he held that post for twenty-five years.*

"Closeup: Mississippi Candidate" [Charles Evers]
New York Post 6 February 1968

It would serve Mississippi's late Sen. Theodore Gilmore Bilbo right. For "The Man," as Bilbo loved to refer to himself, predicted it in the first place. Standing on the steps of the county courthouse in Decatur, Miss., one sweltering campaign day in 1937, Bilbo pointed to two little Negro brothers squatting on the sidewalk and said:

"You see them two little niggers sitting down there? If you don't stop them, one of them will be up here on these steps one day trying to go to Congress."

"Not a bad idea," murmured 11-year-old Medgar Evers. "Not bad at all," echoed 13-year-old Charlie Evers.

They stopped Medgar — assassinated him on his Jackson doorstep, June 12, 1963.

But last night, with TV cameras trained on him, Charlie Evers stood on those same Decatur courthouse steps and urged the voters of Mississippi's 3d C.D. [Congressional District] to send him to Congress.

The NAACP Mississippi secretary-on-leave chuckled about the boyhood incident the other day, but made it clear that his candidacy was serious.

"John Bell Williams [the present Governor, whose vacated Congressional seat Evers hopes to fill][7] was the biggest vote-getter in the history of this district. Well, the highest vote he ever racked up was 17,000.

"Now, we've got over 75,000 Negroes registered in the 3d District, not to mention a few hundred white votes I'm pretty sure I'll get.

"So," continued the argument with himself, "what if there *are* 125,000 white voters registered? There are already seven white candidates out for the seat, and two more will announce before the week ends."

The creaking of his Evers-for-Congress office chair was almost audible from his Lynch St. headquarters in Jackson as he leaned back and said over the phone:

"We're out to win this thing the first time out — Feb. 27 — and I think we can do it. We're shooting for a majority of the total vote cast in the primary. Then there can be no ganging up on us in a runoff two weeks later."

But hasn't his candidacy inflamed Mississippi passions?

"Naw. No more than usual. We're keeping race far back in the background, and *all* my supporters accepted this before I announced I would run."

The Evers brothers were born in Newton, Miss. Both served overseas before putting themselves through Alcorn College, Lorman, Miss., on athletic scholarships.

Charlie went into the hotel and funeral business in Philadelphia, Miss., while Medgar tried to make it as an insurance salesman. But when Medgar decided to work full time for the NAACP, Charlie married a childhood sweetheart and migrated to Chicago to "make enough money to keep both me and Medgar going." He did, too, teaching physical education in the public schools and "wheeling and dealing in night clubs and real estate" for "an extra $25,000 or so" a year.

When Medgar was slain, Charlie rushed to Jackson and seized the NAACP secretaryship even while the national NAACP office was debating who could follow Medgar. His wife Nannie and three small daughters followed him home, and they now operate the "Medgar Evers Shopping

Center" (biggest in the county) in Fayette, Miss., while Charlie is out campaigning.

He has come a long way from Newton, Miss. He intends to go farther.

HARLEM'S TROUBADOUR

A cultural era ended for Poston when Langston Hughes died. This piece is reminiscent of Poston's farewells to other notable Harlemites, for example, James Weldon Johnson, composer of the Negro national anthem, "Lift Every Voice and Sing" ("Harlem Buries Johnson"); Bill "Bojangles" Robinson (see section 15, above); Walter White ("2,000 Attend Funeral"); W. C. Handy, who wrote "St. Louis Blues" ("On a Harlem Street Corner"; "Mama Remembers"); and pianist-singer Nat King Cole ("Nat King Cole").

"Langston Hughes: A Poetic Farewell"
New York Post 26 May 1967

> When you come to my funeral
> Come dressed in red;
> Cause I ain't got no business
> Being dead.
>   From the early poems of Langston Hughes [8]

Of course, no one did. Those who showed up yesterday were the survivors. Somehow, like Hughes, they had made it. Fur coats. Fame. But their suffering was not necessarily less than his.

And, in the neat recesses of Benta's Funeral Home at 630 St. Nicholas Av. — "the best funeral place they have given us in Harlem," an old lady said yesterday — they sat there more entranced than they had ever been with the magic of the man who had made life more livable for them, too.

The nearest to this early admonition was a white dowager, Mrs. Amy Spingarn, widow of a founder and second president of the NAACP.

She laid down her furled umbrella, looked at her red scarf and opened her coat, still damp from the gentle afternoon rain, and said:

"I'm glad I wore the scarf. I'm even more glad I helped publish one of his books of poems. He called it 'Pumpkin Yellow,' I think."

The service was well on its way. And what a service.

For who else but James Mercer Langston Hughes could write and direct his own funeral?

"I never saw anything like it in my whole life," said producer, director, ex-standup straight man and comedian Dick Campbell later in the Red Rooster.

(Lang dropped into the Red Rooster often. Especially on Wednesdays. That's the only night they offer chitterlings *and* champagne at the same price on the same night.)

But the service was going on then. And how else would a poet, dramatist, short story writer, novelist, anthologist do it?

It had started out with this groovy number by the Randy Weston Trio. Lang had narrated one of their albums once. Real groovy. The piano in command but nurtured by the combination.

And then Arna Bontemps, Lang's longtime friend, associate and collaborator, had come on to speak—briefly—of the death wish which had haunted this gentle man all his life.

"But Lang was not only occupied with death," he said, "but also with life."

And while the trio beat the drums and strummed the piano behind him, Bontemps recited a few lines from Hughes' "Beat the Drums for Me."

Arna recited a few biting lines from "Night Funeral in Harlem." (Where do they get the money, how can they afford it? but finally: They love their own.)

Mrs. Spingarn said, "Listen" as Arna mentioned "Dear Lovely Death." The room was silent as he read:

> Death is a tower
> To which the soul ascends
> To pass a solitary hour
> Which never ends.[9]

Ralph Bunche had come in earlier. But even earlier than that he had wired the family:

"He had a remarkable type of genius, expressed through his natural ability to establish communion with and to reflect the thinking of the common man, the simple man, who also is frequently the thinking man."

Nora Holt Ray had come in right behind him. And Henry Lee Moon director of public relations for the NAACP, had introduced her to Mrs. Spingarn.

"She was the Lena Horne of her day," he whispered of those dark days when no Negro aspired to Broadway and the well-paying rooms all over town.

And, at that moment, Lena Horne walked in and joined Nora Holt Ray at the other end of the row. They sat sobbing together.

Moon — once a press agent, always a press agent — was assuring Mrs. Spingarn that Lang's first prize-winning poem, "A Negro Speaks of Rivers," was published in The Crisis, the NAACP's long-lived periodical, and that his last poem, "Backlash," would appear in the June Crisis. [. . .]

But the Bunches, the Hornes, the Nora Holt Rays were not alone. There were others who had survived. Not all, but mostly, Negro. Eubie Blake, Noble Sissle, George Meares, poetess Marianne Moore.

"He would have liked this," said Mrs. Spingarn.

And who among us could have questioned it?

"The Legacy of Langston Hughes"
    New York Post 27 May 1967

He created this character and named him Jesse B. Semple and made him America's most caustic commentator on contemporary concerns. But Langston Hughes insisted to last Monday's end that only the name was fictional. [. . .]

But few doubted that Simple — as he became known in practically every Negro ginmill across the nation — was all Langston Hughes. His compassion. His angry humor. His indignation at the foibles of the human species.

Who but Simple (or Langston) could discuss everything. [. . .]

The lack of Negro astronauts in the space program?

"This is serious, because if one of them white Southerners gets to the moon first, COLORED NOT ADMITTED signs will go up all over Heaven as sure as God made little apples, and Dixiecrats will be asking the Man on the Moon: 'Do you want your daughter to marry a Nigra?'"

Why is Simple so sure he will go to Heaven?

"Because I already been in Harlem." [. . .]

Or the time Simple's family whipped him for lying after he'd told them, truthfully, how a kindly old white man "patted me on the head one hot day and gave me a dime, saying, 'Looks like you could stand an ice cream cone.'

"They could not understand," Simple recalled, "that there is some few people in the world who do good without being asked . . . that is why I do not hate all white folks today. Not everybody has to be begged to do good, or subpoenaed into it."

The creation of Jesse B. Simple — first 20 years ago in the Chicago Defender (then a Negro weekly) and last in the New York Post — highlighted one of the many contradictions in the life of one of the most prolific contributors to American literature.

The creation became more widely known than the creator. The Negro masses recognized and loved Simple. Some Negro intellectuals hated Simple — and Hughes. So last March, Hughes told The Post's book editor, Martha MacGregor:

"No more Simple stories . . . the racial climate has gotten so complicated and bitter that cheerful and ironic humor is less understandable to many people. A plain, gentle kind of humor can so easily turn people cantankerous, and you get so many ugly letters."

Simple was all Hughes, but there was so much more to James Mercer Langston Hughes than Jesse B. Simple. Three books of poetry. Four of fiction. Four Simple volumes. Two operas. Five biography-histories. Seven anthologies. Thousands of poems. Like:

> Hold fast to dreams
> For if dreams die
> Life is a broken-winged bird
> That cannot fly.[10]

As late as 10 days ago he told this reporter, an old friend, how amused he still was over his first newspaper story. He was 23 and unknown in 1926 when the old New York Sun told how Vachel Lindsay had discovered a Negro busboy in Washington's Wardman Park Hotel and chanted his poems to an all-white audience. Hughes' first book of poems, "The Weary Blues," was about to be published, and that made news. The headline said: "Negro Boy Sings Some Lyrics."

The title poem began with the music of a Negro blues singer–piano player on Lenox Av., and ended with:

The calm
Cool face of the river
Asked me for a kiss.[11]

[. . .] One of his probable last worries when he was taken to Polyclinic Hospital May 6 for the operation was whether to tell Aunt Toy.

He needn't have worried. We live in an electronic age. Mrs. Toy Harper, his oldest and best friend, closer than any blood relative, heard it on a transistor radio while she was confined to another hospital herself.

She was probably struck with an irony that would have amused Langston. He was laid to rest Thursday from Benta's Funeral Home at 630 St. Nicholas Av. — just two doors from the first real home that Langston had known in Harlem.

That apartment at 634 St. Nicholas Av. had been a big bone of contention between him and Aunt Toy. When he first started making a little money — never made much until the last few years — Aunt Toy discovered a house for sale over on Riverside Dr. and urged him to try to buy it.

"I know that they say the boundaries of Harlem and Bedford-Stuyvesant are exactly where the first Negro moves into an all-white neighborhood," he told her, "but that's not Harlem to me. I'll buy you the house, but I won't live there. I'm going to live and die in Harlem."

So they compromised. He bought a cute little house at 20 W. 127th St. in the middle of Harlem — just up the street from a Negro storefront church named "God's Bathtub," and both were taken from there this month to the hospitals.

It was from there that he wrote the poem which gave name to the late Lorraine Hansberry's Broadway hit: "A Raisin in the Sun." The poem began:

What happens to a dream deferred?
Does it dry up, like a raisin in the sun
Or fester like a sore —
And then run?[12]

Langston Hughes had never lost hold of his dream. But it was deferred for years, long years, [. . .] until he was discovered in the early 20s. [. . .]

But Simple's Boswell always seemed at home with his creation, as when he asked in "Simple's Uncle Sam":

"Uncle Sam, if you is really my blood uncle, prove it. Are we is or aren't we ain't related? If so, how come you are so white and I am so black?"

Or when Simple refused to be disturbed by the possible destruction of civilization in a nuclear holocaust.

"I'm perfectly willing to go myself if my enemies in Mississippi are taken along with me. Greater love hath no man than he lay down his life to get even."

His first poem was published in the NAACP periodical, "The Crisis." His last one, called "The Backlash Blues," will be published there next month. It reads:

> Mister Backlash, Mr. Backlash,
> Just what do you think I am?
> You raise my taxes, freeze my wages
> Send my son to Vietnam.
> You give me second-class houses,
> Second-class schools.
> Do you think that colored folks
> Are just second-class fools? [13]

Langston wasn't. And Simple never was.

SUMMING UP

On 16 October 1968 Professor Luther P. Jackson of the Columbia University Graduate School of Journalism asked Poston to speak on interracial reporting, and Poston presented many of the same ideas he expressed in this essay. Perhaps he saw this speech as a kind of swan song to his race and his profession.

"The American Negro and Newspaper Myths"
Paul L. Fisher and Ralph L. Lowenstein, eds., *Race and the News Media* (New York: Praeger, 1967) 63–72

There is little disagreement that there has been a big change in the content of racial news recently, but there may be some disagreement on the extent and significance of that change. In my opinion, the most welcome change has been in the treatment of racial news in Southern newspapers. I hope this change presages the beginning of the end of one of the most disgraceful decades in American journalism.

There has also been some change in the Northern press. But the coverage in the major newspapers of my area today does not equal the quality of the coverage provided by those papers when the racial problem was regarded as almost solely a Southern problem and not something that might erupt violently in their own back yards.

The majority of the Southern editors and publishers have been cynically defending a myth that they know to be untrue — white superiority, Negro indolence, and a baseless contention that the region's magnolia-scented values would triumph over the moral and legal might of the federal government.

At the same time, during my thirty-five years in this business, I have observed Northern editors and publishers creating and perpetuating a subtler myth: that Northern Negroes really are a monolithic mass, not plain individual Americans, and that they must be viewed and reported in that context. Both interpretations may seem harsh, but I am prepared to defend these theses if necessary.

In terming recent years "one of the most disgraceful decades in American journalism," I am not making a blanket attack on the whole Southern press. There have always been, and there still are, some fine and courageous Southern papers. As a native Kentuckian, I was reared from my earliest days on the Louisville *Courier-Journal.* As a college student, Pullman porter, and dining-car waiter, I received a valuable adjunct to my education through the Nashville *Tennessean,* The Atlanta *Constitution,* the St. Louis *Post-Dispatch,* and other pillars of liberal journalism in the South.

Not all the courageous papers have been large and prosperous. I am sure that most journalists are familiar with the crusade that has been and is still being waged, at great cost, by Hazel Brannon Smith, the editor of the Lexington (Miss.) *Advertiser,* against bigoted local officials, the White Citizens Councils, and the resurgent Ku Klux Klan.

A brief review of another paper of the same name — the Montgomery (Ala.) *Advertiser* — might furnish the classic example of what I regard as a betrayal of trust by most Southern papers. Under Grover C. Hall, Sr., one of the great editors of his era, the *Advertiser* stood as a beacon light in the darkness of the 1920s, when the forces of reaction and prejudice threatened not only the South but much of the North.

When the Klan was finally routed and run out of Alabama, it was not an accomplishment of the old New York *World,* which had done yeoman service toward that end. It was the courage of Grover C. Hall, Sr., who castigated and ridiculed the hooded riders in his newspaper, who met their daily threats by wearing his holstered pistol to his office, and who mobilized the responsible citizens of the community by citing the very real threat to lawful government. This Pulitzer-prize winner not only had the courage to fight against what he regarded as wrong but also had the courage to admit his own mistakes and to apologize publicly for such mistakes.

When Montgomery's Negro community became incensed after Hall had editorially castigated nine young Negro youths accused of raping two white girl hobos as "beasts" and "apes," the editor stuck to his guns until the court testimony itself proved that the Scottsboro boys were the victims of a monstrous frame-up. He then not only changed his editorial position but also went publicly to a mass meeting of the Negro community and apologized for his earlier intemperate remarks. I believe he would have done this even if his Negro readers, the circulation backbone of many a Southern newspaper, had not quietly invoked an effective boycott against the *Advertiser.*

The Montgomery *Advertiser* is still in existence and is still edited by a Grover C. Hall—this time by Grover C. Hall, Jr. A handsome, immaculate, articulate young man, whom I was to meet and get to know well during the year-long Montgomery bus boycott, Hall seemed destined to follow in his father's footsteps when he said in a speech on April 26, 1953: "A newspaper has great potential for both mischief and beneficence, for being worthy or unworthy of its opportunities and obligations. A paper is a temple and not a resort for a bully, a knave, or a clod."

Two years later, in the wake of the 1954 Supreme Court desegregation decision, Alabama found itself faced with a new spearhead of reaction, the burgeoning White Citizens Councils. The Negro community, which had loved and respected Hall's father, enthusiastically hailed young Hall when he assailed the White Citizens Council members as "manicured Ku Klux Klansmen." But the joy was short-lived. Senator James O. Eastland of Mississippi came to Montgomery and addressed a cheering meeting of some 15,000 current or potential members of the White Citizens Councils, and the Montgomery *Advertiser* did a sudden and complete about-face.

Most wcc meetings, even those that attracted only a handful of people, became front-page news. The *Advertiser's* letters-to-the-editor column became almost an exclusive forum for the WCC. On the day that a rising young leader, Martin Luther King, Jr., addressed 12,000 people in the Cathedral of St. John the Divine in New York City, the *Advertiser* reported the event in a three-paragraph shirttail to one of the five separate stories on WCC meetings in that single issue.

Later, in one of our numerous friendly conversations during my extended stay in Montgomery at the time of the bus boycott, I gently chided young Hall, whom I still regard as a friend, about the paper's about-face. He asked a cynical question that sums up the abdication of responsibility by many Southern editors: "Well, what the hell would Jimmy Wechsler [editor of the New York *Post*] [14] have done in a small community like this when most of the important people in town had joined the White Citizens Council and when it had mustered a fifteen-thousand membership?"

There is no intention here to single out the Montgomery *Advertiser*. I could cite far more glaring examples from personal experience. I was in Decatur, Alabama, in the 1930's for the third trial of the Scottsboro boys. The local paper made no editorial suggestion on what should be done with the nine young Negroes. It just devoted its whole front page to an eight-column picture of the naked, swinging bodies of two white men who had been lynched in California two days before for kidnaping the nephew of Bret Harte. I was in Birmingham, Alabama, when the Birmingham *News* headlined the bloody riots in Cyprus while finding only brief space at the bottom of page four to make passing mention — without many details, of course — of the local rioting then going on between Birmingham's Negroes and Bull Connor, with his police dogs and fire hoses.

It should be noted that my criticism has been directed mainly at the editors and publishers of Southern papers and not at the working newspapermen I've met during my many years on the racial beat. Nowhere else have I met a more knowledgeable, decent, and frustrated group of newspapermen than those with whom I worked down South. I can say truthfully that I owe my life to several of these men. Without their warnings and assistance, I could have been lynched on any of the three occasions when I was chased out of town by mobs — the last one led by three sheriff's deputies.

I sometimes feel apologetic when I glance at the Heywood Broun or George Polk awards I won for coverage of racial developments in the South. For the facts in the cited series were not always a result of my reportorial brilliance; they were usually given me by frustrated young reporters on the scene who knew what was going on, but whose editors would never let them print it. If the changing content of racial news in the South is to have any significance, the shackles will have to be removed from those who would like to practice honestly the craft they have chosen.[15]

But enough of the sins of the South. Let us consider the sophistries of the North. I have been a working newspaperman on the daily press in New York City for more than a quarter of a century, and the only thing that surprises me is that there have been only *three* Harlem riots — and those mainly against property.

There has been hardly a single year since I escaped from the South that the New York dailies — and this includes my own New York *Post* — haven't had at least one season of Negro "scare" stories that aroused such intra-community tensions that bloodshed could well have resulted. One paper may pick up a legitimate and dramatic story of racial conflict, and then the season is on. A competitor will seek a "new angle" on the story, only to be topped by a third or fourth rival, and pretty soon the whole city will seem to be fighting the Civil War all over again.

When real conflict is threatened between a resentful black community and a frightened white community, the New York papers — liberal pro–civil righters all — wash their hands of any responsibility, except to demand, if violence breaks out, "Why doesn't Roy Wilkins — or Whitney Young or A. Philip Randolph — control his people?" Not one of these papers would dare demand such control or impute such responsibility to the leader of any other ethnic or racial group in the city. The last time this demand was raised, one of the Negro leaders pointed out that on another front, the federal government was investigating the New York Cosa Nostra, or Mafia. "Every name that has come out so far is Italian," this Negro remarked bitterly. "Paul Screvane is an Italian and president of the City Council. When are they going to demand that Screvane 'control his people'?"

A couple of cases will document my charge. Months before the rioting of July, 1964, broke out in Harlem and in Brooklyn's Bedford-Stuyvesant section, the annual scare season had been opened — and from a rather unexpected source. The staid *New York Times* — which has given the country its most distinguished coverage of the Southern racial scene through the work of Ray Daniell, Johnny Popham, Claude Sitton, Ben Franklin and other great reporters — suddenly made a great discovery in its own back yard. It proclaimed that it had uncovered the existence of a sinister Harlem organization composed of Negro teen-agers and pre-teen-agers who had pledged to maim or murder every white person found in Harlem. Then it cited four recent isolated and unsolved slayings of white persons during apparent holdup attempts and credited them all to the new organization — the Blood Brothers.

Every responsible social, civic, youth, and antidelinquency agency in Harlem not only denounced but disproved the preposterous story. But *The Times* continued to pursue it, with its competitors panting in its path — and with the Blood Brothers' membership growing from 30 to 400 and then dropping to 90 in successive editions.

In Queens, a white student who wanted to quit college read of the Blood Brothers and got a big idea. He slashed himself with razor blades and told the police that he had been assaulted by two Negroes who called him "white man" (obviously Blood Brothers). The story got a big play in all the local dailies and made a big hit with everybody except the police. They called the student in for questioning, and he broke down and confessed to the hoax.

All the papers seemed willing to drop the story except the New York *Journal-American*. In "news" stories that really should have run in the editorial column, the *Journal-American* intimated that the only "hoax" in the case was the youth's confession. Didn't everyone know the Blood Brothers were around?

The Times buried the Blood Brothers as abruptly as it had created them, but the scare returned in the form of stories about a group of youthful assassins called the Five Percenters, said to believe that 95 per cent of all Negroes are either cattle or Uncle Toms and that only the remaining 5 per cent are courageous enough and determined enough to try to kill all white people and Negro policemen.

This new group was publicized editorially by the New York *Herald Tribune*, the same paper that sent Bob Bird and Bill Huie into the South for some of the nation's best coverage on the civil-rights revolution. *The Times* denounced the Five Percenter scare, compared it with the Blood Brother myth, which, it said, was properly protested by Negro leaders. *The Times* didn't seem to recall where the Blood Brothers were born.

During the 1964 pre-Harlem-riot season, the New York *Post* got a telephone tip that a fight had broken out on a Harlem River excursion boat taking about a thousand high-school pupils up to Bear Mountain. The new-angle-seeking assistant city editor yelled excitedly to me, "Find out how many Negroes are on that boat and who started the race riot." It turned out that only ten Negroes were among the students and that the "race riot" was only a fist fight between two Italian youngsters. The whole story was dropped later, but not before hundreds of white parents had been frightened that their children were being slashed up by rampaging Negroes on a school outing.

There have been some changes in the content of racial news in the Northern press, but at times I yearn for the good old days. The old myths were less dangerous. In the 1930's the New York dailies fell in love with a little Negro cultist named Father Divine and appointed him the spokesman for *all* Negroes. When the Board of Elections refused to let Divine's angels register under such celestial monikers as "Heavenly Light" or "Serene Sarah," Divine made the front pages when he ordered his followers not to register at all. On the day after the election in 1936, *The Times* had two stories on its front page. One double-column exclusive at the top of page one proclaimed: "Polls Deserted in Harlem as Father Divine Orders His Followers Not to Vote." The other story was a routine statistical account of the election. The figures showed that Harlem's four assembly districts had just produced the greatest Negro vote in the city's history.

The myths are still with us, but they are not so amusing these days. It might be rightly said that because of one current Negro myth, New York City has the first Republican mayor since Fiorello LaGuardia. The myth is that Adam Clayton Powell is the most powerful political leader in Harlem and that only he can deliver the Negro vote. True, my own paper did raise some doubts about Powell's ability to do this. But a glance through the morgue of any of the other New York dailies would have shown that Powell has never been able to deliver a Negro vote for anyone except himself. The Democratic candidate, Abraham Beame, believed the myth. Didn't he read it in every paper? So he concentrated his campaign in the other ethnic areas and ignored the Harlem and Bedford-Stuyvesant communities. After all, hadn't Powell promised to deliver *that* vote?

Apparently, the Republican candidate, John Lindsay, didn't believe it. He spent most of the last three days of his campaign on the streets of Harlem, Brooklyn, Jamaica, and South Bronx—wherever Negroes and Puerto Ricans were concentrated. As a result, Lindsay racked up the greatest vote among Negroes of any Republican candidate since Mayor LaGuardia and left Beame with only press clippings on the invincibility of Adam Clayton Powell.

Despite the admittedly fine job many Northern papers have done on the racial struggle in the South, few of them have met their responsibilities to those of their readers who are hemmed in, hopeless, and sometimes helpless in their own back yards. This is true partly because the editors and publishers really don't know or wish to know that part of their larger community. They know the Roy Wilkinses, the James Farmers, the Whitney Youngs, and the Martin Luther Kings—many of them personally—and they treat these acknowledged leaders with great respect in learned and liberal editorials on national issues or on brutality in the benighted South. But there is an increasing and dangerous tendency for Northern papers to create their own versions of Negro leaders in the Harlems of this country. How do they do this? Simply by giving front-page coverage to and designating as a "leader" any nonwhite citizen who makes preposterous statements about race relations. Giving respectability to irresponsibility seems to me the greatest crime of many of our Northern papers in these times of national stress.

The silken curtain between the major Northern newspapers and their Negro readers hasn't been noticeably pierced, in my opinion, by the sporadic hiring of a handful of Negroes. Since editors regard their Negro fellow citizens as a monolithic mass that only they, in their superior wisdom, can understand, why should they listen on the big issues to reporters who are themselves part of that mass?

I would be derelict if I did not report that the Blood Brothers were a creation of a Negro reporter hired—but since fired—by *The New York Times*. He was not the first Negro reporter to justify distortion by saying, "Man, you've got to give these white folks what they want!" The Negro reporters on white dailies must bear some responsibility for this sad state of affairs in Northern journalism. Many of them—and I plead a certain guilt—were so anxious to prove that they were hired not as "Negro reporters" but because of their all-around skill that they avoided assignments where their special knowledge might have been of benefit.

It is a matter of both pride and regret to me to acknowledge that today there are fewer of the handful of Negro reporters on white dailies than there were at the time of the Harlem riots. For many have seen the hopelessness of trying to change the blindly abstruse minds of their editors and have fled to the more flexible—and better-paying—fields of radio and television.

It is quite possible that I am too pessimistic on the subject of the changing content of racial news. If someone else can support a more optimistic outlook, I can only invoke an old Missouri slogan: "Show me!"

NOTES

Introduction

1. "Representatives and direct Taxes shall be apportioned among the several States which may be included within this Union, according to their respective Numbers, which shall be determined by adding to the whole Number of free Persons, including those bound to Service for a Term of Years and excluding Indians not taxed, three fifths of all other Persons."

2. The full text of the poem reads:

> Numbered among the common herds
> That answered the nation's call to arms
> Were men of science and of words,
> Some of fiber green as palms.
> Sandwiched in this complex array
> Was lanky Private Jack McKay.
>
> Dark of color and of habits,
> Rough as new pig iron from the mold;
> His past training was of such
> That orders he could neither give nor hold.
> But when clothed in the dress of the USA
> There came a change in Jack McKay.
>
> Army discipline harnessed his soul,
> Changed his habits and his form.
> Directed his aim toward the ideal goal
> Of brotherhood, and to hate the storm
> Of prejudice, the sin of yesterday
> In the life of Private Jack McKay.
>
> When we crossed the pond in war unkind
> Against the atrocities of the Hun,
> In the American line he raced the Rhine
> As did Jackson at Bull Run.
> The historian in his war essay
> Lauded the record of Jack McKay.

Having been touched by the souls of men
From all parts of the universe,
McKay is not the same as when
He entered camp to rehearse
His vision has been broadened with the day
So the world has to deal with a new McKay.

3. The full text of the poem reads:

When you meet a member of the Ku Klux Klan,
Walk right up and hit him like a natural man;
Take no thought of babies he may have at home,
Sympathy's defamed when used upon his [form?]
Hit him in the mouth and push his face right in.
Knock him down a flight of steps to pick him up again.
Get your distance from him and then take a running start,
Hit him, brother, hit him, and please hit the scoundrel hard.
Pour some water on him, bring him back to life once more.
Think of how he did your folks in the days of long ago:
Make a prayer to heaven for the strength to do the job,
Kick him in the stomach, he, a low, unworthy snob.
Call your wife and baby out to see you have some fun.
Sic your bulldog on him for to see the rascal run.
Head him off before he gets ten paces from your door.
Take a bat of sturdy oak and knock him down once more.
This time you may leave him where he wallows in the sand,
A spent and humble member of the Ku Klux Klan.

4. The full text of the poem reads:

Lord God, look down on Thy poor soul:
Each passing breeze says I am man;
An hundred times I have been told
By babbling brooks I'm of Thy plan.

I'm of Thy plan, to breathe, to think
And watch the sunset o'er the hill,
I'm of Thy plan, O God, to drink
Deep of Thy loves to fill.

None holier, O God, all heavens teach,
Than I when on Thy bosom bask;
None worthier, none whene'er I reach
Thy vantage ground to ask.

Did all alike see this, O God,
I'd have no cause to seek Thee now;
But Oh, some think I'm apart,
And trifle with Thy power.

Teach them, O God, to see my worth,
To know that I'm of thee;
Oh, pave the way unto the birth
Which makes Thy children free.

But if they've strayed and love's not rife
Within the barren hearts of men,
Oh, teach me then to live the life
Complete and not offend.

5. Only the part of the poem printed in Dunnigan, *Black Woman's Experience* 142–43 has been preserved; also see Dunnigan, *Fascinating Story* 186. Dunnigan had met "Professor E. Poston" "some years earlier at M. & F. College at Hopkinsville." She lauded "Professor Poston's ode" for bringing "to public attention some of the sacrifices made by our elders to provide better opportunities for those who followed."

6. Ersa Poston says that Ted told her it was a common-law marriage (Poston interview), but see marriage certificate #36390, 1923 (Hauke 303).

7. FBI Report 77–1244 was completed on 31 January 1942, when Ted Poston sought clearance for secure government work. People who knew him in childhood, at his schools, and at every place he resided were interviewed to see whether he was a security risk, a stable person.

8. Frank R. Crosswaith, "The Pioneering Pullman Porter," mimeographed speech, n.d. [ca. 1938], box 5, folder 24, Crosswaith MG100, Schomburg Center, New York Public Library (hereafter NYPL).

9. Ted Poston, lecture, "Interracial Reporting," 16 October 1968, audiocassette tape made by Luther P. Jackson Jr., Columbia University School of Journalism (copy at Auburn Avenue Research Library on African American History and Culture, Atlanta, Georgia).

10. Weaver (1907–97) went from his studies at Harvard directly to government service. He served as Ickes's adviser on Negro affairs in the Department of the Interior from 1933 to 1938, managed the integration of Negroes in industry and government in the National Defense Advisory Commission from 1940 to 1942 and went to the War Manpower Commission in 1943. Weaver became the country's first black cabinet member when President Lyndon B. Johnson appointed him secretary of the Department of Housing and Urban Development in 1966.

11. Patricia J. Williams, "Reflections: Notes from a Small World," *New Yorker* 29 April–6 May 1996: 92.

12. Tierney to Thackrey, 20 August 1945; Thackrey to Tierney, 24 August 1945, box 82, Schiff Papers, NYPL. The enthusiasm for Poston, at whatever salary, did not last. He never received a merit increase (Frank Daniels to Dorothy Schiff, 13 October 1965, box 57, Schiff Papers, NYPL). In 1965, when Poston pleaded for a raise, Sann, perhaps annoyed at Poston for not writing the series on black society that Sann had suggested, said, "Ted is not among those who has the barest claim on a merit raise. He is overpaid at $229.27 a week. . . . He is one of the most impeccable OT [overtime?] men in our little family (sometimes I think he uses a stop watch). . . . He hates this newspaper and everybody on this floor . . . and he is up to his neck in inside Negro politics and cannot tell on the club. If he went away, it would not disturb me at all." When Poston was sick in 1971 and inquired about severance pay if he should retire on his sixty-sixth birthday (July 1972), he was told he would get $24,500, or $174 monthly, as an annuity.

Blair Clark, who was managing editor for a short time, looked at the records and discovered that Poston "started at $125 (way over [Newspaper Guild] scale) in '45," and "now gets $51 over scale." Then Schiff tried to save the *Post* money on Poston's severance, noting that "there is a $2,000 difference in the amount of severance Poston would get if he resigned before March 31, 1972, than if he resigned, as he wishes to do, in June, 1972. . . . Offer Poston the full amount of the severance earned before March 31st if he will retire before March 31st, thus saving the *Post* his salary for part of the second quarter, plus the additional $2,000" (Schiff, file report on Poston, 2 March 1972, box 57, Schiff Papers, NYPL). In addition, the business department failed to tell him that he would not actually receive the $22,116 he could expect as of 31 March 1972; because of taxes, he would only get $13,385 (Leonard Arnold to Mrs. Schiff, 8 March 1972, box 57, Schiff Papers, NYPL).

Sann himself complained about *Post* pay. He got a $5,000 bonus in 1949 that soon became salary, but in 1955 he "expected a much better break and didn't get it" (Sann to Schiff, box 66, Schiff Papers, NYPL). When another of the *Post's* fine writers, Helen Dudar, approached Sann for a raise, he turned her down with "You're already earning a lot for a woman." She says now, "The pay was really crummy. It was Guild level" (Dudar interview). For the *Post* branch of the Guild newsletter, an anonymous poet wrote of the poor pay at the *Post* when Schiff moved the paper from its grimy West Street headquarters to the shiny newly refurbished former *Journal-American* building at 210 South Street: "Half truths, distortions, untruths, misleading information and rumors to the contrary, notwithstanding, The Post United Poet . . . is alive and well and settling in at South St. He was overheard mumbling . . . last night as follows:

> "Millions of bucks worth of concrete and stone,
> Employes, however, nary a bone.
> 'We've arranged for a bus, right to the door'
> (It only costs a dollar more).

"Maybe we've done them a 'serious disservice,'
Maybe we are all uptight and nervous.
An air-conditioned plant to keep us all cool
(Eighty-Two degrees, as a general rule).

"Modern wash rooms they're really terrific.
(But now about paper, to be more specific.)
Space and facilities, what a treat.
(You can walk for an hour, bu. nothing to eat.)

"Telephones and lights, at these you can't sneer.
(Will all of you scoffers please step to the rear.)
Everything's wonderful, we're in the clover.
(But some of us were told, 'The Party's Over.')

"Improved environment, with this we're replete.
(Same old desk, same old seat.
Same old song, same old dance.
Equitable settlements, Fat Chance.)"

"At this point, the Poet drained his glass and wandered off into the night" ("The Poet's Return," *West Street Other, New York Post* Unit, Newspaper Guild of New York [vol. 20, no. 5], 9 April 1970, box 126, Schiff Papers, NYPL).

13. Ten years later Marie married a kindly, Harvard-educated, prominent, and elderly Chicagoan, Alexander L. Jackson, and was finally happy in marriage (Adams letter; R. Reed interview).

14. A few years after Ted's death, Ersa became vice chair of the U.S. Civil Service Commission under President Jimmy Carter.

15. For example, see Schiff to Wechsler, 19 November 1963, box 57, Schiff Papers, NYPL: "I want to remind you that we offered Ted Poston a column several years ago and you reported that Ted didn't want it."

16. "Robinson at Bat Again," *Editor and Publisher* 2 May 1959: 72; Jean Gillette [Schiff's secretary] to Wechsler, 20 April 1959, box 63, Schiff Papers, NYPL.

17. Wechsler to Marvin Berger, 20 April 1959, box 63, Schiff Papers, NYPL.

18. Poston to Sann, 11 March 1963, box 57, Schiff Papers, NYPL. Poston reiterated that the *Post* should be trying to "attract as much Negro circulation as we can, but also Negro-oriented circulation . . . the readership of persons who are interested in broad issues which encompass not only the matter of Negro rights but of civil rights. At this moment we are in the fortuitous position of being the paper that might well attract more of that audience. During the recent dispute, our publisher stressed repeatedly that we were the only liberal paper in town. We are, at the moment, the darling of the labor movement. We do have a history of being the paper of the underdog in this city. And I would like to see our record continued."

Then Poston compared what the *Post* was not doing to attract black readers with what other papers were doing: "Even before the current difficulty [the newspaper strike], several of the other papers were making studied and sustained efforts to attract more Negro readers. The Herald-Tribune was devoting more space to civil rights stories, I think, than all the rest of the papers combined. The World-Telegram, especially in its Brooklyn editions, doubled its coverage of such matters. . . . I do not believe that any of these papers are necessarily endowed with any spirit of crusading liberalism in pushing such circulation. I think that they are only recognizing one fact that I hope we do not lose sight of. And that is this: Negroes and Puerto Ricans comprise the only *growing* population in New York City. . . . I am not suggesting in this memo that we try to copy the efforts of other papers, although some of their efforts may be worth emulating. I am asking only that we be aware of what is happening, and that we take our own steps to protect our own interests. Neither am I asking The Post to take on its shoulders the sole burden of solving the so-called Negro question. I think that the fight for civil rights and human rights will continue if The Post decides never to carry another line about it. But I do feel that we would be silly not to try to profit from an atmosphere which this newspaper, over the years, has helped create. . . . The fact is that Negroes will buy The Post anywhere if it is the kind of paper they want."

19. Various correspondence between Wechsler and Schiff, Schiff Papers, NYPL, and James A. Wechsler Papers, State Historical Society of Wisconsin (hereafter SHSW); Ephron letter.

20. Hamill claimed that the *New York Post* was "the newspaper that gave me my life" (1). Poston and Murray Kempton "improved all of us [reporters] just by showing up." Poston "endured the usual stupid slights, North and South, but he remained a man of grace and generosity, particularly to those of us who were young" (5).

Hamill characterized Poston as a "proud, funny" newspaperman; Hamill can "hear him still." Poston told Hamill once, "This is the best gahdamned business in the world. . . . We help more gahdamned people than any gahdamned government. So don't you ever disgrace it, you hear me?" (5).

21. Poston cited Anderson in his history of the *Amsterdam News*, "Inside Story."

Poems

1. For Poston's review of the first volume, see "Truly." Linda K. Kerber describes Murray as "the feminist intellectual hero of our time. . . . Murray wrote some of the key legal analyses that targeted . . . the system of 'Jane Crow.' . . . She was the quiet, steely, brilliant great-great-granddaughter of a slave, a poet who became a lawyer so that she could fight for social justice, a lawyer who left the law to become an Episcopal priest because she thought the world needed more spiritual guidance

and less litigiousness" ("Moving beyond Stereotypes of Feminism," *Chronicle of Higher Education* 23 April 1999: B-6). The Arthur and Elizabeth Schlesinger Library on the History of Women in America at Radcliffe College holds some of Murray's papers.

2. Dingy (i.e., black) person.

Articles, 1930s

1. Moon wrote of the value of the Russian experience in "A Negro Looks at Soviet Russia," *Nation* 28 February 1934: 244–46.

2. See section 26 below.

Articles, 1940s

1. See section 22 below. Robert Poston wrote in the *Negro World*, "After I left the Army, with the spirit of fight for the right permeating my soul . . . I went to the city of Detroit [where] they had a Civil Rights Law, but no colored man in the city of Detroit had ever been protected under [it] and we were told . . . that it would be impossible to win. Nevertheless, we tackled it, and we won. The records in Michigan will show that the first conviction was that in the case of R. L. Poston versus John Bazoulas, a Greek" ("I'll Be Back").

2. Rowe was a regular weekly columnist for the *Pittsburgh Courier*. When he became ill on the trip, Poston pinch-hit, writing Rowe's "Out of Billy Rowe's Harlem Notebook" for the week of 6 April 1940.

3. Reprinted later in *The Negro Caravan*, ed. Sterling A. Brown, Arthur P. Davis, and Ulysses Lee (Salem, N.H.: Ayer, 1991) 96–100. This story also appeared as "We Gonna Make This a Union Town Yet! . . ." in *In Their Own Words: A History of the American Negro, 1916–1966*, ed. Milton Meltzer (New York: Crowell, 1967) 140–49.

4. These brackets appear in original.

5. These brackets appear in original.

6. Fourteen-year-old Emmett Till of Chicago was lynched in Mississippi in 1955 for flirting with a white store clerk. Poston covered the story for the *New York Post*. James Baldwin based his 1964 drama, *Blues for Mr. Charlie*, on that lynching. James Chaney, Andrew Goodman, and Michael Schwerner were civil rights workers who were murdered on 21 June 1964 during the Freedom Summer in Mississippi, where they had gone to help register blacks to vote (see Poston, "Mississippi"). Viola Liuzzo, a white Detroit housewife, was ferrying freedom marchers when four Klansmen shot her to death on the road between Selma and Montgomery, Alabama, on 21 March 1965 (see Stanton).

7. "The $500 [Geist] first prize went to Mrs. Roosevelt for her newspaper

columns opposing discrimination in all forms, while Post reporters Ted Poston and Oliver Pilat shared the $400 second place award for outstanding reporting on the subject of group friction. . . . The [annual] awards were established by Irving Geist, New York business man and philanthropist, in co-operation with the Newspaper Guild of New York to 'encourage a greater interest among newsmen in the problems of interfaith and interracial understanding'" ("Mrs. F.D.R., Poston, Pilat Win Awards for Fighting Bias," *New York Post* 23 January 1950).

"The Polk Memorial Award for 'the most distinguished reporting in the national field' has been conferred on Ted Poston . . . by the Journalism Dept. of Long Island Univ. . . . The Florida series . . . typified the 'stick your neck out attitude' which led to George Polk's [death]. The awards, gold plaques, were first established in 1948 in memory of Polk, American correspondent who was murdered while on duty in Greece" ("Poston Gets L.I.U. Award—Wins 2d Honor in Month," *New York Post* 5 February 1950).

"Washington, Feb. 24—Ted Poston, New York Post reporter whose coverage of a Florida 'rape' trial last year attracted national attention, has been adjudged 1949 winner of the Heywood Broun Award of the American Newspaper Guild. A duplicate award was made to Herbert Block, New York Post cartoonist. . . . Broun awards were presented . . . by Alan Barth, an editorial writer for the Washington Post and one of the three judges. . . . Barth [said], 'Heywood Broun would have read with tremendous pride and enthusiasm the work Ted Poston did in covering that story. . . . I had to do some work on this case for my newspaper. I went to the Dept. of Justice, and was told there that if I wanted to get a complete, accurate and factual background of the case, I could do no better than look up the stories of Ted Poston in the New York Post'" (Charles Van Devander, "Post Writer, Cartoonist Win Broun Awards," *New York Post* 24 February 1950; reprinted in *The Bulletin: Tennessee A. and I. State College*, March 1950: 6).

"Ted Poston, Post staff writer, today held the 1951 Unity Award of Beta Delta Mu fraternity for 'efforts to promote inter-faith amity, brotherhood and understanding.' In presenting the gold statuette and plaque, Alden Norman Haffner cited the efforts of the reporter and The Post to promote better understanding among ethnic and religious groups through newspaper stories and campaigns" ("Ted Poston Wins 2d Award in Single Month," *New York Post* 31 December 1951).

See Hauke 116, 246 n.45, for the Pulitzer story.

8. Richard Pyle, "Latest Top 100: Century's 'Best American Journalism,'" AP Wire, 2 March 1999. This list of books, articles, columns, collected works, famous photographs, and television reports was selected by a panel of experts assembled by the New York University School of Journalism.

9. These brackets appear in original.

10. The *Nation*, a liberal weekly, compared what the American wire services were reporting on the Tavares case with what an objective British reporter learned:

"The wire services made something of a hero last month of a sheriff in Lake County, Florida, who, unarmed, was reported to have dissuaded a lynch mob from taking out of his custody two of four Negroes suspected of raping a white woman. True, the wire services added, the incident was followed by rioting in and around the town of Groveland, but none of the community's 400 Negroes had been hurt because conscientious whites had moved them out of town on trucks.

"When Terence McCarthy, a British economist with a special interest in the South, went to Groveland for the *New Leader* to verify the story, this is what he found. Far from receiving protection, Groveland's Negroes had hidden in swamps and woods for three nights while white marauders burned and shot up their homes, stores and restaurants. The sheriff's heroism smacks of a deal — security of the prisoners in exchange for free reign to terrorists beyond the confines of the jail.

"According to sworn affidavits in McCarthy's possession, the sheriff has for years insured a cheap labor supply for the region's citrus fields and packing plants by arresting, beating up, and jailing Negroes who fail to show up for work [on] Saturdays. McCarthy makes it clear that the real root of the 'disorders' is not a rape that may or may not have occurred but the anger of Lake County whites — and whites in central Florida generally — over the attempts of a few Negroes to raise themselves out of peonage and into the ranks of private farmers.

"He also learned that the local press had crusaded for 'justice' before the details of the 'crime' were publicly known and warned 'outside' lawyers to steer clear unless they wanted to 'bring suffering to many innocent Negroes.' Finally, he writes, the three captured 'suspects' have been cruelly tortured, and the fourth, a man resented for his college education, [was] killed by a posse. Trial of the survivors is scheduled for this week. Trial of their white 'superiors' is not scheduled at all" ("The Wire Services Made Something. . . ." *Nation* 3 September 1949: 214–15).

11. Langston Hughes, "The Negro Artist and the Racial Mountain," *Nation* 23 June 1926: 692–94.

Articles, 1950s

1. The day before the election, Robinson "received a note from the [*New York Post*] management informing him that he had been fired," Falkner says, even though Robinson only shortly before had been the luncheon guest of publisher Dorothy Schiff and executive editor James A. Wechsler, and "both indicated how pleased they were with the column and with its reception from readers" (281–82). See also Branch 306.

Assisting Robinson in writing his column was not a big event in Poston's career, but although Robinson has been the subject of a number of biographies, the journalistic phase of his life has not been documented elsewhere. The column-writing venture had begun with the highest hopes. In a letter to Robinson, Wechsler said that he would do his best to make Robinson's column and its syndication "an adventure of which we can both be proud" (Wechsler to Robinson, 23 April 1957, Wechsler Papers, SHSW). In promoting Robinson's work to other papers, Wechsler claimed to be impressed with Robinson "as a human being. He is intelligent, independent, articulate. . . . He will have a guy working with him on the writing, but this will be Robinson talking; he doesn't want the conventional ghost job" (Wechsler to Milburn P. Akers, 22 April 1959, Wechsler Papers, SHSW).

Poston wrote a profile of Robinson to introduce the column ("Daily Closeup"). Then Sann and Wechsler both attempted to sell the column around North America and enlisted the *Chicago Sun-Times* and the *Philadelphia Evening-Bulletin* (Sann to Les Cook, 27 April 1959, Wechsler Papers, SHSW). *Editor and Publisher* announced the column's inception, adding that Robinson would be "given some help . . . by William Branch, a young Negro and Guggenheim Fellow, whom he employs for his radio activities. Jackie dictates his copy and Mr. Branch edits it" ("Robinson at Bat Again," *Editor and Publisher*, 2 May 1959: 72). The *Post* was "trying to create some kind of newspaper history by making Jackie the first syndicated Negro columnist in America" (Wechsler to John Block, 16 June 1959, Wechsler Papers, SHSW).

There was no groundswell of support for syndication. The *Toronto Telegram* found the column "too American" (J. D. MacFarlane to Wechsler, 8 May 1959, Wechsler Papers, SHSW). The *Montreal Star* was tempted since "Mr. Robinson broke into first class baseball in Montreal," but "our racial situation here is less acute than in the United States and our politics are totally different" (Walter O'Hearn to Wechsler, 8, 13 May 1959, Wechsler Papers, SHSW). The *Northern Virginia Sun* foresaw "a problem in establishing Jackie Robinson as an authority on world affairs and on political matters" but believed that it was "a fine thing to have a Negro columnist appearing outside of the Negro press" (Philip M. Stern to Wechsler, 8 May 1959, Wechsler Papers, SHSW). The *Miami News* found Robinson's writing "stiff": it was not clear "what he was aiming at," and there would be "trouble bridging the gap of a man who is a baseball personality to general and perhaps philosophical comments" (William C. Baggs to Wechsler, 12 May 1959, Wechsler Papers, SHSW). The managing editor of the *Milwaukee Journal* discussed the column around his city room. Some editors found it wordy. One said that "Robinson had returned to the bush leagues if this was his best effort as a columnist." The editor's own reaction was, "I boil inside whenever a paper brings in an amateur in a top spot. . . . A lot of the public doesn't think too much of the press. So how are we going to encourage the growth of professionalism and high competency among newspapermen if we make big splashes when we turn some of our space over to amateurs." However, "I'm not in New York. Maybe what you need there is more amateurs to get closer to the people" (Wallace Lomoe to Wechsler, 19 May 1959, Wechsler Papers, SHSW).

Poston placed Robinson's column in the black *Chicago Daily Defender* (L. Alex Wilson to Wechsler, 8 July 1959, Wechsler Papers, SHSW). By summer the column was appearing in two more papers, the *Detroit News* and the *Bridgeport Herald*. Even so, the column was not well received. The Bridgeport editor found it "windy and dull . . . a pity because every now and again he has something worth saying — but somehow it gets loused up in the writing, and there aren't many readers who will stay with him all the way" (H. R. Wishengrad to Wechsler, 10 September 1959, Wechsler Papers, SHSW). Robinson's latest biographer, Arnold Rampersad, considers Robinson's writing in general "stiff and artless, but sincere" (82).

Poston was called to Robinson's final rescue. Wechsler wrote Wishengrad that Robinson's first helper had not been "the man for the job" and that Wechsler was "hoping to put Ted Poston on it for a while," which should "produce a notable improvement" (Wechsler to Wishengrad, 11 September 1959, Wechsler Papers, SHSW). The *Bridgeport Sunday Herald* agreed that "Ted Poston will pep" it up (Leigh Danenberg to Wechsler, 17 September 1959, Wechsler Papers, SHSW). But during the summer of 1960, the *Post* was receiving a plethora of letters against Robinson's views. The presidential election campaign was on. The *Post* was leaning toward endorsing Kennedy, whom Robinson found "a phony on civil rights" (Robinson to Wechsler, 1 June 1960, Wechsler Papers, SHSW). Robinson's autobiography was published that year, and the *Post* thought of serializing it, but Wechsler found some of the book "banal" and worried that serializing it might "build [Robinson] up" when he was "on the verge of endorsing Nixon." Furthermore, "whatever circulation he can bring us is provided by his column" (Wechsler to Schiff, 6 June 1960, box 63, Schiff Papers, NYPL). The *Post* broke with Robinson over the story of Vice President Richard Nixon and his refusal of State Department funds to transport 250 African students to America for college. All the students' other educational expenses had been underwritten privately by prominent American blacks such as Harry Belafonte and Sidney Poitier. When Nixon turned down the subsidization of their air travel by the U.S. government, the Kennedy Family Foundation offered to pay the bill. Nixon did an about-face and said the U.S. government would pay the transportation expenses after all. Robinson knew the sequence of events and of Nixon's initial refusal but wrote that Nixon and the State Department were picking up the costs and said, "I congratulate Vice President Nixon [and others] for the vital roles they played in bringing it about" ("Jackie Robinson," *New York Post* 17 August 1960: 76; William V. Shannon, "Too Late," *New York Post* 17 August 1960: 39). But the Kennedy Foundation was already paying the bill. *Post* readers were irate. Schiff received one telegram: "If you do not have Jackie Robinson's ghost writer William Branch deny the story of Vice President Nixon's aid to the African students . . . your paper needs a new mistress" (Dora Maugham to Schiff, 17 August 1960, box 63, Schiff Papers, NYPL).

Poston was summoned to investigate and explain the incident, resulting in one of the longest single stories he ever wrote for the *Post* ("Behind the Row"). Robinson's column continued briefly but letters to the editor only worsened. An anonymous reader threatened "on behalf of 100 Democrats," "If you continue to allow Jackie Robinson to endorse Nixon through the columns in your paper we will stop buying the Post and boycott all the merchandise advertised" ("A Democrat" to Wechsler and Schiff, n.d. [August 1960], box 63, Schiff Papers, NYPL).

In the midst of these exchanges, Schiff called Robinson in to talk with him on the dangers of being too partisan, the importance of stating the facts as they are, and the dangers of half-truths. He replied that he trusted Nixon but not Kennedy because Kennedy would not look him in the eye (Schiff, report for file, 25 August 1960, box 63, Schiff Papers, NYPL). Schiff defined her position in a letter to Robinson: "Our columnists are free to support whichever presidential candidate they choose even if the paper should endorse his rival. But we do care very much about the integrity of the editorial content of this newspaper. . . . I had invited you to lunch to warn you about the danger of becoming the tool of one side or the other. . . . You had been aware that the Kennedy Foundation was going to pay the bill [for the African students]. You confirmed this at lunch. Nevertheless you had withheld the information. . . . You are a novice in journalism and politics. . . . This sort of thing must not happen again. The newspaper, not the politicians, must come first" (Schiff to Robinson, 29 August 1960, Wechsler Papers, SHSW). She quoted to him Walter Scott's *Marmion*: "Oh what tangled webs we weave, when first we practice to deceive" (Schiff to Wechsler, 30 August 1960, box 63, Schiff Papers, NYPL). Schiff was articulating an informal credo of the journalistic craft that a popular NBC television reporter, John Chancellor, later voiced in a law school forum, "Journalists do their best as observers of society — as scorekeepers at the game, guests at the banquet, outsiders looking in," rather than as determined adversaries of the political power structure ("Journalists Do Their Best Work as Observers," *Harvard Gazette* 19 April 1985: 2).

When the *Post* ceased carrying Robinson's column, the *New York Times*, noting the brouhaha, called Sann to learn what was going on. Sann said that Robinson would be on leave only until the presidential campaign was over (Sann to Schiff, 2 September 1960, box 63, Schiff Papers, NYPL; "Columnist Takes Leave of Absence: Jackie Robinson to Work for Nixon," *New York Post* 4 September 1960, clipping in box 63, Schiff Papers, NYPL). Robinson was paid through the period of his contract, but he complained about his forced leave in an address to the Urban League ("Jackie Robinson," transcript of speech to National Urban League, 4 September 1960, box 63, Schiff Papers, NYPL). His column was picked up by the *Citizen-Call*, a violation of his *Post* contract, the *Post* business department told Wechsler, advising him not to make an issue of the matter because "in addition to giving Robinson a platform from which to vituperate against us, by the time a temporary injunction could be handed down, we would have reached the end of our contract period" (Marvin Berger to Wechsler, 30 September 1960, box 63, Schiff Papers, NYPL).

Robinson later talked with Poston about the incident; Poston reported that Wechsler was "pretty unhappy" about Robinson's appearance in the *Citizen-Call* and the promotion it was doing for him. Robinson telephoned Wechsler, and Wechsler said that the *Post* found itself in the position of "1) first learning that he had joined the Nixon team from the New York Times and 2) first learning that he had joined the Citizen-Call from the columns of that paper." Robinson asked whether the *Post* would resume his column after the election, saying that he had gone to the *Citizen-Call* because he needed an outlet. Wechsler "suggested that he had a much better outlet here and that he had destroyed it by formally joining the Nixon staff" (Wechsler to Schiff, 7 October 1960, box 63, Schiff Papers, NYPL). On the evening of election day, Wechsler officially canceled the column, telling Robinson, "This was neither an easy nor pleasant decision. . . . But I cannot in good conscience urge an extension of [the column]. . . . [Y]our personality never came through precisely because your views and attitudes were filtered through another writer. . . . I do not want to disparage Bill [Branch] whose writing talents may be very great. . . . The simple truth is that the column project did not work" (Wechsler to Robinson, 8 November 1960, Wechsler Papers, SHSW).

Robinson was angry, castigating Wechsler for his "feeble attempt to justify [his] actions" (Robinson to Wechsler, 14 November 1960, Wechsler Papers, SHSW). That Robinson also lost his job at Chock Full o'Nuts caused Schiff to look into the situation concerning the "Negro girls" working there. Schiff then reported to Wechsler that Robinson "admitted they received little more than minimum wages, averaging about $1.15 an hour. . . . [T]he company couldn't afford to do any more." Schiff consulted *Post* economics columnist Sylvia Porter on Chock Full o' Nuts's financial condition. Porter replied, "It just split four to one. . . . It was a spectacular success in the market of last year" (Schiff to Wechsler, 7 September 1960, box 63, Schiff Papers, NYPL).

One of Robinson's biographers tried to encapsulize Robinson's work in the media: "Like it or not, Jackie Robinson was a spokesman for black people even though he had no formal training in the area and no legitimate credentials. He had learned from life. . . . He was often, as he had been as a ballplayer, controversial" (Allen 216). A second biographer concluded that Robinson's decision to support Nixon had "cost him prestige with the public — and did so without gaining a place for him in the Republican party or with the movement. In liberal political circles, the sense of disenchantment with Robinson was inevitable" (Falkner 282).

Poston was involved in the saga of Robinson and the *New York Post* at both beginning and end. He could see that intraracial political camps were splintering and subdividing. It was the end of the age of black intellectuals being automatically liberal and supporting the Democratic Party because of its pro-black stance.

2. These brackets appear in original.

3. Nat King Cole was beaten by racists while performing on a Birmingham stage in 1956 (Poston, "Nat King Cole").

4. These brackets appear in original.

5. Hughes to Poston, 20 September 1961, Langston Hughes Papers, James Weldon Johnson Collection, Beinecke Rare Book and Manuscript Library, Yale University.

6. These brackets appear in original.

Articles, 1960s

1. See Poston and Kahn; Poston, "Harlem Quiet"; Poston, "Violence Flares"; Poston, "Rioting Ebbs."

2. These brackets appear in original.

3. These brackets appear in original.

4. These brackets appear in original.

5. These brackets appear in original.

6. These brackets appear in original.

7. These brackets appear in original.

8. "Wake," in Hughes 39. Poston misquoted Hughes's poem. The correct version reads:

> Tell all my mourners
> To mourn in red —
> Cause there ain't no sense
> In my bein' dead.

9. "Tower," in Rampersad and Roussel 128. Poston again misquoted Hughes: the original has *meditative* where Poston used *solitary.*

10. "Dreams," in Rampersad and Roussel 32.

11. "Suicide's Note," in Hughes 85.

12. "Harlem," in Hughes 268. The full text reads:

> What happens to a dream deferred?

> Does it dry up
> like a raisin in the sun?
> Or fester like a sore —
> And then run?

Does it stink like rotten meat?
Or crust and sugar over —
like a syrupy sweet?

Maybe it just sags
like a heavy load

Or does it explode?

13. "The Backlash Blues," in Rampersad and Roussel 552. Poston quoted only part of the poem, and he again misquoted Hughes. The full text reads:

Mister Backlash, Mister Backlash,
Just who do you think I am?
Tell me, Mister Backlash,
Who do you think I am?
You raise my taxes, freeze my wages,
Send my son to Vietnam.

You give me second-class houses,
Give me second-class schools,
Second-class houses
And second-class schools.
You must think us colored folks
Are second-class fools.

When I try to find a job
To earn a little cash,
Try to find myself a job
To earn a little cash,
All you got to offer
Is a white backlash.

But the world is big,
The world is big and round,
Great big world, Mister Backlash,
Big and bright and round —
And it's full of folks like me who are
Black, Yellow, Beige, and Brown.

Mister Backlash, Mister Backlash,
What do you think I got to lose?
Tell me, Mister Backlash,
What you think I got to lose?

I'm gonna leave you, Mister Backlash,
Singing your mean old backlash blues.

You're the one,
Yes, you're the one
Will have the blues.

14. These brackets appear in original.
15. This observation is reinforced by Bradlee 125–28.

SELECTED SUPPLEMENTAL
ANNOTATED BIBLIOGRAPHY

Books

Allen, Maury. *Jackie Robinson: A Life Remembered*. New York: Watts, 1987.

Bates, Daisy. *The Long Shadow of Little Rock*. Fayetteville: University of Arkansas Press, 1987.

Bradlee, Ben. *A Good Life: Newspapering and Other Adventures*. New York: Simon and Schuster, 1995.

Branch, Taylor. *Parting the Waters: America in the King Years, 1954–1963*. New York: Touchstone, 1988.

Dunnigan, Alice Allison. *A Black Woman's Experience: From Schoolhouse to White House*. Philadelphia: Dorrance, 1974.

———. *The Fascinating Story of Black Kentuckians: Their Heritage and Traditions*. Washington: Associated, 1982.

Falkner, David. *Great Time Coming: The Life of Jackie Robinson, from Baseball to Birmingham*. New York: Simon and Schuster, 1995.

Hamill, Pete. *News Is a Verb*. New York: Ballantine, 1998.

Hauke, Kathleen A. *Ted Poston: Pioneer American Journalist*. Athens: University of Georgia Press, 1998.

Hughes, Langston. *Selected Poems*. New York: Vintage, 1974.

Martin, Tony. *Literary Garveyism: Garvey, Black Arts, and the Harlem Renaissance*. Dover, MA: Majority, 1983.

Poston, Ted. *The Dark Side of Hopkinsville*. Ed. and annotated by Kathleen A. Hauke. Athens: University of Georgia Press, 1991.

Rampersad, Arnold. *Jackie Robinson*. New York: Knopf, 1997.

Rampersad, Arnold, and David Roessel, eds. *The Collected Poems of Langston Hughes*. New York: Knopf, 1994.

Stanton, Mary. *From Selma to Sorrow: The Life and Death of Viola Liuzzo*. Athens: University of Georgia Press, 1998.

Articles by Ted Poston

"Alexandria Library Opening Resulted from Fight." *Pittsburgh Courier* 16 March 1940.

One facet of society that annoyed Poston from the time he was a small boy was the exclusion of citizens of color from public libraries in the South. Here Poston acknowledges progress but notes how limited it is; the whole idea of separate facilities is ridiculous.

"Althea Gibson." *New York Post* 25 August 1957–1 September 1957.
Profile of first black Wimbledon champion and her rearing on the streets of Harlem.

"Althea Would Love All the Acclaim — If She Could Only Get Some Sleep." *New York Post* 10 July 1957: 2.

"America's Negro Problem to Be Depicted in Social Science Exhibit at Chicago Exposition." *Pittsburgh Courier* 29 June 1940: 13.

"At Home with the Poet" [Langston Hughes]. *New York Post* 11 June 1962.

"At Last, a Good Novel from Himes." Rev. of *The Third Generation*, by Chester Himes. *New York Post* 16 March 1954: n.p.

"Autherine Lucy's Life Story." *New York Post* 5–11 March 1956.

"Back to Ol' Virginny . . . First Class." *New York Post* 7 September 1956: 1, 47.
Martin Luther King Jr. echoed the biblical "Truth crushed to earth will rise again." Poston describes a small dialogue in his own neighborhood when federal troops upheld school integration; a little old lady could not believe the apparent government about-face. Buoyant Poston casts himself here in a subdued listening mode and captures rhythms of the vernacular.

"Beckwith Goes on Trial for Murder of Evers." *New York Post* 27 January 1964.

"Beckwith's Day in Court: A Smile Suddenly Fades." *New York Post* 28 January 1964.

"Behind the Row on the African Students: The Kennedy Foundation, $100,000 and the GOP." *New York Post* 18 August 1960: 5, 57.

"The Bell Rings in Powell's School." *New York Post* 20 May 1958: 5, 31.

"Bells Toll and Negroes Pray in Montgomery." *New York Post* 6 December 1956.

"Big Turnout at Polls by Alabama Negroes." *New York Post* 3 May 1966: 5.

"Black Poet Now More Militant: Gwendolyn Brooks." *New York Post* 2 April 1971: 13.

"A Book on Harlem." Rev. of *Harlem: Negro Metropolis*, by Claude McKay. *New Republic* 25 November 1940: 732.

"Bread Fifteen Cents in Most Shops Here as Wheat Soars." *New York Post* 10 March 1947: 5.
On post–World War II inflation.

"Breathless Reporter Gets His Story as Dodgers Hit Town." *New York Post* 3 October 1949: 3, 19.

"Bronx Hard Hit by Raging Storm." *New York Post* 26 November 1950: 1, 2.

"A Brother's Eulogy: The Cause He Died For." *New York Post* 27 January 1964.
Charles Evers on Medgar Evers.

"Bus Boycott Leader Hailed as Symbol of Hope in Bias Fight." *New York Post* 26 March 1956: 5, 37.

"The Cab Drivers: Hacking in Harlem." *New York Post* 29 July 1955: 4, 20.

"Chappy Gardner Makes 'Princess' out of Harlem Home Relief Client." *Amsterdam News* 20 July 1935: 1, 2.

"Charge Rocky Betrayed Vow to Bolster Rent Law." *New York Post* 1 March 1961.

"C.I.O. vs. A.F. of L." Rev. of *Labor on the March*, by Edward Levinson. *Crisis* June 1938: 185.

From the time of his co-founding of the Newspaper Guild, Poston promoted black inclusion in labor unions in all industries. He praises this book written by a New York Post colleague, the labor editor, but wonders where is the thorough coverage of Negroes in the labor movement.

"City Scrams out of Town by Air, Bus, Rail, Jalopy." *New York Post* 2 July 1950: 4.

"Clay in Malcolm X's Corner." *New York Post* 3 March 1964.

"Closeup: Black, White and Brown." *New York Post* 26 July 1967.

On militant Rap Brown, new leader of Student Nonviolent Coordinating Committee.

"Closeup: Carl Rowan, The Next 'Voice of America.'" *New York Post* 26 January 1964.

Carl Rowan, still going strong in American journalism at the end of the twentieth century, followed Poston to Tennessee State University a generation later; Poston hails Rowan's personal and professional successes.

"Closeup: Embattled Editor, Harry S. Ashmore." *New York Post* 21 September 1967.

"Closeup: 'Equal'" [Clifford L. Alexander]. *New York Post* 2 August 1967.

"Closeup: The Evers Judge." *New York Post* 31 January 1964.

"Closeup: In the Running, Jesse Owens." *New York Post* 22 March 1968.

"Closeup: Kenneth Clark, Civil Rights Front-Runner." *New York Post* 22 March 1964.

Harlem-born Kenneth B. Clark administered the doll test in the Brown v. Board of Education *case, demonstrating that with segregated education, black children grow up with a poor self-image. (Poston did not know that as a boy, Clark had studied art with Poston's sister-in-law, Augusta Savage.)*

"Closeup: Mrs. Peabody." *New York Post* 1 April 1964.

An elite northern white woman goes to jail over civil rights.

"Closeup: Unseated Legislator" [Julian Bond]. *New York Post* 19 January 1966: 24.

Poston surveys the field of rising blacks and anticipates that the future is in good hands although old problems remain.

"A 'Clumsily-Great Government' in Action." Rev. of *Frontier on the Potomac*, by Jonathan Daniels. *New York Post* 31 October 1946.

In 1941 Poston went to Washington. Roi Ottley says Poston was the most vocal and colorful member of President Franklin D. Roosevelt's Black Cabinet. Jonathan

Daniels was a key friend and associate of Poston's when both were at the White House in 1945. When Daniels wrote of the war years, Poston reviewed the book.

"Comeback-Hopes of Garvey Fade: Ex-Followers Will Devote $300,000 Legacy to Co-operative Work." *New York Post* n.d. [ca. June 1937 or 1939].

"Congo Conquests: Will the New King Leopold Atone the Sins of the Old?" *Amsterdam News* 2 February 1935: 1.

"CORE Warns Sit-Ins Will Go on in South." *New York Post* 18 October 1960.

"Dad Tells Why He Turned in Dope-Addict Son." *New York Post* 5 September 1952.
Drug addiction spread into the broad general community in the 1950s; American youth seemed to lose their innocence en masse. Poston depicted how drugs undermined families and communities.

"Daily Closeup: Jackie Robinson, New Post Columnist." *New York Post* 27 April 1959: 42.

"The Day Mama Put the Whammy on the Yankees." *New York Post* 10 October 1956: 9, 34.

"Death Takes No Holiday in Harlem's Firetraps." *New York Post* 13 December 1954: 4, 22.

"Depression Brings Harlem Better Food." *Amsterdam News* 4 November 1931.

"Diane — Portrait of a Leader, Twenty-two." *New York Post* 24 May 1961.
Poston encouraged nonviolence in the turning-militant 1960s by featuring its leaders; nonviolence mirrored his own chosen modus operandi.

"Dick Gregory: Not Only Laughter." *New York Post* 14 April 1963.

"A Different Kind of War Novel." Rev. of *And Then We Heard the Thunder,* by John O. Killens. *New York Post* 31 March 1963.

"Dixie Cites Frameups Like Scottsboro Case: Staff Writer Hears Tales of Horror Which Never Found Way into Newspapers." *Amsterdam News* 29 November 1933: 1, 2.
The false accusation of the Scottsboro boys is typical treatment of black youth. For a sense of immediacy, Poston uses the present tense and the conversational second person you so that readers can identify with the accused Scottsboro boys and with the many other incidents similar to theirs. Poston's assertion that the black South "will not long be content" simply "to pray" foreshadows the situation of the black militants of the 1960s whom he described by his career's end.

"Dixie's Negro Leaders 'Hazy' on Scottsboro." *Amsterdam News* 22 November 1933: 2.
The case of the Scottsboro boys became known internationally. Eight of the boys were sentenced to death, the thirteen-year-old to life in prison. Before the sentences could be carried out, the communist-backed International Labor Defense took up their cause, hiring a leading criminal lawyer, Samuel Leibowitz, as attorney, for which Leibowitz accepted no pay. Here Poston castigates southern Negro leadership for its ignorance of the case and for turning toward it a blind eye.

"The Don Newcombe Story: Closeup." *New York Post* 12 June 1955, sec. M: 2.

"Eisenhower Asked to End Lily-White Fellowships." *New York Post* 13 November 1949: 5.

"Epic of Our Time." Rev. of *Stride toward Freedom*, by Martin Luther King Jr. *New York Post* 28 September 1958.

"Exalted, Exhausted, Althea Hides Away." *New York Post* 10 July 1957: 82.

"Ex-Slave Sees Endless Riches in U.S. Ersatz" [George Washington Carver]. *New York Post* 21 September 1939.

"Family of Boy, Ten, Convicted in Kissing Case Faces Eviction." *New York Post* 10 December 1958.

"Fast on Again for Harry Wills." *New York Post* 1 April 1937: 16.

"FBI Investigating Squeeze on Tenn. Negro Voters." *New York Post* 1 July 1960.

"Federal Writers' Project to Issue Achievement Book." *Pittsburgh Courier* 22 June 1940: 5.

"FEPC March on Washington: Backers of Legislation to Parade." *New York Post* 1 March 1946: 51.

"Fight Fans Jam Harlem, Create a Housing Crisis." *New York Post* 22 June 1938: 3. *Joe Louis fight ambience.*

"Fighting Editor: Fights for the Same Old South." Rev. of *Where Main Street Meets the River*, by Hodding Carter. *New York Post* 24 May 1953.

"Fighting Pastor: Martin Luther King." *New York Post* 8–14 April 1957.

"The First Million Is the Hardest: Closeup of William J. Trent." *New York Post* 2 April 1947, sec. M: 1.
First executive director of National Negro College Fund.

"For Rev. King, Get-Well Wishes—and a Trickle of Hate Mail." *New York Post* 25 September 1958.

"A Foster Child's Plea: Please Let Me Go Home." *New York Post* 15 February 1967.

"Fresh Air in Dixie." Rev. of *An Epitaph for Dixie*, by Harry S. Ashmore. *New York Post* 26 January 1958.

"From Shakespeare to FEPC: Closeup of A. Philip Randolph." *New York Post* 13 February 1946.
As a railway porter, Poston had admired A. Philip Randolph's forming of a railroad workers' union. When Poston moved to Harlem following his graduation from college and lived with his brother and sister-in-law, Ulysses and Sybil Poston, Randolph was his neighbor in the fashionable Dunbar Apartments. Randolph inspired Poston again in his attempts to bring the black press into the Newspaper Guild when Poston was city editor of the Amsterdam News in 1935.

"Garland Patton, Gigolo." *Amsterdam News* 16 December 1931–9 March 1932.
Popular Harlem series on how wealthy white Carleton Curtis was bilked by a woman of color, Letitia Brown, who conveyed Curtis's gifts and money to her black lover, Garland Patton, who, unknown to her, was already married.

"Glamour Girl No. 1 Makes Her Bow to Harlem's Elite: Physician's Daughter, Eighteen, Has Debut — Six Hundred Attend Party." *New York Post* 22 June 1939: 3.

"Graduation Ceremony — for a Class and an Era." *New York Post* 3 June 1957: 7.
When Poston was a child, his father taught at Kentucky State College (then Kentucky Negro Industrial Institute). His brother, U. S. Poston [1914], sister, Roberta [1916], and third wife, Ersa Hines Poston [1942], graduated from Kentucky State. Ted attended the school's 1957 commencement, at which Martin Luther King Jr. was principal speaker.

"Grandma and Little Boy Lost All Night." *New York Post* 23 December 1947.

"Hailing a New Talent from Barbadoes." Rev. of *In the Castle of My Skin*, by George Lamming. *New York Post* 30 August 1953: n.p.

"Haiti President Called Dictator by Two Exiles Here." *New York Post* 5 June 1939.

"Harlem Buries Johnson, Beloved Negro Composer." *New York Post* 30 June 1938: 30.

"Harlem Buries the Brick in Tammany Fight." *New York Post* 11 May 1939.

"Harlem Emerges as Stronghold of Trade Unionism." *New York Post* 13 May 1938: n.p.

"Harlem Honors Its Arctic Hero after Thirty Years" [Matthew Henson]. *New York Post* 19 May 1939.

"Harlem Limps on Bunions after Battle of Ballrooms." *New York Post* 29 October 1939.

"Harlem Quiet but Tense; Riot Toll: 1 Dead, 122 Hurt." *New York Post* 20 July 1964: 3+.

"Harlem Reacts to the Explosion." *New York Post* 18 September 1963.

"Harlem Shadows." *Pittsburgh Courier* 24 January; 7, 14 February; 28 March; 11 April 1931.

"Harlem Shadows." Rev. of *Battle of the Bloods*, by John Louis Hill. *Pittsburgh Courier* 21 March 1931, sec. 1: 1.

"He'd Outlaw His Own Good Job: William H. Hastie." *New York Post* 12 November 1948: 55.

"Heil Huey! Harlem Minister Would Make Kingfish Dictator of Nation." *Amsterdam News* 15 December 1934: 1.

"Here's a Primer on Desegregation." Rev. of *Now Is the Time*, by Lillian Smith. *New York Post* 13 February 1955.
Poston delighted in pointing out such white leaders in the desegregation struggle as Smith.

"Himes Writes of Prison Life: Novel Highlights Unconventional Love Story." Rev. of *Cast the First Stone*, by Chester Himes. *New York Post* 8 February 1953.

"His Goal: Jobs for Blacks" [Whitney Young]. *New York Post* 11 March 1971: 2.

"Horror in the Sunny South." *New York Post* 1, 4, 6, 7, 9, 11, 12, 19, 24 September 1949.

"How It Feels to Be Negro in America." Rev. of *On Being Negro in America*, by J. Saunders Redding. *New York Post* 21 October 1951.

"Huey Long to Fight Costigan Bill: Would Let Negroes Vote — in North." *Amsterdam News* 19 January 1935: 1.

On a popular Louisiana politician; Poston illustrates how Negroes of every age and station were called by their first names. Poston is thirty and identifies with the thirty-year-old man who was lynched. Poston dogs Long's steps to get an interview, then reveals that Long's promises to blacks are empty at best. The moral: Be wary of the rhetoric of a demagogue.

"A Hughes Omnibus." Rev. of *The Langston Hughes Reader: The Selected Writings of Langston Hughes*. *New York Post* 6 April 1958.

"Hughes Tribute: 'He Knew Us.'" *New York Post* 25 May 1967.

"'I Hope Joe Win,' Says No. 1 Louis Fan: Daughter Jackie." *New York Post* 19 June 1946.

"'I Taught Father Divine' Says St. Bishop the Vine." *Amsterdam News* 23 November 1932: 1.

"Island of Nassau Now Woos Negro Tourists." *New York Post* 2 September 1955.

"It's a Tough Job — He Likes It" [Robert C. Weaver]. *New York Post* 4 March 1956: 2.

"JFK Urged to Visit Miss. to See 'Spreading Violence.'" *New York Post* 12 October 1961: 5.

"Jim Crow in New York." *New York Post* 22 April 1956: 4, 5.

"Josephine Baker Threatens to Picket Stork Club over 'Discourtesy.'" *New York Post* 18 October 1951: 3, 6.

"Judge Lynch Presides." *Amsterdam News* 9, 23 March 1935: 9.

Series on lynchings through the years.

"Judge Waring Cited for Long Battle for Negro Rights in South." *New York Post* 27 November 1950: 1, 2.

"The King Murder: A Mystery Telephone Call." *New York Post* 15 March 1969: 1, 57.

"Law and Order in Norfolk." *New Republic* 7 October 1940: 472–73.

Reminiscent of Rudolph Fisher's 1925 story, "City of Refuge," in which a country boy is amazed to reach Harlem and see a black policeman. The hope kept alive here is also reminiscent of the Jews of the Diaspora who uttered annually, "Next year in Jerusalem," believing that one day they would have a homeland. The "reckless eyeballing" in this story foreshadows Emmett Till's southern visit and subsequent murder fifteen years later.

"LBJ a Surprise Visitor at Rights Talks." *New York Post* 2 June 1966.

"Leading Harlem's War on Poverty: Livingstone Wingate, Arthur C. Logan." *New York Post* 12 July 1964: 24.

"A Letter from a Miss. Jail: The Fight Goes On." *New York Post* 16 June 1961: 11.

"Letter to an Alabama Editor." *New York Post* 24 June 1956: 5, 16.

"Like Father, Like Son? Young Ben Davis Seeks to Destroy Life Work of His Parent." *Amsterdam News* 30 June 1934.
How black lives are programmed for failure: Ben Davis Sr. and Ben Davis Jr. illustrate why the communists in the 1930s presumed that the black population constituted a fertile field for planting their doctrines.
"Little Rock, Four Months After . . ." *New York Post* 27 January 1958: 2, 22.
"Little Rock High Schools Reopening; Gang Fires on Home of Daisy Bates." *New York Post* 12 August 1959: 3.
"Little Rock—Where Minnie Jean Fights Back." *New York Post* 7 February 1958: 4. 10.
"Love and Vigilance in the South: The Case of Ruby McCollum." *New York Post* 29 August 1954, sec. M: 10.
"Madrid Teems with Literati Says Returning Novelist" [Langston Hughes]. *New York Post* 27 January 1938: n.p.
"Mahalia Jackson Sings and Montgomery Rocks." *New York Post* 7 December 1956: 10.
"Mail to Help Evers Family Irks Barnett." *New York Post* 10 January 1964.
"The Making of a Judge: Closeup of Harold A. Stevens." *New York Post* 14 August 1955.
Another example of survival against the odds, Judge Stevens proved that a black person can reach the playing fields of the judiciary.
"Malcolm and the Muslims." *New York Post* 22 February 1965.
Uncompromising militant Malcolm X knew he was a marked man.
"Mama Remembers Mr. Handy . . ." *New York Post* 3 April 1958: 2.
"Mama's Whammy Runs into Poston's Jinx." *New York Post* 11 October 1956: 3, 81.
"The Man from Ghana" [Kwame Nkrumah]. *New York Post* 27 July 1958, sec. M: 4.
As Africa began throwing off colonialism in favor of independent nationhood, African Americans rejoiced that the first leader of the new Ghana had been educated in the United States. Poston portrayed Nkrumah as an amazing one-time resident of Harlem.
"Man in the News: George F. Kennan. Time to Defrost Our Cold-War Policy?" *New York Post* 4 February 1967.
Poston's wide-ranging assignments included an interview with Kennan, diplomat and expert on the Russians. This piece shows Poston's breadth of mind, impressive for a reporter whose career was in decline and who had concentrated on black affairs through so much of it.
"Man in the News: Thurgood Marshall, LBJ's Choice for Solicitor General of the U.S." *New York Post* 18 July 1965.
"Martin Luther King: Where Does He Go from Here?" *New York Post* 14 April 1957, sec. M: 5.
"Meet Mahalia — Gospel with a Beat." *New York Post* 12 April 1959.

Profile celebrating a woman who, over the years, generated love. Poston elicits from Jackson a definition of blues, spirituals, and gospel songs and an explanation of what church music has meant to people whose forebears rose from slavery.

"Minnie Jean Will Attend School Here." *New York Post* 18 February 1958.

"Minnijean Wants to Be 'Just a Teen-Ager.'" *New York Post* 24 February 1958: 5, 21.

"A Minority Report." Rev. of *Brown Girl, Brownstones,* by Paule Marshall. *New York Post* 23 August 1959.

Elements of the African Diaspora conjoin in this review of a first novel on Barbadian immigrants transplanted to New York City.

"Mississippi: Tragic Anniversary." *New York Post* 20 June 1965.

"Mother's Day Reflections." *Blue and Gold* (Nashville: Tennessee Agricultural and Industrial Institute) June 1927: 7.

A fictional memorial to Poston's mother, Mollie Cox Poston.

"Moton Talks! I Wouldn't Serve the Lord If He Were against My People." *Pittsburgh Courier* 13 April 1940: 13.

"Mrs. Evers on Stand: 'Loud Blast, Silence.'" *New York Post* 31 January 1964.

"Mrs. Medgar Evers Waits to Confront the Accused." *New York Post* 29 January 1964.

"Mrs. Roosevelt in Harlem to Draw Overflow Crowd." *New York Post* 22 October 1937.

Eleanor Roosevelt counted as friends National Council of Negro Women founder Mary McLeod Bethune, singer Marian Anderson, and novelist Richard Wright. Mollie Lewis, one of the twenty-two "actors" who traveled with Poston and Moon to Russia in 1932 and who married Henry Lee Moon in 1938, was on the Crisis committee that helped arrange this appearance of Mrs. Roosevelt.

"Muslims — Myth or Menace?" Rev. of *The Black Muslims in America,* by C. Eric Lincoln. *New York Post* April 1961.

"NAACP Fears Bloodshed as Till Trial Aftermath." *New York Post* 5 October 1955.

"NAACP to LBJ: Take over Miss." *New York Post* 26 June 1964.

"NAACP to Little Rock: Don't Expect Minnie Jean." *New York Post* 14 February 1958: 7.

"Nat King Cole: As They Remember Him." *New York Post* 16 February 1965.

"The Negro and His War: He Didn't Sit It Out in 1860–65." Rev. of *The Negro in the Civil War,* by Benjamin Quarles. *New York Post* 9 August 1953, sec. M: 12.

"Negro Minister Slain in Mississippi: Refused to Take Name off Voter List." *New York Post* 20 May 1955: 4, 40.

"The Negro Press." *Reporter* 6 December 1949: 14–16.

A historical sketch on the necessity for a black press and ways it must improve. Poston identifies himself as a liberal who condones interracial marriage, which many black periodicals do not. He draws on personal experience when he served as an interface during World War II between the War Manpower Commission and man-

ufacturers and unions that resisted integrating the war industries; at the Office of War Information, he took flack from Congress for publishing too much black news and from black readers for not publishing enough.

"Negro Voters Feeling the Squeeze in Tennessee." *New York Post* 29 June 1960: 8.

"Negroes Assail Nazis, Ask Fight on U.S. Fascism: Urge Americans to End Race Discrimination in Own Country." *New York Post* 25 November 1938.

"Negroes for Willkie: They Succumb to His Charm." *New York Post* 25 June 1940: 2.

"The Negroes of Montgomery." *New York Post* 14, 15, 18, 19, 20, 21, 24 June 1956.

"A Negro's Vivid Report on Jim Crow Land." Rev. of *South of Freedom*, by Carl T. Rowan. *New York Post* 3 August 1952, sec. M: 12.

"New Man on the Bench" [Thurgood Marshall]. *New York Post* 7 October 1962.

"New York, New York." *New York Post* 8, 9, 10 December 1952.

"News (Good News) about the Negro in the Armed Forces." Rev. of *Breakthrough on the Color Front*, by Lee Nichols. *New York Post* 7 February 1954, sec. M: 12.

"Nine Kids Who Dared." *New York Post* 20 October–1 November 1957.

"The Nineteen-Day Ordeal of Minnie Jean Brown." *New York Post* 9 February 1958: 3.

"A Novel of Africa." Rev. of *Mine Boy*, by Peter Abrahams. *New York Post* 12 June 1955.

"N.Y. Group Plans Aid to Negroes in Tenn. Boycott." *New York Post* 7 July 1960.

"Ode to a Harlemite." *Pittsburgh Courier* 11 April 1931.

Also capturing the joys of Seventh Avenue was James Weldon Johnson in Black Manhattan, *saying that a stroll on the avenue "is not simply going out for a walk; it is like going out for an adventure" (163). Carl Van Vechten opened his novel* Nigger Heaven *with a description of that broad, tree-lined street and its denizens.*

"Oil Firms: Can't Stop Squeeze on Tenn. Negroes." *New York Post* 30 June 1960.

"On a Harlem Street Corner, W. C. Handy's Blue Notes." *New York Post* 2 April 1958: 3, 47.

"On the Passing of House-Rent Parties." *Pittsburgh Courier* 25 April 1931.

On Friday evenings, to pay rent, tenants would cook soul food and provide music — live musicians in the beginning, eventually phonograph and radio — and partygoers would pay about fifty cents each for all they could eat and a night of dancing. Tenants would thus garner sufficient money to pay the week's rent.

"Out of the Past: Willie Reid Speaks . . ." *New York Post* 6 January 1960: 5, 56.

"A Page from the War to End Wars." Rev. of *Paths of Glory*, by Humphrey Cobb. *Amsterdam News* 20 July 1935.

War produces no winners. "Can we just get along?" Rodney King beseeched after his videotaped March 1991 beating by police touched off a 1992 Los Angeles race riot. A jury cleared the police of wrongdoing even a generation after Poston's death and forty years after his book review.

"Pickets Fight Rent Boost as House Is Opened for Negroes." *Amsterdam News* 13 July 1935: 1, 2.

"Policy Bankers Mutter Darkly about Mr. Dewey." *New York Post* 28 September 1938: 6.

"Pope Calls U.S. and Palestine DP's Only Hope, Traveler Reports." *New York Post* 3 January 1947: 18.

"Porters Hail Roosevelt." *New York Post* 17 September 1940.

"The Post's Reporter Gets to See Gov. Talmadge — by the Back Door." *New York Post* 25 May 1954: 5, 32.

"Powell Cuts His Tour, Heads for P.R. Home." *New York Post* 6 September 1962. *African Americans who came out of "the best foot forward," "don't disgrace the race" school of social interaction fretted at antics of Harlem minister-congressman-playboy Adam Clayton Powell Jr. Poston was a lifelong friend of Powell, but when Powell incurred State Department wrath, Poston reported it.*

"Powell's Harlem Threat to Tiger Grows." *New York Post* 6 August 1958.

"Prejudice Is a Two-Way Street, Negro Learns." Rev. of *The Seekers*, by Will Thomas. *New York Post* 5 July 1953, sec. M: 12.

"Protection for Colored Workers: Social Security Board Declines to Act against Employment Bias in State Administered Agencies." *Pittsburgh Courier* 6 January 1940: 24.

"A Quiz for Two Returned Freedom Riders." *New York Post* 14 June 1961: 76.

"Randolph for Powell, Cites Seniority." *New York Post* 28 May 1958.

"Retreat to Harlem: Communist Party Purges Ford as Scapegoat for Failure among Negroes." *New Leader* 30 March 1940: 4.

"Rev. King Continues to Gain: Takes First Steps since Stabbing." *New York Post* 23 September 1958: 4, 17.

"The Rev. King Hails Kennedy for His 'Courageous Stand.'" *New York Post* 1 November 1960.

"Rev. King Wants to Go Back to Work." *New York Post* 24 September 1958: 4, 30.

"The Revolt of the Evil Fairies." *New Republic* 6 April 1942: 458–59.

"Rioting Ebbs in Harlem." *New York Post* 22 July 1964: 2, 30.

"The Rise of Colored Democracy: Black GOP Begins New Tammany Hall Organization." *Amsterdam News* 6 April 1932: 1, 6.

"Robert C. Weaver, Sec. of Housing." *New York Post* 23 January 1966: n.p.

"Rockefeller Orders Willie Reid Sent Back to Florida Prison." *New York Post* 23 November 1959.

"Rocky's Daughters Keep Baldwin's 'Blues' Onstage." *New York Post* 28 May 1964.

"Scholarships for Negroes: A Program That Works." *New York Post* 19 April 1964.

"Scottsboro Boys Framed, Says Girl Who Named Them." *New York Post* 19 July 1937: n.p.

"Scottsboro's Fugitive: A Victim's Tale of Alabama 'Justice.'" Rev. of *Scottsboro*

Boy, by Haywood Patterson and Earl Conrad. *New York Post* 4 June 1950.
Haywood Patterson's life indicates a source of black rage as it built through the twentieth century: African Americans continuously becoming more conscious of their situation in relation to the whole.

"Seven Kids Who Tried." *New York Post* 1 November 1957, sec. M: 2.

"Seventh Ave. Finance: Harlem Shadows." *Pittsburgh Courier* 10 January 1931.
Anti-Jew here, Poston would come to spend the majority of his career on the Jewish-owned New York Post *and would become an admiring, loving friend to many Jews as colleagues. The World War II Holocaust stunned and sickened him, says fellow reporter Fern Marja Eckman.*

"Simon Not So Simple: Harlem Polemicist a New Dooley." Rev. of *Simple Speaks His Mind*, by Langston Hughes. *New York Post* 30 April 1950.

"The Simple World of Langston Hughes." *New York Post* 24 November 1957, sec. M: 2.

"Singapore Goes It Alone." *New York Post* 15 August 1965: 24.

"Social Security Act Bars Most of Us." *Pittsburgh Courier* 23 December 1939: 24.

"Socialist Uncovers Something New in Harlem — the House Rent Party." *Amsterdam News* 16 March 1935: 2.

"Sorry, Father, but It's Not Wonderful." Rev. of *Fr. Divine, Holy Husband*, by Sara Harris. *New York Post* 1 November 1953, sec. M: 12.

"South Takes School Bias Ban Calmly, Negro Leaders Move to Widen Fight." *New York Post* 18 May 1954: 5, 40.

"Southern White Woman Is 'Angel' of Savannah." *Pittsburgh Courier* 8 June 1940: 12.

"The Soviet Fair — a Mixed Bag of Goods and Not-So-Goods." *New York Post* 30 June 1959.

"A Statement on Racism — by Beckwith." *New York Post* 31 January 1964: 11.

"Station Throngs Listen to Negro: Tenor, Out of Job, Sings Nightly to Thousands for His Supper." *New York Post* 8 January 1940: 1, 6.

"The Strength of Non-Violence" [Close-up of South African Professor Z. K. Matthews]. *New York Post* 28 September 1952.
An early African National Congress fighter against apartheid who did not live to see that regime fall and Nelson Mandela — incarcerated for twenty-seven years — become head of state.

"Suicide in the CHA: Feared Loss of Job Over Race Issue." *New York Post* 13 January 1958.
A white housing administrator cannot take the abuse when he obeys the law and integrates public housing.

"'Take Me to Bellevue' Begged Heights Youth before Killing." *New York Post* 11 June 1948: n.p.

"Evil" may be a genetic abnormality, Poston suggests, or simply a reaction to the insidious nature of racism.

"There Are No Seats in the Colored Section." *New York Post* 12 June 1959: 5, 17.
The intransigence of southern ways represents a regression for a black reporter who had left the South.

"They'll Shoot Me in the Back of the Head." *New York Post* 26 August 1959: 5+.

"This Columnist Racket," in "Harlem Shadows." *Pittsburgh Courier* 25 April 1931.
How hard it is for a columnist to come up with ideas; editors are never satisfied.

"Three Flights up to the Fourth Estate." *New York Post* 11 June 1959: 5.

"Timeworn Rusty Chain Binds Novelist's Miss. Negroes." Rev. of *Chain in the Heart,* by Hubert Creekmore. *New York Post* 26 July 1953, sec. M: 12.

"The Tolling Bells and the Prayers." *New York Post* 25 November 1963.
Ordinarily cynical newspeople are surprised to learn how many people had cared for President Kennedy.

"Town Finally Honors Ignored Negro PWS." *New York Post* 11 September 1953.

"The Tree of Hope Will Be Spared as City Improves Seventh Avenue." *Amsterdam News* 31 January 1934.
In the "laughing to keep from crying" tradition, Poston relates that when opportunities are few, actors rely on a magical lifeline. The slang with which "the boys," Harlem denizens, talked with each other is illustrated here.

"A Truly American Family." Rev. of *Proud Shoes,* by Pauli Murray. *New York Post* 21 October 1956.

"Two New Yorkers Ready for Appeal of Conviction in Greyhound Case." *Pittsburgh Courier* 13 April 1940.

"2,000 Attend Funeral for Walter White." *New York Post* 24 March 1955.

"Vet Spurns Desperately-Needed Apartment over Jim Crow Rule." *New York Post* 17 September 1948: 19.

"Violence Flares for Third Night: Fifty Injured in Harlem." *New York Post* 21 July 1964: 2, 53.

" 'We Are Neglecting Our Manners,' Dr. Charlotte Hawkins Brown Admonishes." *Pittsburgh Courier* 20 April 1940.
Educator Dr. Charlotte Hawkins Brown taught southern courtesy as well as academics in her finishing school. Young women of color received training there that enabled them to function with poise in both the black and white worlds. To Brown's Palmer Memorial Institute, Langston Hughes brought his poems on some of his first tours of the United States, thrilling the listeners. Nat King Cole's wife, Maria Ellington, attended Palmer Memorial Institute; Charlotte Hawkins Brown was her aunt.

"We Have So Much to Say" [Lorraine Hansberry]. *New York Post* 22 March 1959, sec. M: 2.

A creative African American woman borrowed Langston Hughes's metaphor for black rage, "a raisin in the sun." Hansberry died of cancer at age thirty-four, six years after this piece. Her husband, Bob Nemiroff, assembled her autobiographical writings in a dramatic production, To Be Young, Gifted, and Black.

"Weaver Set for Top U.S. Housing Job." *New York Post* 30 December 1960.

" 'We've Got to Go Back to Cicero,' Say Victims of Race Riot." *New York Post* 9 August 1951: 2, 21.

"Widow Leads King March." *New York Post* 8 April 1968: 1+.

"Widow Talks of Her Life with Malcolm." *New York Post* 23 February 1965.

"Wife Slays Pastor Who Boasted of Conquests." *Pittsburgh Courier* 10 August 1940: 1.

"Willie McGee Dies — and Rebel Yells Ring Out." *New York Post* [date illegible]. *Poston recognized McGee as a typical black male whose fate was foreordained. Many African Americans cheered in 1995 when football legend O. J. Simpson was acquitted of the murder of his ex-wife because so many black Willie McGees had been lynched without reason before him.*

"Wright's Terrible Reality in a Violent, Explosive Novel." Rev. of *The Outsider*, by Richard Wright. *New York Post* 22 March 1953.

"You Can't Win!" *Amsterdam News* 14 April–19 May 1934. *Series demonstrating that crime does not pay.*

"Young Bob's a Chip off the Old Block." *New York Post* 20 January 1947. *The heir of the man responsible for the Wagner Act — the National Labor Relations Act of 1935, which affirmed labor's right to organize and bargain collectively through representatives of its own choice or to refrain from such activities — illustrates a theme of Poston's through the years, how some scions carry on the work of their forebears. The Ben Davis, Jonathan Daniels, and Thurgood Marshall pieces all show this theme.*

Articles by Ted Poston and Collaborators

Arzt, George, and Ted Poston. "He's a Pusher at Age Twelve." *New York Post* 26 February 1970: 1, 4.

Caldwell, Earl, and Ted Poston. "CORE Sets Separate Harlem School Board." *New York Post* 1 March 1967.

——. "Harlem Reaction Worries City." *New York Post* 10 January 1967.

——. "Harlem Vows to Vote Him Back." *New York Post* 2 March 1967.

Grove, Gene, and Ted Poston. "CCNY's Hello and Good-Bye to Gov. Ross Barnett." *New York Post* 21 May 1964.

Hendricks, Alfred D., and Ted Poston. "Survey Reveals Heavy Support for Powell in Harlem." *New York Post* 23 May 1958: 4+.

Kahn, Joseph, and Ted Poston. "After a Harlem Fire: The Homeless and the Helpless." *New York Post* 21 December 1954: 4, 26.

Massolo, Arthur, and Ted Poston. "Jack Says Powell Stirs Hooliganism in Effort to Scare off Political Foes." *New York Post* 19 May 1958: 5+.

Milne, Emile, and Ted Poston. "Mayor at the Carey Funeral." *New York Post* 7 July 1969.

Moon, Henry Lee, and T. R. Poston. "Amsterdam News Reporters Tell Why Soviet Russia Dropped Film: American Prejudice Triumphs over Communism." *Amsterdam News* 5 October 1932: 1.

Pelleck, Carl J., and Ted Poston. "I Try to Explain . . . Santa Won't Come . . ." *New York Post* 23 December 1955: 5, 33.

Poston, Ed [sic], and William Greaves. "Tells Why City OKd Nude Fair." *New York Post* 14 December 1970.

Poston, Ted, and Joseph Kahn. "Negro Boy, Fifteen, Killed by Cop; Students Riot." *New York Post* 16 July 1964.

Poston, Ted, with Joseph Kahn, Henry Beckett, and Joseph Cotter. "Life in the Slums: New York's Shame." *New York Post* 7–13 November 1955.

Poston, Ted, and Irving Lieberman. "Inside the Dope Racket." *New York Post* 24 October–2 November 1949.

Poston, Ted, and Louis Martin. "Detroit Is Dynamite." *Life* 17 August 1942: 15–23.

Poston, Ted, and Stan Opotowsky, with Irving Lieberman, Edward Katcher, and William Haddad. "Graft in the Buildings Department." *New York Post* 25 June–7 July 1957.

Poston, Ted, and Roi Ottley. "New York vs. Chicago: Which City Is Better Place for Negroes?" *Ebony* December 1952: 16–24.

Poston, Ted, and Carl Pelleck. "No Heat for Year — So for Yule, Water's Cut Off." *New York Post* 25 December 1954.

Smilon, Marvin, and Ted Poston. "Ex-Fong Aide Gets Eighteen Months." *New York Post* 4 January 1972.
Ted Poston's last byline.

Articles about Ted Poston

DeKnight, Freda. "Date with a Dish: Barbecued Squab; Succulent Birds Are Ted Poston's Favorite Dish." *Ebony* August 1955: 96, 99.

Dreyfuss, Joel. "The Loneliness of Being First." *Washington Post* 19 January 1974: B1, B3.

Eckman, Fern Marja. "Ted Poston — Newspaperman." *New York Post* [parody for retirement party] 14 April 1972: 1.

Eckman, Fern Marja, and Roberta B. Gratz. "Ted Poston Dies at Sixty-seven; a Legendary Reporter." *New York Post* 10 January 1974: 2, 58.

Fraser, C. Gerald. "Ted Poston Dies." *New York Times* 12 January 1974: 1.

"Guild Honors Poston." *New York Post* [retirement issue] 14 April 1972: 1.

"Harlem Agog over Newspaper 'War.'" *Pittsburgh Courier* 25 April 1931: 3.

"NAACP Honors Ted Poston." *New York Post* 7 December 1951: 3.

"Noted Newspaper Reporter Ted Poston and Wife" [advertisement for Smirnoff]. *Jet* 28 March 1962: 42; *Ebony* May 1963: 127.

"Poston of the Post." *Newsweek* 11 April 1949: 62.

Powell, Bill. "Yesteryear with Bill Powell." *Louisville Courier-Journal* n.d.

Writings by and about Other Poston Family Members

"Augusta Savage, Sixty-two, Sculptor, Is Dead." *New York Times* 27 March 1962: 37.

"Distinguished Workers Whose Names Will Adorn Our Honor Roll. No. 6. Robert L. Poston." *Negro World* 23 October 1923: 4.

Dudar, Helen. "Woman in the News: Mrs. Ersa Poston." *New York Post* 13 December 1964: 25.

"Ex-Newsman Services Held at Concord" [U. S. Poston]. *Amsterdam News* 21 May 1955: 9.

Fax, Elton C. "Augusta Savage — an Appraisal." *AMSAC Supplement* 18 October 1962: 4–5.

"Forrest-Poston." *Hopkinsville (Kentucky) New Age* 25 April 1924: 1.

"Jet Profile: First Woman Director of EEOC Regional Office" [Marie Byrd Poston]. *Jet* 20 July 1967: 10.

Johnson, Greenleaf. "Thriving Business Enterprises of the Universal Negro Improvement Association" [profile of Ulysses S. Poston]. *Negro World* 8 July 1922: 3–5.

"Miss Augusta Savage Finds No Bread Line in Gay Paris." *Amsterdam News* 2 September 1931: 3.

Poston, Ephraim. "The KNEA." *Kentucky Negro Education Association Journal* January–February 1940.

Poston, Robert L. "I'll Be Back," in "The Reason Why I Accepted the Garvey Program." *Negro World* 12 May 1923: 4.

———. "Is There a Race Question in America?" *Negro World* 31 March 1923: 4.

———. "The Negro Prayer." *Negro World* 2 September 1922.

———. "When You Meet a Member of the Ku Klux Klan." *Negro World* 21 October 1921.

———. "The 'Why' of It" [editorial]. *Negro World* 8 October 1921: 4.

Poston, U. S. "Harlem Economist Tells Needs of Community." *Pittsburgh Courier* 15 October 1927, sec. 1: 4.

Poston, Ulysses S. "How Some Presidents Expressed Their Attitude toward the Colored Man." *Inter-State Tattler* 13 March 1925: 4.

———. "An Ideal Ticket." *New York Contender* 22 October 1932.

———. "The Political Buzz-Saw: An Open Letter to Negro Voters." *Inter-State Tattler* 9 June 1932: 4.

———. "The Political Buzz-Saw: Communism and the Negro." *Inter-State Tattler* 19 May 1932: 4.

———. "The Political Buzz-Saw: Georgia Goes Lily-White." *Inter-State Tattler* 31 March 1932: 4.

———. "The Political Buzz-Saw: Herbert Clarke Hoover." *Inter-State Tattler* 21 January 1932: 4.

———. "The Political Buzz-Saw: Mayor James J. Walker, Whole Life and Works Symbolize the Spirit of New York." *Inter-State Tattler* 11 February 1932: 4.

———. "The Political Buzz-Saw: Negro Women in Politics." *Inter-State Tattler* 12 May 1932: 4.

———. "The Political Buzz-Saw: Silhouette: Abraham Lincoln." *Inter-State Tattler* 18 February 1932: 4.

———. "The Political Buzz-Saw: The Democratic Party." *Inter-State Tattler* 16 June 1932: 4.

———. "Private Jack McKay." *Negro World* 15 October 1921: 7.

———. "Relief Ahead for Home Owners." *Amsterdam News* 19 July 1933: 3, 9.

Savage, Augusta. "An Autobiography." *Crisis* August 1929: 269.

———. "My Soul's Gethsemane." *Negro World* 26 December 1922: 3.

———. "The Old Homestead." *Negro World* 26 December 1922: 3.

———. "Supplication." *Negro World* 18 November 1922.

"Seeks Exhibition of Augusta Savage Work." *Amsterdam News* 7 March 1936: 5.

Interviews

Banks, Ruth. Personal interviews, 22 August 1983; 29 June 1984. Telephone interviews, 23 October 1983; 17 July 1991.

Bourne, St. Clair T. Personal interviews, 6 January, 16, 22 July 1993. Telephone interview, 5 December 1990.

Dudar, Helen. Personal interview, 3 February 1998.

Duncan, James, Jr. Personal interview, 11 February 1985.

Duncan, James, III, and Doris Duncan. Personal interview, 11 February 1985.

Eckman, Fern Marja. Personal interview, 13 October 1984. Telephone interview, 24 September 1984.

Eckman, Irving. Personal interview, 13 October 1984.

Elliot, Mollie Lee Moon. Telephone interview, 2 November 1982.

Evers, Charles. Personal interview, 15 January 1997.

Jackson, Barbara Loomis. Telephone interviews, 25 August 1983; 15 March 1994.

Jackson, Luther P., Jr. Telephone interviews, 15, 20 October 1982.

Kahn, Joe. Personal interview, 5 July 1984.

Lewis, Diana Bonnor. Personal interview, 29 December 1984. Telephone interviews, 16 September, 29 November 1983.

Moon, Henry Lee. Interviews with Luther P. Jackson Jr., 11 January, 12 July 1979; 16 January 1980, Columbia University Oral History Project.

———. Personal interviews, 15 July, 4, 14 August, 16, 28, 30 September, 28 November 1983; 29 June 1984. Telephone interviews, 13 July 1982; 27 May 1983.

Poston, Ersa H. Personal interview, 5 July 1983. Telephone interviews, 3 March 1985; 1 May, 27 October, 16 November 1991.

Reed, Eloise Scott. Telephone interview, 9 November 1991.

Reed, Rosemary. Telephone interview, 5 November 1991.

Sann, Paul. Telephone interview, 24 October 1984.

Tarry, Ellen. Personal interview, 12 June 1991. Telephone interviews, 9, 16 March, 5, 17 October 1991.

Weaver, Robert C. Personal interview, 18 August 1986.

Williams, Allison. Personal interviews, 3 July, 3, 8, 9, 10, 11, 12, 13, 14 October 1983; 4, 7, 13, 14, 18, 19, 20, 24 January, 7, 18 February, 29 March, 27 April, 1 May, 3 July, 17, 25 November 1984; 22 January 1985. Telephone interviews, 3, 10 September 1983.

Wilson, Clifford. Personal interview, 9 October 1983.

Wilson, Mary Duncan. Personal interviews, 9 October 1983; 10, 11 February 1985. Telephone interviews, 10, 28 September 1983; 29 January 1985.

Correspondence

Adams, Lea, and Ruth Adams. Letter to author, 26 February 1992.

Banks, Ruth. Letters to author, 13 September, 17 October, 7 December 1983; 2 January, 3, 21 February, 10, 15 March, 16 April, 18 May, 5, 21 August, 15 September 1984; 23, 31 January, 20 February, 2 April 1985; 1, 10, 15, 23, 25 March, 15 May 1991.

Bourne, St. Clair. Letters to author, 6 May, 5 July 1991; 16, 22 July 1993.

Eckman, Fern Marja. Letters to author, 24 September, 31 October, 8 November 1984; 16 June 1985; 10, 18 April 1986; 20 February 1988; 5, 18 March, 7 May, 11 July, 1 August, 22, 29 October 1991.

Ephron, Nora. Letter to author, 20 July 1987.

LaNier, Carlotta Wells. Letter to author, n.d.

Lewis, Diana Bonnor. Letters to author, 9, 19 September, 29 November, 5 December 1983; 21, 30 January 1984; 2, 4 February, 4 March, 18 September 1985; 18 January 1987.

Maynard, Robert C. Letter to author, 25 June 1987.

Moon, Henry Lee. Letter to author, 11 January 1984.

Poston, Ersa H. Letters to author, 21 April, 4 May, 26 August 1982; 27 June, 30 August, 1 December 1983; 1 March, 19 November 1984; 28 May 1985; 16 June 1989; 31 December 1990; 4 November 1991; 25 February 1994.

Tarry, Ellen. Letter to author, 4 March 1991.

Williams, Allison. Letters to author, 3 July 1983–11 February 1985.

Wilson, Mary Duncan. Letters to author, 28 September, 14, 24 October, 15 December 1983; 12 January, 15 February, 30 April 1985.

INDEX

Horace Mann High School, 139–40
Horne, Lena, 192–93
Hotel Theresa, 160
Housing, 33, 53, 178
Houston, Charles, 56–57, 158
Howard, Curtis, 73–74
Howard University, 3, 56–59, 151, 158
Hubert, James H., 30
Hudson River, 10
Hughes, James Mercer Langston, xx,
    xxvii, 22, 77, 100, 153, 191–94, 196,
    218 (1950s n. 5, 1960s nn. 8–13)
Hugo, Oklahoma, 55
Huie, Bill, 201
Humphrey, Hubert, 86, 172
Hunter, Jess, 64, 67–68, 72
Hutchinson Street Baptist Church, 133
Huttig, Arkansas, 144

Ickes, Harold, xxii, 207 (n. 10)
Illinois, 96
Illinois Central Railroad, xx
Indianapolis, Indiana, 120
"Inside U.S.A." (Gunther), 116
Interstate Commerce Commission
    (ICC), 169
"Invisible Man" (Ellison), 119, 180
Irish, 19–20, 173, 177–78
Irish Post, 164
Irvin, Walter, 64–75
Isolationism, 92
Ivie, Ardie, 186, 188

Jack, Hulan, 121
Jackson, Alexander L., 209 (n. 13)
Jackson, Jesse, 77
Jackson, Luther P., Jr., 196, 207 (n. 9)
Jackson, Marie Byrd Tancil Poston
    (Ted's second wife), xxiii–xxv, 112,
    209 (n. 13)
Jackson, Mississippi, 144, 173

Jackson Heights, New York, 120
Jamaica, 182, 202
James, Alberta, 133
Jane Crow, 210 (n. 1)
Jefferson Davis Highway, 43
Jesus Christ, 27, 31
Jet magazine, 128, 156, 167
Jews, 53, 111, 139, 164
Jim Crow, 40–41, 52, 56, 59, 65, 68, 94,
    96–97, 112–13, 115, 168
"Jim Crow in New York," 123
Jim Crow laws, 130
Johnson, James Weldon, 156, 191
Johnson, John H., 167, 169
Johnson, Lyndon B., 185, 207 (n. 10)
Jones, C. H., 145
Jones, Moses W., 135
Josephs, David N., xxiv
Justice Department, 179–80, 212 (n. 7)

Kansas City Call, 157
Kefauver, Estes, 172
Kelley, William M., 21
Kempton, Murray, 168, 210 (n. 20)
Kennedy, Jackie, 159–61
Kennedy, John F., xxv, 86, 159–61,
    171–75, 216 (n. 1)
Kennedy, Robert F., xxvii, 173–74
Kennedy Family Foundation, 215–16
    (n. 1)
Kentucky, 37, 63, 113, 115
Kentucky Negro Industrial Institute,
    xviii
Kerber, Linda K., 210 (n. 1)
Kid Chocolate, 12, 86
King, Martin Luther, Jr., xxv, xxvii, 3,
    51, 60, 122, 127–28, 135–37, 150, 172,
    185, 188, 199, 203
Knudsen, William, 90
Ku Klux Klan, 45, 64, 122, 160, 197–98,
    211 (n. 6)